The VICTORS
and the
VANQUISHED

The VICTORS
HEDA KOVÁLY

and the

ERAZIM KOHÁK

VANQUISHED

HORIZON PRESS NEW YORK

-Preface-
"Remembrance of Things Past"

"We need poetry, not fantasy"—the quote is from Thomas G. Masaryk, three quarters of a century old, but it has lost none of its bite. Facts and fantasies abound, and the poetic sense of life that fuses vision and reality remains the rarest of commodities.

We have not set out to tell a story and add to the store of facts. Nor did we set out to moralize about the past. We set out to relive the unfinished age of hope and fury, but to relive it consciously, both living events and discoursing meanings.

In a divided world, truth is stereophonic. It emerges in a dialogue in which foes come to know each other and the victors and the vanquished recognize their common humanity.

In our time, there has been little dialogue. We have pinned our hopes on Victory, intent on the defeat of our various foes far more than on understanding. Time and again, our victories have turned to defeats, yet even that did not lead us to dialogue. We were too convinced of our victorious, vanquished truths. There is more than one autobiographical volume by liberals describing their "radicalization"; there are many more volumes by disillusioned Communists, describing their disillusion. Each follows the twists and permutations of one monaural truth.

This book is the product of dialogue. Heda Margolius Kovály is the widow of a high-ranking Communist official: when the Communists seized power ïn Czechoslovakia, she was on the side of the victors. I was one of the vanquished whom the Communist coup in 1948 and again the Soviet occupation in 1968 made aliens in their own land.

When I first met Heda Margolius Kovály, I was not eager to work with her on a common volume. I was too immersed in my own truth, preoccupied with writing my own book. When I read the first fragments of her reminiscenses, written in the vivid Czech of a recent exile, with all the intensity of a participant, I began to realize how partial and incomplete my truth was—and how partial and incomplete was what she considered the truth. I started responding, asking for accounts of periods and events I remembered, even if from a very different viewpoint. The dialogue that developed as the book grew was not a confrontation, but a common search for the unity of a truth that each of us had lived and found differently. That dialogue continued through the process of selecting and ordering episodes and topics, through the many stages of translating and editing, in the margins of manuscripts. What emerged from it is a truth that, though it is one, is stereophonic: it requires two speakers.

Heda Margolius Kovály writes of a period in history through which I, too, have lived—the war, the postwar ferment, the triumph and the thermidor of Communist revolution, and the slow rebirth of freedom that bore its fruit in the Czechoslovak Spring. She began her adult life behind the barbed wire of Lodz and Auschwitz in the Second World War. She escaped from a forced march to occupied Prague, took part in the resistance and the uprising. In the postwar years, as the wife of the young Communist idealist Rudolf Margolius, she lived at the center of the intellectual ferment that preceded the coup of 1948. After the coup, her husband became a prominent Communist official, and Heda Margolius made a firsthand acquaintance with the revolutionary elite. Four years later, Rudolf Margolius was executed by those whom he had helped bring to power and conspirator in one of Stalin's purge trials, and Heda Margolius faced the peculiar vengeance of true believers. During the liberalization of the 1960s, as an active literary figure, she participated in the rebirth that culminated in the Dubček Spring of 1968. That fall, in the wake of the Soviet occupation, she found herself in exile.

The life of Heda Margolius Kovály had been a microcosm of human experience in a revolutionary age, lived with intimate intensity. Yet it was still only half of the story. She had lived the cycle of revolution from the vantage point of the victors; both in triumph and defeat, she was one of the active participants of our history. For most of us, the perspective was different. We were the vanquished, excluded from participation, condemned to reflection.

I was not arrested during the war, as most of us were not. Nor did I become a Communist after the war, as, again, most of us did not. When the Communists seized power, I did not share in that "victory," as most of us did not. During the years of triumph and disaster, I was in exile, as most of us were—whether the overt exile in a foreign country or the internal exile of our private minds and lives. The perspective from the receiving end of a revolution, whether in triumph or in disintegration, is significantly different from that of the giving-out end—and that perspective is the other half of the truth in a polarized age.

In retrospect, it is easy to make a virtue of having been one of the vanquished. The vanquished can quite truthfully claim a freedom from blame. We did not contribute to the Communist victory. We were not guilty of the destruction of our freedom, of the trampling of justice, of the sacrifice of a whole generation and of the loss of our independence, still not regained. It is easy for us to yield to the self-righteousness of the vanquished, matched only by the self-righteousness of the victors who even in defeat and exile still proclaim the righteousness of their cause. They, after all, had acted. Though they eventually failed, at a horrendous cost, they can and do claim to have been idealists, fighters for the future of humanity.

The truth of our age, throughout the world, is neither that of the victors nor that of the vanquished. The pride of the victors and the innocence of the vanquished each tell only a part of the story, incomprehensible in itself. The truth emerges only in dialogue, and that is the truth we have sought in this book. For Heda Margolius Kovály, this is the first exile, and a time to remember. For me, it is the second exile in one lifetime, and a time to reflect. Those are the two perspectives which merge into a whole book and they tell the story.

The two perspectives become one in the Epilogue, as the perspectives of the victors and the vanquished merged in the socialist democracy of the Czechoslovak Spring. That Spring was the triumph of the realization that truth cannot be won by victories and defeats, that truth is reconciliation. The socialist democracy of the Spring bridge for our nation the divisions that continue to plague the world—the division between socialists and democrats, between freedom and social justice, between the victors and the vanquished. The Spring gave us something for which all the world is still searching—the unity of people of divergent views who meet one another as human beings, in common work, instead of confronting each other in the struggle of hostile, anonymous blocs.

We are writing in exile, but it is an exile from our land, not from our nation. Today all Czechs and Slovaks are vanquished, and the victors who rule our land speak a foreign tongue. We shall resist them: to acquiesce to violence is as antihumanistic as to perpetrate it. But we have learned, and our hope is that they, too, will learn: as long as there are people who are vanquished, all victory is self-destructive. The only lasting victory is the reconciliation of human beings in freedom and justice.

ERAZIM KOHÁK

21 August 1972, four years after
the occupation of Czechoslovakia

Contents

Preface—"Remembrance of Things Past"   5

	PART ONE *The Victors*	PART TWO *The Vanquished*
I—Preparing the Ground	13	177
i. The Descent	13	178
ii. Defiance	23	181
II—Sowing the Seed	44	192
i. A War Ends	44	193
ii. Uneasy Peace	58	201
iii. The Party	66	210
III—Bitter Harvest	76	220
i. The Revolution	76	221
ii. Faith and Doubt	91	228
iii. On Trial	120	236
IV—The Shoots of Hope	144	246
i. Stagnant Water	144	247
ii. The Spring	162	255

Epilogue—Promise of Things To Come   264

The VICTORS
and the
VANQUISHED

Part One

THE VICTORS
Memoirs of
Heda Margolius Kovály

(Edited and translated by Erazim Kohák)

-I-

Preparing the Ground

i. The Descent
I do not want to write, I do not want to remember. My memories are not simple recollections. They are a return to the bottom of an abyss; I have to gather up the shattered bones that have lain still for so long, climb back over the crags, and tumble in once more. Only this time I have to do it deliberately, in slow motion, noticing and examining each wound, each bruise on the way, most of all the ones of which I was least conscious in my first headlong fall. But I know I have to do it. My future stands aside, waiting until I find meaning in all that has been. I feel as if I had to overcome some almost physical obstacle, and, feel drained, breathless from the effort.

It was long ago, but to me everything seems even sharper, more painful in the perspective of remembrance. When we lived those events, the intense, tortured spasm of will that let us survive also brought us partial anaesthesia. You live the horror, you lose your sense of it. Only afterward you realize that it all has happened, and that you survived. What you lived remains planted in you like a jagged crystal that starts growing, slowly, slowly, until there is no room for anything else and you become one searing pain, bursting its shell. And then you survive that, too. After that you only want to let it lie where it belongs, in the past.

Now I bear the past within me, stored away like a picture-postcard folder brought from a foreign land, all neat and tidy. But it all takes is to lift one corner and an endless snake, the sign of the viper, reaches out. One picture tumbles out after another and they start forming a sequence, crowding into the present, living time. They linger and come into focus. Sometimes a second of that past wedges so deeply into the workings of my internal time that it brings it to a halt. My time skips a beat, and a second of that irreplaceable, irretrievable present time is lost.

The mass deportations of Jews from Prague began in the fall of 1941. We had been ordered to report for transport, with no idea of our destination. The order was simply to report to the Trade Fair Hall, with food for several days and essential baggage. No more. When I got up that morning, my mother turned away from the window and said, almost childlike, "Look, the sun is rising. I thought not even the sun would rise today." But it rose, and on the streetcar people around us rode to their jobs as if it were just another day.

The scene in the Trade Fair Hall overwhelmed us. Our nerves were stretched to the breaking point. Several of the severely ill, brought there on stretchers, died that morning. There were women screaming in sheer hysteria—a Mrs. Tausig tore her dentures from her mouth and threw them at out lord and master, Obersturmbannführer Fiedler. She raved for several hours until the sounds she made were no longer human. There were small children and babies, too, weeping ceaselessly, while next to us a short, fat man with a shiny bald head sat on his suitcase as if it all did not concern him, playing Beethoven's Concerto in D major on a violin, practicing the difficult passages over and over again.

I wandered about, searching out familiar faces among those thousand people. That is where I first saw him. To this day

I think he was the handsomest man I ever saw. He sat upright, composed, on a black suitcase trimmed in silver, wearing a dark suit, a white shirt with a pearl gray tie, and a black overcoat. He had on a handsome black hat and was leaning on a stick-thin, tightly rolled umbrella. His eyes were gray, and so was his faultlessly trimmed beard. The hands folded on the handle of his umbrella were slender and well-groomed.

Amid the chaos of people bundled up in sweaters, heavy boots, and quilted jackets he stood out as if he were stark naked. I stopped before him, startled. He rose, bowed with a smile and offered me a place on the suitcase next to him. He was a professor of classical philology from Vienna. When the Germans had overrun Austria, he had escaped to Prague, and there the Germans caught up with him. I asked him why he had not selected something a bit more practical for a journey to God knew where, but he replied that he had always dressed like this and did not like to change his habits under the pressure of circumstances. In any case, he considered it most important to retain equanimity *"rebus in arduis."* Then he spoke of ancient Rome and classical literature. I sat there spell-bound. Later, I went to see him whenever I got a chance, and he never failed to welcome me with that courteous smile and, it seemed, with pleasure.

Two days later we were put on a train. In the following years I lived through infinitely more cruel transports, but this trip still seems the worst, perhaps because it was the first. If every beginning is hard, the beginning of something hard is hardest.

We had not become used to the sounds of blows and shots and to the anguished cries that always followed. We had not become used to the agonizing thirst, the unbreathable air in overcrowded freighters, to the cramps in a stiffened jaw.

When we arrived in Lodz it was snowing hard. It was only October, and all through the following three years I never saw such a snowstorm, even in the dead of winter.

We plowed laboriously through the snow from the railway stop. There we first saw all those who were dying of hunger, small children almost naked and barefoot in the snow. . . .

Several days later I wandered into a basement. There was

a group of young people from our transport sitting around a kerosene lantern on the floor. Someone was playing Czech folk songs on a mouth organ. The ceiling was course and vaulted, and the lamp cast long, pointed shadows as in a cathedral. And then I thought an angel should appear and mark in blood the foreheads of those destined to die. . . .

The concentration camp in Lodz, officially the Litzmannstadt Ghetto, was originally a tumble-down slum, without sewage, which the Germans walled off with a board fence and barbed wire. For some time after our arrival our transport group remained together in one of the few undamaged buildings, and I still occasionally saw the Viennese professor. Then another transport arrived, and we were ordered to find other housing. We scattered through the half-crumbled buildings where almost a hundred thousand Polish Jews were already crowded together, surviving in unimaginable conditions, and after that we lost sight of each other.

Our transport included our family physician, a fine old gentleman who had known me since birth. He was over seventy, but each day he would venture out, walking with even pace, cane in hand, to seek out those who needed help. We had little in the way of medicines, but he used to say that often it is enough for a doctor to come in, and the patient feels some relief. I was glad when he accepted my offer to help. After that, we wandered together from hovel to hovel, climbing countless stairs, often to give the sick no more than a kind word. Frequently I had to fetch a pail of water, wash the patient and clean up around him before the doctor could even examine him.

Once we walked into a room, almost completely bare but scrubbed clean, where a child was lying on a pile of rags, a boy of about four, by now no more than a tiny skeleton with huge eyes. His mother, very young and so thin that she herself looked like a child, was weeping quietly in a corner. The doctor pulled out his stethoscope, listened for a while, then caressed the boy's head and sighed. There was nothing more to do. Then the child turned to his mother with a stern expression and said calmly, factually, like an adult, "You see, mother? I kept telling you I was hungry but you would not give me anything to eat. And now I must die."

When we walked out, an old woman stopped us and asked us to go into the house next door. She told us to go and see a sick man there who had not come out in several days. The house was split from the roof to the ground, and looked ready to collapse, entirely deserted. It took us quite a while to find the one room with a door. We knocked but there was no answer. Finally the doctor opened the door and we went in. On the floor of the narrow room there was a torn mattress, in a corner a heap of rags and broken utensils, in another an open suitcase full of books. A dead man lay on the mattress, an open book on his chest. The book was a superb, illustrated study of ancient art, of the beauty that was Greece. Droves of white lace crawled over the dead man's face and over the face of the Venus of Milo, smiling serenely from the page.

I bent over him. It was my professor. The doctor said, "He hasn't been dead for more than a few hours."

About a year later, I was at work when I heard the fire bell. Though the fire alarm was among the daily events, I sensed that this time it was our house that was burning. Leaving work was strictly forbidden, but I sneaked out and ran along the walls to the half-crumbled tenement where we had a room. My mother, who had grown very frail, was anxiously throwing a few essentials into a suitcase. A while later my father came running. He, too, had little strength left, but he tried to help. My cousin Jindřišek lay immobile on his straw pallet on the floor, his young body gnawed out by tuberculosis. He could only follow us helplessly with his intense, sad black eyes.

The firemen encircled the house, and there was smoke and shouting. It was freezing, bitterly cold, there was no water—but still there was no panic. Even then we all had a sense of resignation. I helped my father drag out our two suitcases, then wrapped mother in a blanket and sat her down on them. Then we ran in to get Jindřišek. The firemen tried to stop us; one of them swung at me with his stick. My father blocked him and I ran in. Jindřišek tried to raise himself but couldn't; I shouted at him, furiously, desperately. He seemed terribly heavy, though he was bone thin. With one of his arms around my shoulders I dragged him out, shouting at him brutally. I wanted to give him something of my will, of my energy, just to get him out, over the threshold, across the yard, into the street. He collapsed at every step, but we finally managed it. I sat him down on a suitcase, mother covered him with a blanket and put his head on her lap. They sat there as after the crucifixion. I leaned my head on my father's shoulder and sobbed with relief.

In the end the firemen did put out the fire, and we all dragged ourselves back into the building with our suitcases. By then people started to help, though we all were exhausted from the effort and the excitement. When all was back in place, I heated a huge pot of water. Jindříšek was lying on the floor, facing the wall. His eyes were closed but there was a trace of a smile on his lips. I undressed and scrubbed myself slowly, thoroughly, and combed my hair. I dressed carefully, cleaned my shoes, and went back to work.

Jindříšek died some three weeks later. I came home at night and my mother whispered to me that he had asked her to sing the wistful national anthem, "Where Is My Home," and the folk song, "Whither Have Gone the Times of Old." Jindříšek was already in agony. I sat next to him on the floor and tried to cram a bit of food into his mouth. He was barely conscious, but the urge for food was so strong that he clamped down on the spoon and fought me when I tried to take it out of his mouth. I put my hands under his head. Soon afterward he stopped breathing.

My mother was praying, but I kept asking myself what reason there could be for praying for someone who died at sixteen, after suffering so much. There is nothing more pointless, nothing more cruel than dying before we can be guilty of anything that would justify death. For a long time I kept seeing those black, wistful, forlorn eyes in the corner that had been his.

Sometimes I think that when people speak of time past, they do not know what they are saying. The real past is what Jindříšek thought of when he was lying on his straw on the ground and watched me walk out into the sun and the bitter frost, and what was in my mother's mind as she sang "Where Is My Home" to her dying nephew behind the barbed wire in Lodz. The real past is whatever leaves no touchable memory behind.

People have often asked me about the Stalin years. Didn't

you know? Didn't you know that the Communists had reopened the concentration camps, that people were again being beaten and tortured, that humanity had again become a privilege—and a stroke of luck?

No, we did not know. If someone had told us, we would not have been capable of believing it. In the 1950s foreign broadcasts used to speak of what was happening behind the official facade in our country, but to us it seemed simply proof that "the imperialists" lie about us. It isn't hard for a totalitarian regime to keep people ignorant. Once a man decides to believe, it becomes difficult for him to know. Once he exchanges freedom for understood necessity, for socialism, for the glory or greatness of the homeland, for any of the substitutes that often seem so persuasive, he gives up truth. Slowly, a drop at a time, life begins to drain out of him as surely as if he had slashed his veins, and he becomes incapable of knowing.

Let me tell you one other episode. In the last concentration camp I passed through we worked in a brick kiln, owned by a civilian, far from the camp. It was late autumn, beautiful but cold. In the morning, when we stood for roll call long before dawn, the ground was covered with a heavy blanket of hoarfrost, which would not melt until noontime. We had nothing to wear except our brief shifts made of burlap sacking, no underwear, no shoes. We used to collect scraps of paper at the work site, especially the heavy cement sacks, and even though it was strictly forbidden we used to wrap them around our bodies, under our shifts, so that we would freeze a little less. The morning roll call took two hours, then a grotesque little train made up of flatcars with two long benches carried us the hour's distance to work. Then a half-hour march to the brick kiln, where we passed along bricks for twelve hours, then the trip back to the camp, another roll call, a bowl of weak turnip soup and a piece of bread, and finally a short and restless night.

For most of the girls the trip on the train was the worst part. In the course of the hour we would freeze through and through; at the end of the ride, we did not so much get off as fall off, and it would take us half a day's work to warm up a bit. But I used to love those trips. The track led over an underground factory complex. In many places steam rose from the ground, and the forest was broken up by mysterious iron structures and fantastically tangled pipes. The sun would just be rising, and because a heavy fog blanketed the ground, the sun's rays broke in and dyed it now deep pink, now orange, now gold or blue. Out of that glowing mist dark silhouettes of trees and bushes emerged, flowed toward us, passed by and disappeared again. There were several clusters of trees that seemed especially beautiful. I used to wait for them each day: I still remember one small mound where a young pine lay uprooted and a second, a handsome, symmetrically shaped tree stood upright and serious beside it, as if it were standing guard over the body of a fallen comrade.

On Sundays we would work inside the camp, but usually there were no meals because the woman commandant had calculated that even turnips for a thousand people could be turned into a pretty penny. So on Sundays we held fast until the managers of the factories where we worked started complaining that on Mondays the girls kept fainting and were not worth their cost.

The brick kiln, which rented about fifty of us from the camp, belonged to an odd character. I think he must have been Russian or German-Russian by origin. He was thin, grey-haired, and wore a Russian-style, black, belted shirt. To our amusement, he constantly threatened that if we did not work for the victory of the Reich, the Russians would come and kill us all. One Monday, after another Sunday fast, a trainload of coal arrived at the kiln and we were ordered to unload it as fast as possible. The coal came in huge chunks and was mixed with heavy stones. Few of us were strong enough to pick up a shovel. After several hours most of the girls had fallen down on the piles of coal, exhausted to a state of unconsciousness. Then the owner of the brick kiln arrived furious. "What kind of workers are you, anyway? Don't you even know how to hold a shovel? I am not paying for you to have you lie around here!"

I don't know what got into me. Perhaps I was beside myself with hunger, but I threw down my shovel and started shouting at him. I demanded what right he had to scream at us, that we were students and educated women and if he wanted us to do pick-and-shovel work he should at least make sure we were treated as well as laborers. The girl lying on the coals nearest me grabbed my ankles and tried to drag me down to the ground to silence me, but I could not stop screaming. The man looked at me for a while, but to everyone's amazement did not reach for his pistol, did not call a guard, just turned around and left. For the rest of the day we worked in terror, wondering what my mad scene would mean for us all. But nothing happened.

The following day, as soon as we picked up our shovels, the owner showed up. *"Wo ist die Studentin?"* he asked. The fury was long since gone out of me, I was stiff with fear and preparing myself to die as he led me out of the kiln. But that strange man simply announced, drily and almost courteously, that from now on I would work at the furnace, bringing coal from the piles in a wheelbarrow and firing the furnaces. To work under a roof, in warmth, was the greatest dream of all inmates, but this work was heavy labor even for two men. I could never have managed were it not for my fellow workers at the furnace, POWs, Frenchmen, good lads who came to my aid again and again and often did most of the work for me.

One evening the owner came in with two Frenchmen and ordered them to help me bring in a supply of coal. About an hour later he came back, chased them out and asked me to sit beside him on a stone ledge by the wall of the furnace and then said only, "Tell me about it."

For the rest of my life I shall not forget that dark cavern, the black walls flashing with the rays from the fire, the old man, dressed in black, who listened and listened and seemed to shrink away as if with every sentence a piece of him withered. I have lived through something like that only once more, one other time—with my own child, when I finally dared tell him how his father had died.

And so I spoke of the camp in Lodz, where cesspool cleaners whistled Beethoven at work and where a hundred thousand human beings died of starvation or were murdered; I told of the trains arriving constantly from Polish villages, bringing men with bloody heads and women wrapped up in scarves. When the trains left, the women started unwrapping their shawls and pulling out babies, many already suffocated but some still living, saved from German bayonets. Several months later the SS would come, pile those same babies into wagons and drive them off to the gas chambers. I told of the public executions and men left hanging on the gallows for weeks while we walked by on our way to work; of freightcars full of bloody clothes, which we tore into strips and wove into mats for German tanks so that the soldiers would not freeze their feet. And I told of the time when the front lines finally came so close that we could hear the noise of the battle and a German colonel, all decked out in gold braid, calling us together and declared, "You have nothing to fear. The camp must be evacuated but I give you my German officer's word of honor that nothing bad will happen to you and that you will be well cared for. . . ." A week later those who survived the transport in sealed cattle cars walked through the gate in the electrified wire fence, straight into the black smoke of Auschwitz.

By then I had forgotten where I was, to whom I was speaking. I saw once more the barracks of Auschwitz, a former horse stall, where a thousand completely shaved, half-insane girls were packed together, howling under the whips like a pack of wolves. The women in charge, as insane with fury as we with pain and horror, dashed back and forth in the path in the middle of the block and struck aimlessly with their whips at the girls crammed in the stalls. Over it all, Mrs. Stein from Prague stood, shaved bare like the rest of us, singing "The Fireflies Gather Around my Golden Hair" at the command of the block commandant who ordered that her barracks must be happy. I saw us all again kneeling on hard, sandy ground, supporting those who fainted because whoever fell would never rise again. It was a time when a girl had attempted escape and all of Auschwitz had to kneel all day and all night until she was caught. Then we had to stand at roll call and watch as they broke her arms and legs before hauling her off to a gas chamber.

I did not speak much of Auschwitz. Words can express only what a mind can hold, no one can describe hammer blows that dash his brains to tatters. But I explained in detail how we lived in the concentration camp from where we came daily to work. I told him that there were among us girls brought in recently, straight from their homes, and several dozen of them proved to be pregnant. One evening the matrons called them together, locked the main barracks after them, and we never saw those girls again. But in the morning the commandant ordered out a special detail to wash pools of blood from the barrack floor.

I don't remember what else I told him, but I know that all that time he did not say a word, and when I heard shouting and orders outside and got up to join my fellow prisoners for the return trip to camp, he remained sitting there, huddled with his head in his hands. That man lived in Nazi Germany, came into daily contact with the inmates of the concentration camp, and still he knew nothing—I am quite sure of it, he knew nothing. He thought we were common criminals, duly sentenced by a court of law for proven crimes. . . .

ii. Defiance
In the last months of the war, the Germans could no longer spare railway cars to transport slave labor. When the front inched close to our last concentration camp, our guards herded all the thousand inmates together, issued us an extra ration of bread, and set out with us, day after day, week after week, toward the heart of Germany.

Our column moved slowly through the frozen snow; few of us had enough life left to turn around when our redheaded guard, Franz, fired a shot. He was an ordinary soldier who spent most of his time hovering around one of the girls—her name was Eva, she was barely more than a child and wept through each night. Franz fluttered around her, almost fatherly in his concern, and even managed to procure some food for her. Only now and then, usually when we rounded some convenient turn, he would spin around and fire at random toward the stragglers at the rear. If he scored a hit, he would run off with one of the other guards and the two of them would dig perfunctorily for a bit. Then he'd be back, dancing around terrified Eva.

For days I walked with my head bent, watching my bare feet in the frozen slush on the road and speaking quietly with Hanka, the girl next to me; speaking about freedom, about the possibility of escape. One day, when we passed a crude wooden road sign with the legend PRAG in black, we clasped hands and solemnly swore we would not turn off from that road: come what may, we would make it to Prague. It was a bit ludicrous, especially since we didn't believe it ourselves, but it was a good feeling.

We had thought of nothing else from the moment we left the concentration camp, accompanied by the echo of pistol shots as the SS finished off the girls in the hospital barracks. Many of us had the same idea. Some of the girls even made a tentative attempt: they would hide in the hedges and wait for the column to pass. But invariably they rejoined us at the end. It was just too difficult to face unknown danger alone.

Hanka had spoken of it—"You see, if we keep walking in a herd, there is nothing anyone can expect of us except to walk and walk and finally let Franz shoot us at some turn. We don't have to reproach ourselves, no one could expect us to do more. But if we were free, it would be up to us. We'd have to act."

That was just it. Shuffling along together we had a sense of belonging, the knowledge that we were all equally frozen, starved, and abused. We had a common fate, a common road underfoot and somewhere along that road even a common death. But if we broke free . . . and then it would dawn on me: at this moment it would take no more than a single act, a single decision, to win the greatest freedom one could have in our age, in our corner of the world. As soon as I slipped out from under the bayonets, I would be standing outside the entire system. I might win only a few days, more likely a few hours, but it would be a freedom millions didn't even dare dream about. I would belong nowhere, I would belong to nothing. No one would know I existed, all the rules and prohibitions would no longer apply to me. I would be outside, outside of it all. When they caught me, I would be like a wind trapped in a sail, a bird shot in flight.

Most of the nights on the march we slept in the open, under guard. But one evening, when our column came closest to the Czech border, we halted in a village. We waited for a long time in the muddy square, sensing the eyes examining us behind the curtained windows. Then our guards marched us off to a large farm complex at one side of the village, past a picket fence, through a narrow door in a brick wall to an old barn. That meant sleeping under a roof, and Hanka whispered to me, "At least we don't have to agonize tonight—two fences and a locked barn—not even a mouse could slip away."

We stomped our feet in the mud and waited for the two warm potatoes the villagers provided from their own supply. Then we surged into the barn, trying to capture a spot where it would be less likely that someone might step on our faces with a wooden clog in the total darkness. I stood casually by the door. Toward morning no one would be watching; the guards always took a nap when they could lock us up. The lock was an ordinary padlock, hinge hanging on two rusty nails. Ridiculous.

"Listen," someone grabbed my hand and drew me behind the open door. "I heard tomorrow we'll turn north. We'll never again be so close."

There—did everyone know what I had in mind?

"And look, I managed to get shoes. They don't match, and the soles are wired on, but they'll be better than nothing."

I hid the shoes gratefully under my coat. One more glance at the lock—better pull out one of the nails now. For just such a chance I had hoarded my greatest treasure, a small pocket knife. The nail came out easily; it was the decision to pull it out that was hard. Before going to sleep, we whispered about it vaguely with Hanka. But the leap to freedom was too enormous, too dizzying. It demanded a clear decision, and we had almost forgotten how to think and decide. We fell asleep in the middle of a word, without a plan.

I woke up early with a start, dimly aware that I would miss something crucial. Something I had to do, right now. Oh, yes. Around me there was the quiet rustling of straw, the sound of many human beings breathing, as if some great, tired animal were stretching in the dark. But lighter strips showed through the cracks in the wall; it would soon be daylight. I shook off the knee digging into my ribs from the right. "Hanka, what about it?"

Hanka awoke at once; she knew what I was asking but could not grasp it either. "I feel so dreadfully chilly," she whispered and burrowed deeper into the straw. I got up—the half-torn lock proved no obstacle. The guard was still off somewhere, snoring. It was still dark, but not for long: there was a promise of light in the black sky.

I put a piece of cloth on my head in place of a kerchief to cover my stubby hair. Less than half a year ago, my head had been shaved bare at Auschwitz. Then I stomped my feet idly, picking pieces of straw off my coat. Still no one came. At long last the door opened and Hanka slipped out. I gave her no time to think but ran off toward the wall. It was broken down in places and not hard to cross. Then quickly over the fence. Behind us another head appeared over the wall. I climbed the fence without difficulty, Hanka after me, and we ran a few steps to hide in a nook formed by the wall of the neighboring farm. Another girl came running breathlessly. It was Zuzka: "Máňa and Andula are coming, too."

Then we saw Máňa running and almost at the same moment heard a rifle shot. Andula was too late. We pressed in our corner, shaking almost audibly. Someone was saying, "Come on, let's go back."

"Nonsense. Now that I'm out, I'm not crawling back. There'll be chaos, and the old man will give the guards hell for killing a girl in the middle of a village. You know he does not like that. Then they'll call the roll, and before they've counted the girls and figured out how to explain to the old man that they are four heads short, we've got to be gone."

This seemed logical, and calmed us all. It was dawn now, and from our nook we had a good view of the flat countryside and the hills lining the horizon. There was not much snow; the dominant colors were those of the earth and the bare trees. The country was open as a palm, without a trace of a forest or any other cover. In the distance we could see groups of men, marching under bayonets; probably prisoners of war.

Now there were footsteps around the corner. We crouched in our hiding place. Then, suddenly, a tiny, thin girl of about twelve stood before us, holding out two big slices of bread.

"Don't be afraid of me, I know who you are."

When I managed to tear my eyes away from the bread, I said, "You must not speak with us, little girl. Run on home." The Germans shot whole families without trial on suspicion of contact with escaped prisoners. The girl smiled and thrust out the bread at us.

"Go ahead, take it. We have enough. I'll lead you away from here. I know you want to go home and you don't know the way."

With my mouth full of bread I whispered in near panic, "Run away! What would your mother say?" But the child just pointed off to the side where an older woman in a shawl emerged around the corner and nodded to us.

"That's my mother. She sent me. We're Czech, too."

We could comprehend none of it. All we knew was that it was high time to be gone, and so we set out, ripping off the concentration camp squares of striped cloth from each other's back as we walked after our little guide.

The countryside was completely awake by then. Fortunately the roads were full of people. Bands of slave laborers marched under bayonets; wagons with evacuees rattled on, piled high with the odds and ends of households; local people hurried by to work. Many people looked at us. But we walked on, tense and choking with mad joy. For the first time in years without bayonets, without electric or barbed wire! Hanka, a reflective soul, plodded purposefully beside me, meditating out loud:

"You know, the only thing I don't like about this is that now we really are completely outside the law. . . ." I looked at her and broke out laughing, roaring until tears flowed from my eyes. I laughed as I hadn't laughed in five years.

It grew dark early on this wintry day. Our little guide had left us long ago, but she had given us advice—where to go, who might help, whom to avoid. Thanks to her we managed to walk almost to the demarcation line separating the parts of Czechoslovakia that now were annexed to the German Reich from the truncated rump known officially as the Protectorate of Bohemia and Moravia. We were cold, hungry, and desperately tired. But those few hours of freedom had transformed us. The apathetic, deathly worn shadows that had escaped more out of despair than hope had been seized by a wild determination to live. We began to believe there might, after all, be not only a way out of bondage, but even a way back to life. Fear and hope drove us along the narrow path that heavy-handed reason would never have attempted to follow—fear and hope, which saved us so many times in the years when there were few opportunities for courage and reason.

The road turned down into a valley, toward a village and a large factory. We stopped a young boy: "Where does Mr. Čermák live?"

"There is no Čermák here."

"Oh . . . I must have the wrong name. But he is Czech. Is there a Czech living somewhere here?"

The lad sounded hostile. "There are no Czechs here."

We stared at each other, taken aback. Then we heard the siren; the end of the shift at the factory. A group of women came walking toward us, workers from the plant. They spoke loudly as they came. Thank God, Poles. We stood aside, waiting for a woman walking alone. She had blonde hair, and looked worn, though she couldn't have been much older than we were. Zuzka got up her courage and stepped toward her:

"Prosze pani. . . ."

Yes, she was Polish. She led us to a tumble-down shack where a tiny girl, almost a baby, was waiting for her. We recited a story about having been assigned to work in the Reich, having been bombed out and lost our documents, and concluded with the question, how can we cross the demarcation line.

Our hostess gave no indication of believing or doubting our tale. But she did offer to lead us to a Czech woman who lived in the village. We waited until it was completely dark and then tiptoed fearfully after her through the whole long village. Finally we stopped at a small, neat house. Our guide knocked, a woman's voice replied, and the door opened wide. From the speed with which our Polish friend disappeared in the darkness I knew she had not believed our story, and realized what a chance she had taken in accompanying us.

Mrs. Němcová, our new hostess, chubby and energenic, frankly paid no attention to our story. She seated us at her table, that was covered with a sparkling white cloth, in the beautifully clean kitchen and placed a loaf of bread in the center. We stared in disbelief: no one could be that lavish. But Mrs. Němcová took a knife and cut us each a slice so big that half the loaf disappeared. For a moment everything melted away, the whole world stood respectfully aside and there was nothing but the four of us, soaring through space with that huge, sweet-smelling, fabulous hunk of bread.

Mrs. Němcová seemed familiar with people of our type. By half past ten she led us out, explaining that there would be dancing at the tavern and everyone, including the police, would be drunk. We could hear the music from the village, dogs barking and distant voices.

Mrs. Němcová took Hanka's hand and mine; Zuzka with Máňa followed close behind. We sneaked past the blacked-out houses, the bare, silent gardens, and then ran barefoot across the frozen furrows of the fields, holding on to our shoes to avoid losing them in the darkness. I could hear Hanka sobbing quietly and Mrs. Němcová whispering encouragements. We ran faster and faster, not knowing where. Just as we thought we could not manage another step, Mrs. Němcová stopped. "There, you are almost home. You can run a bit slower now, but don't linger. The watchman by the barrier is all right, don't be afraid of him, but watch out for the next village—there the policemen have dogs."

We embraced her and ran on, alone again. Hanka moaned that she could go no further, but I dragged her by the hand, whispering, "On all fours if we have to, but we will make it home."

At last we reached the barrier at the frontier. We crawled cautiously under it, but still the guardhouse door opened. We could hear a cross voice behind us, "Just some god-damned women. You'll get no smokes from them." Then the door closed again and we ran on along the road. We decided to avoid the dangerous village with the police dogs and to go on through the fields instead. Zuzka, whose home was nearby, invited us all with a flourish. She was only half Jewish, and some of her family had not been deported. Gratefully, patiently we crept through the silence full of sounds, through the darkness full of shadows.

For the first time since I opened my eyes this morning I felt the tension leaving me. I was still trying to pierce the darkness ahead, still registered every whisper, but something in me began to relax. It seemed to me that I held freedom cupped in my hands, wondering what I would do with it, what I would make of it. It might be for a short span only, there was no time to waste.

At that point I did not dare to think of what I'd do when I reached Prague—I knew I might never reach it. But my life was no longer torn in two. There was continuity; I was no longer a prisoner, I was a human being, a woman with a past and a future.

The first step had succeeded, I had escaped. Now I faced a different problem: to find a home once more, to find a place where I would belong. But homecoming takes more than a return. The second step, from the lonely freedom of an escaped bird to freedom among people, proved to be the hardest. Not only for us former prisoners, but for all our people. Sometimes I think that for many of the idealistic, dedicated people the revolution was an attempt to fight their way home, to fight their way back to being human.

The beginning of my homecoming was hopeful enough. Zuzka's relatives gave us food, found shelter for Máňa, and even found a ride in a truck most of the way to Prague for Hanka and me.

We walked the last few miles and caught a streetcar at the outskirts of the city. We were painfully aware of the risk we were running. If the Germans caught us, it would mean death not only for us, but for anyone who helped us or associated with us. In the city the police were constantly searching houses, checking identity papers—and anyone could denounce us. One close look told anyone who cared that there was something not quite in order about us.

In the center of the city, Hanka shook my hand for the last time and went off. I remained alone, standing in the corner at back of the streetcar and watching my fellow passengers. They, too, had their cares, God knows what they had been through. It may not have been as dramatic as what I had lived through, but any suffering can be unbearable; these people around me could be as worn out by running for the air-raid shelter and waiting in endless food lines as I was by life in the concentration camps.

Prague had changed over the years, perhaps more than I had.

Most of the people I had known, friends and relatives, had been deported. My one hope was Jenda, who had been our closest friend, almost one of the family. I felt confident that if he had changed, it could only be for the better. On the eve of out deportation, Jenda came to our apartment, gave each of us some memento and declared, a bit formally: "No matter what happens, no matter where they send you, my place shall always be your firm rallying point. Send messages to me if you can, when you return you will all meet again at my place. And if anything happens to me, I shall arrange for someone to take this over for me. Rely on me in everything, I will always be prepared, I will always be waiting for you. You will always have a place to come back to."

It was getting dark when I reached Jenda's apartment. My legs ached; just walking up the stairs became a struggle. If only Jenda was home! I arranged the scarf on my head and smiled as I pressed the bell. The door opened, my heart leaped to my throat—it was Jenda! I had won!

He did not seem to recognize me, but that was hardly surprising. I smiled again. Then Jenda's eyes flashed recognition, but what followed was not happy surprise, but an expression of such horrible shock, such terror that the smile froze on my lips. Without a word he drew me inside, threw a terrified glance at the stairs, and closed the door carefully. "In God's name, what brings you here?"

I stared at his pale face: this pathetic, frightened wretch who does not dare look me in the eye, could this be Jenda? I looked around the room, searching for something familiar, intimate. Yes, there was his library, the easy chair by the window, all that was familiar. There was also a new red rug, a new record player, and some paintings I had not seen before.

We stood in silence, facing each other. Then he spoke. I did not let him explain overmuch, it was all clear without words. I could see how hard it was for him—but fear, fear was stronger than all else. He could not think of anything but to keep clear of the deadly danger that had walked in with me—had anyone seen me on the stairs? He had to make sure I would never come back, I would let him live. He had to shut out the death and despair of others. But I think that as he spoke he knew his peace was gone. He might never see me again, but his life would not be the same.

Then I was out in the street again. It was dark, the streets were deserted. I had nowhere to turn. I thought of an old woman who had been my father's secretary and a friend of the family. We had left some clothes with her for safekeeping when we left. Perhaps she could keep me overnight.

I was sorry to give her such a shock, but she proved a brave old woman. As soon as I pressed the bell, I could hear her slippered feet shuffling down the hall. When she got over her first shock, she welcomed me, weeping, and sat me down on the old velveteen sofa, by the wall covered with old family photographs.

"Let me stay just one night, Auntie," I apologized. "Tomorrow I'll find a place to stay." She nodded, her eyes full of tears. Movement seemed to be her antidote to excitement: she wandered around the room, opening every closet, and found me a complete set of clothes from prewar days to make me less conspicuous in the street. Then she bedded me down on the sofa, covering me with a checkered blanket. She sat down by the door, her hands folded, as if her vigil could preserve us from all evil.

In the morning I walked out again into the empty streets. I felt better: I had warm clothes, I had slept and eaten breakfast. But my situation had changed: up to now I had only the police apparatus of a fascist state to contend with. Now I had to face a far worse enemy, human fear and indifference. Up to now I had a clear, precise goal— to reach Prague and find Jenda. Now I was striking out toward an indefinite possibility—I had to find a human being whose humanity would be stronger than his fear.

I walked the familiar streets, waiting for the morning and relishing the sense of having come back. Franta, another friend, lived nearby. If he could not help me himself, at least he could tell me what others were doing. He had been an ambitious, conscientious lad, struggling through the university while supporting his mother. He had slaved from morning till night, working on farms during vacations, tutoring less bright students and accepting even the hardest work to earn something to help his mother. He never doubted his ability or his goals. The war must have crossed his plans, too.

Franta faced me, unshaven, dressed in a pair of shapeless old trousers. He stared at me without a word, then stepped back and let me into the hall.

"Franta, I escaped from a concentration camp. I need help. Do you know any place where I could hide for a few days and rest up? Do you know anyone who has contacts with the underground? The war is almost over. It's a matter of a few months at most."

I could not see his face in the dark hall, and he did not speak a word. Finally he opened a door and motioned for me to come in and sit down. I watched him pacing nervously for a moment. Then he sat down opposite me, pulled out a cigarette, examined it, laid it down, and finally picked it up and lit it. He scrutinized me carefully.

"I have to look you over. I have to look at someone who escapes from a concentration camp, wanders around without papers, has no place to lay down her head—and thinks she can survive. That is really exciting. Ever since the occupation I have tried in vain to win a sense of personal freedom, at least for an hour, at least for a moment. Frankly, I don't think it can be done. You freed yourself from outright bondage, and now you find yourself in something worse. You must hide, run, and in the end they'll catch you anyway. Sorry, but I can't imagine how you could save yourself. You did what seemed best to you, but it goes against all reason. Look, I could pretend I'll try to help you. I could make promises and tell lies. But there is no point to it. If you look at it rationally, you'll see it's hopeless. I'm sorry, but I can do nothing."

I got up without speaking and started for the door. Franta leaped up and barred my way.

"Please don't leave yet," he pleaded. "I want you to understand. This is something I have puzzled over endlessly. Is it right to risk one's life if you can help it? You escaped because you probably thought you'd die anyway. But I think that you're much more likely to be killed here than in the concentration camp. Somebody, after all, has to survive even there. Now you have much less hope. Is it right for me or anyone to risk his life for something that is that hopeless? What is the point of risking one life for the sake of another? Life is the only thing I have left. What right do I have to throw it away?"

I stepped back and tried to make him look me in the eye. Franta tossed away his cigarette. He was silent for a moment, then he said hoarsely,

"Yes, you are right. All right, I'm scared."

I trudged across Prague once more. There was another friend, Marta. She did not live in an apartment, but in a small house with a garden, high up near the top of the Břevnov district, on the opposite end of Prague. It might be less conspicuous.

The air-raid alarm sounded twice before I got there. Alarms were as dangerous as streetcars: the police and the air-raid wardens checked the identity papers of anyone caught in the street—and they frequently checked them in the shelters as well. Each time, I managed to slip inside a doorway, hiding in a corner and passing the time wondering what Marta would be doing. It was not hard to imagine. She'd be painting, that is the better side of her life. And waiting for Vláďa, her husband —because that is the other, worse side of her life. Just now, close to noon, she has probably put down her brushes and is fixing Vláďa's lunch. I'd better hurry to reach her before he got home.

Marta stepped back in surprise when she saw me at the

garden gate, but then her face lit up. She did not embrace me, did not fuss, but sat me down in her warm kitchen and showed no trace of fear. Fatigue settled on me and I could barely manage a few sentences. But that was enough for Marta.

"It's marvelous you've come," I heard her saying. "It will be a while yet before Vláda comes, and so listen, I have a lot to tell you. You have no more worries, Vláda will help you. Don't look so surprised, it is true. I know what you and all our friends thought of Vláda. And I have to admit I was coming to agree with you. About a year ago I told him I would leave him. He pleaded, promised to change. And he changed, completely. You will see. He started working with the resistance, and is doing just what you need. He is helping conceal refugees and partisans, he even helped some across the border. At first he did not want to tell me about it, but you know how hard it is for Vláda to keep from saying something good about himself.

"I can see you think I've made the whole war into a private affair; I'm terrible, and you are right. But this war, which hit you so hard and destroyed so many people, actually brought me happiness. It is a horror and a shame, but that is how it is. I am dreadfully afraid for him, and still I am happy. He's coming now—let me meet him and tell him about you."

Marta disappeared in the hall. She came back soon, followed by Vláda. He really had changed. No more the pretty playboy of the prewar years, he was thinner, his face furrowed with wrinkles. Acutally, he was rather more handsome, but there was something in his eyes I could not understand. He shook hands, tried to smile.

"Marta told me you escaped from a concentration camp. You are really quite a woman. I wish I could help you but.. . ."

Marta startled. "What happened?"

"An awkward accident. The man I was to meet tonight will not come. The connection broke down somehow. It's hard, but it is the sort of thing we have to expect."

"Contact someone else. You've told me how you have everything covered. You can rebuild your contacts."

"Sure, sure, but it takes time. Today is out of the question. It will take a week, perhaps ten days."

"In that case we'll hide Heda here for a few days. Vláďa, we'll put her in the cubbyhole by the attic; she'll be out of sight and warm there."

"Marta!" Vláďa's face contorted in terror and beads of sweat broke out on his forehead. "Don't you know they shoot people for helping escapees?"

"But you've been doing it for almost a year . . . or . . . you said you were doing it . . . Vláďa. . . ."

Vláďa collapsed on a chair, his knees shaking. Marta raised her hand to her lips, so white that her black hair and eyes seemed painted on the wall behind her. I pushed back my chair, got up and tiptoed out of the kitchen. Neither of them noticed my leaving.

It was a long way to Vinohrady; again I walked all across Prague. I feared that my aching legs would no longer carry me. I decided to risk a streetcar, at least for a few stops. By late afternoon I managed to reach Milena's apartment. She had always been my best friend, ever since grade school. Later, when we were in our late adolescence, Ota, the man she was to marry, used to wait for her after school and walk us both home.

Ota opened the door. He looked incredulous at first, but then he drew me into the apartment and in a moment I felt Milena embracing me.

"I am so glad you are here! I was so afraid I'd never see you again. You can stay here, I won't let you leave. We'll fix up a place for you. You have to tell us everything, but no, first rest. I'll fix you something to eat. Yes, we have food, you know, grandmother has a farm. Now just come see my son and daughter. We'll talk about it later, first lie down and get some rest."

I let her lead me to a sofa and tuck me in as if I were her third child. Her mother covered me and drew the curtains, then sat beside me, stroking my hair—it had been so long since anyone had done that. I closed my eyes. So something has not changed, something has survived. Here I can catch my breath, start a new life. A day or two of rest, then I'll go somewhere, perhaps into the forests. . . . Milena and Ota can find me contacts. . . . All will be well . . . I'm lucky. . . . I don't have to drag my aching body over the pavements tonight. . . . Milena . . . so brave . . . even though she had her mother to think of . . . and her children . . . those two tiny babies. . . .

I jerked myself awake, my mind suddenly clear. Those two children! And the old woman! If Milena and Ota were alone, I would not have hesitated for a moment. But those small children! Lucky no one had seen me on the stairs! I must get away, right now.

For just a moment I closed my eyes and forgot I had to go on, that nothing was over, nothing resolved, and it would be night in a few hours. I lay with my eyes closed, listening to the clock. In the kitchen Milena, Ota, and Grandmother were whispering like conspirators. Ota was drawing a sketch—they probably wanted to wall in some corner for a hiding place.

I had to talk first, trying to speak concisely and, for the sake of the old woman, to leave out my worst memories. Then at last I got to ask about other friends. How many were left? Two, Zdenka and Ruda. Zdenka had married, she and her husband shared her parents' apartment. Ruda, Milena told me, would be hard to find: he was constantly away from Prague, only once in several months he'd show up for a weekend. Then he would come in alone, unannounced, tired and silent. He would sit for a while, listen, then leave again.

Finally I forced myself to tell Ota and Milena that I was leaving. They argued, tried to persuade me, but they could tell my mind was made up. Milena, troubled and worried, prepared a huge bag of food for me, clothes, odds and ends I might need. I promised to let them know and to come back if I found no other way, but I knew that I must not and would not come back.

Outside it was growing dark. I could no longer think of anything but that I must not be caught in the streets at night, that I must find shelter. I remembered Mrs. Machová, who helped raise me before the war. She lived with her husband in Pankrac, in an apartment house where he worked as a janitor. She welcomed me as a long-lost daughter. She did not want to let me go, but there was no room to hide me in her one-room apartment, with tenants coming in at all hours. In the end she sat down at her table and started to weep. Then she had an idea: one of the tenants was away and his apartment would be empty until the next day. I could sleep there, if I got away before dawn. The whole house was asleep when I tiptoed up the dark staircase, slipped into the empty apartment, and quietly, alert as a stray cat, huddled on a strange sofa.

It was still dark and very cold when I was again walking on the deserted streets. When the day came, it turned into a nightmare. Once again I wandered from friend to friend and even to stranger—perhaps the criminal underworld could hide me. But my one contact, a Czech policeman, thought willing, knew of nothing. In the end I had only one hope left, my friend Zdena. When I rang her doorbell, her mother opened the door for me—chubby, glowing, with a baby on her arm. She stood there, looking at me, and her face grew pale, her body trembled. She held out the child toward me like a crucifix and screamed, "For God's sake, go away! Can't you see? This child. . . . For Christ's sake, go away! For the sake of the child, go away. . . !"

I ran down the stairs, darkness in my eyes. Damn it, damn it, damn it, this is too much, this is the end of it, no more, no more! If it goes on like this, there'll soon be no people in my world. I'll lose what even the concentration camps and the war could not take away.

I passed along some streets, to the edge of the city. Out in the field I tripped on lumps of frozen soil and thought back to three days ago, when I was tripping on frozen ground, running and repeating to myself, "On all fours if we have to, but home. . . ."

The sky was clear and high above me. In two, three months it would be spring, all the colors would change and perhaps the war might be over. But three months was too long. My dash for life just hadn't worked out, for reasons other than I had feared, but in the end the difference was not much. I still had one freedom left, the freedom of dying my own way. It had been a magnificent try even if it had failed. Even if dying would be harder now.

Then I saw a small church before me, with people walking in. They were not likely to check identity cards there. I slipped in and collapsed in a carved pew. There were only a few people, mostly women, and I could afford to relax. I closed my eyes and thought of nothing. Only a good while later I could feel something running down my cheeks. I felt numb and could not help myself. I sat there, the tears flowing down my face. I felt no special pain, no fear, no regret. I was just endlessly tired, infinitely distant from myself; I could not think or wish anything. I just kept on repeating, life . . . life. . . .

For a while I had been aware that the priest was preaching about something, and finally, managed to concentrate. He spoke of the women who had seen Christ's suffering, felt compassion, but did nothing to help. He spoke of effective repentance, of helping others. What if I went to him after mass and told him I was someone on whom he could practice his preaching? Help me, let me sleep a few nights in some corner of your church: as soon as I recover, I'll move on. I considered it, but finally decided against it. If friends did not help, how would a complete stranger respond? He could report me straight away. His preaching does not mean anything—all who turned me away in the last two days paid lip service to the same ideals.

I did not want to leave, but there was no alternative. The city was veiling itself in a mother-of-pearl dusk, the day was beautiful even when it was dying. The streets were full of people. I wandered slowly back through the city toward the river. It was not frozen; this would be the best way. I am a good swimmer, and had to ensure myself against a last-minute rescue. Milena's bag, loaded with stones, would do.

That took care of the details, and I tried not to think of it any more. But somehow I could think of nothing else. It was not an easy walk. It was evening again, almost dark. My head roared and my whole body burned; I was feverish and the wounds on my feet were festering. Leaning on the bridge railing I could see the river below, black and cold, whispering to itself. The distance seemed immense. Behind me, people were walking on the bridge; I could hear their footsteps and fragments of their conversations. They were quite close and so infinitely far away. I laid my hand on the cold stone rail. I remember thinking quite distinctly, This is the end of my journey. Here is my freedom, the freedom no one even dreams of. And no one really wants. The freedom of a bird, freedom of the wind, freedom without people. Freedom without a way out, lonely, threatening freedom, like the river below me.

At that moment two uniformed men pressed against me from both sides, and deluged me with the drumfire of some German dialect. I stiffened with horror, no, they must not get me! Not now, at the last moment! I broke out with all my strength and one of the men laughed. Only then did I look at them. They were not SS, just ordinary German soldiers. They made no attempt to stop me. I mumbled something indistinct, turned around and tripped away. I was long out of earshot and could still hear their laughter, ever louder behind me. My head resounded with its echo like a thundering bell. I kept seeing sparks before my eyes, my legs seemed to melt under my weight, my heart did not want to return to its usual place. This is really the end, I repeated to myself, I cannot go on. Let the end come, any end, just an end, end. . . .

But there were still too many people along the river, and it was not safe for me to stay too long in one spot. I dragged myself along unthinkingly, the sidewalk swaying under me at every step, the streets, the darkness, shadows, voices, the creeping, stabbing pain in my forehead, the streets, the shadows, voices. . . . I realized where I was only when I stood before the house where Ruda used to live. Did he still use this apartment, or was someone else living there? What if some German had confiscated the apartment?

I had resolved to try no one else, to face no more refusals. But perhaps I should make one last try. Ruda was the oldest, most sensible of all my friends. He'd be most likely to help if he knew I was in Prague. It seemed hopeless in any case, Ruda was bound to be away. But I desperately wanted to do something more, to walk, think, see, speak to someone; I didn't want to die, I wanted to postpone it, if only by a few minutes. I wanted to feel, just for a moment, that I still belonged among people.

I walked through the dark hall and leaning on the railing slowly climbed the stairs. Ruda's name was still there, and a light shone through under the door. Was he home? Was he alone? Should I try once more? Then I thought, why not? all is lost anyway, and I pressed the bell. The door flew open as if someone had been waiting behind it. Marta, pale and dishevelled, stood in the door, whispering, sobbing, and shouting all at once: "Heda! Where have you been all this time? Why didn't you come straight here? I waited for you all day long. I'm going out of my mind! Where did you go when you left us? Where did you spend the night?

"Listen, yesterday, right away—well, not right away but as soon as possible—I phoned here, to talk to Ruda. I thought it would be your next stop—or did you know he was away now? Who told you? He is the right man, the only one of us worth something. He had not been home for several months, but I was lucky and caught him in; he left again this morning. I told him everything. He will take care of you. He waited as long as he could, then gave me the keys and told me to stay here until you came. Since then I've been sitting here, terrified. I'd never forgive myself for letting you leave if something had happened to you. Where were you? What were you doing?"

"I'll tell you some other time, I can't just now." It took all my remaining strength to say that. I clung to the door and felt my knees giving way. "And what of him . . . of Vláda?"

"You saw yourself. He was lying to me all along. I would have forgiven him even that, if at least he had seen you were giving him a chance to do for once something decent in his miserable life. But you saw what happened; he is hopeless. Besides, you matter now, not he, not I. You stay here, and wait. Be very careful, next door they can hear every step. . . ."

Suddenly her face seemed unnaturally close up, shining eyes bending over me, lips moving but I could not hear a word. My head rang and roared, everything spinning and melting around me. At last the roar faded and I could hear Marta's voice again" . . . and I'll let Ruda know. Lie down, you look dreadful."

I watched her close the door, heard the key turn in the lock for the sake of the neighbors, and saw the key slip in through the mail slot. But by then I had already fallen face down on the sofa, my whole body giving way. The tension that had held me together for so long suddenly let go, my stomach seemed to rise up to my throat, and icy shivers ran down my spine like drops of ice water. The walls around me echoed every heart-beat.

I am not sure how many days I lay half-conscious in Ruda's apartment. Then gradually, the fever subsided, my head quieted down and no longer ached, and I could walk again. I found some food in the kitchen, and I began to feel stronger. About two weeks later, someone dropped a letter through the mailslot. I brought it to the table by the sofa and let it sit there, unopened. I had to relish the feeling that someone knew I existed, someone thought of me, someone took the trouble to write to me and even brought the letter. When I opened it, I found a note printed in block letters—

COME AT SIX TO THE PARK BY THE CHURCH. I WILL BE WEARING A BROWN COAT, GREY HAT, AND CARRYING A BLACK BRIEFCASE IN MY RIGHT HAND. SAY, "I THINK WE HAVE MET SOMEWHERE BEFORE."

I spent the whole afternoon getting ready for my first walk. I was still weak from the fever, but I had had some sleep and rest, and the prospect of going out, not just into the streets but to meet someone, made me feel alive.

The evening was wet and gloomy, and patches of snow were melting in the drizzle. I saw him from a distance, standing at the corner of the park. A very young, thin man in a worn overcoat, briefcase in hand. I walked slowly the last few yards, hesitating to speak to him. He looked me over carefully, and then smiled.

"You need not say anything. Ruda sent me. Stop being afraid—we will help you. It will all come out well."

The whisper of the rain stopped suddenly and it began to snow. At the turn of the path, behind the white commotion of snowflakes, I could see the figure of a man. He walked like a machine, his steps falling sharply on the soft path. I could tell it was an SS man even before I could make out the outline of his uniform. I grasped my companion's arm. The SS man came closer, jerked his head in our direction, returned it with another jerk and passed us. I looked up at the young man beside me and felt snowflakes falling on my lips and eyebrows, turning into tiny droplets. He smiled again and pressed my hand.

We walked out of the park and into the street. People passed us, snuggling into their coats. They hurried to get home, to close the door after them and sit by the warm stove. We turned into a street where I had never walked before. It was straight, steep, and I could not see its end in the darkness and falling snow. We walked rapidly, in silence.

-II-

Sowing the Seed

i. A War Ends

The war ended like a journey through a tunnel. For a long time, we could only see a light ahead, continually growing brighter and coming nearer. We crouched in the sooty darkness and longed for that glow outside. The longer it took, the brighter, purer, and more beautiful it seemed to be. Then, when the train finally burst out into the sunlight, we did not see only light ahead. Now we saw the fallow ground, littered with debris, weeds, rocks and the dirt of years.

The final weeks in illegality seemed endless. I was so alone and lonely that I spent my days sitting by the radio just to hear a human voice. What that voice had to say was far removed from everything human, and would give me little comfort. The only broadcasts I enjoyed were readings of children's fairy tales. I used to fall asleep hoping that the next day the radio would speak in the words of children, dwarfs, and animals.

One evening friends from the resistance brought me a wounded Russian partisan, weakened by fever. They laid him on the bed and disappeared quickly, leaving me alone with him and with the icon he pulled out of his pack as soon as they left. I nursed him for two days, shared my few hardened crackers with him, and prayed that he would not die. The third night they took him away and I felt even sadder.

But shortly afterward, foreign broadcasts started giving the call-phrase of Ruda's resistance group. One night Ruda arrived, covered with mud, and dug out the weapons I had cared for all that time. "Next time I come," he told me, "the war will be over." Soon after that I could hear rifle fire, first on the radio, then from the streets. People pinned on badges of freedom and the final battle of the war started, the first and last battle for Prague.

The resistance headquarters for Dejvice was set up nearby in a basement cinema. Dejvice was a fashionable quarter: the gentlemen officers, captains and colonels were mostly out of uniform, marked only by a tricolor on a hat which would be easy to discard. They sat around a table, without any contact with the outside, with no conception of the situation, and issued pointless orders to the eighteen-year-olds whose fathers had been murdered by the Germans and who now fired and died on the barricades.

The first day I took part in the street fighting, but I soon discovered that I had little aptitude for killing and went to work instead where lives were being saved, in the makeshift first-aid station set up in the resistance headquarters. Half-starved pensioners crept through the streets under fire and brought us provisions—loaves of bread squeezed from their meager rations, crumpled packets of cigarettes, bottles of rum. Most of what they brought dissapeared each evening in the shopping bags of our volunteer nurses—mostly Dejvice housewives who devoted their energies to displays of patriotism and flirtations with the officers. But when we got word that two volunteers were needed to bring part of the cache of weapons from the railway station, which was still held by the Germans, no one volunteered except for one worn-out old woman, half-dead with terror, and me. On the way back, carrying a huge laundry basket of weapons, we were stopped by a German patrol and almost shot because that poor old woman lost her nerve. Still, I remember her lovingly. If courage is the ability to conquer one's own fear, she was the bravest person I have ever met.

Among the volunteers who came to pluck a little cheap glory there was a former classmate of mine. She appeared well cared for and elegant. She had obviously been careful to avoid trouble throughout the war and even now stayed carefully out of sight. But the situation in the streets was growing worse by the hour, our underground first-aid station was full of casualties and we were all busy. It was then that she caught me giving water to a dying German soldier. "If I didn't know you had been in a concentration camp," she glowered at me, "I'd make sure you'd pay for this! Didn't you hear the doctor? Bandage the Czechs, let the devil take care of the Germans." I ignored her, but I also realized that war not only kills people, it also corrodes them. It had divided us like a slash of a knife, and the wound will be long healing.

When the Germans finally withdrew, I could go outside again, for the first time in years, without fear. I had a small wound where a bullet had grazed my leg and could not walk without difficulty. Still, I limped out, down the "mouse hole," a path worn along the lilac bushes to the riverbank. The lilacs filled the air with perfume, there was sunshine, and only now and then a shot rang out as people combed the parks and attics for the last remaining Germans. I walked out on Ujezd, to the open space by the bridge. There was not a living soul anywhere, only Prague spread out all around, enveloping me.

It was the moment just before sunset, when all outlines become momentarily sharp and clear, the colors rich and deep, to remind man that night is brief, that darkness comes and then goes. I walked a few steps further and right by the bridge, in a puddle of dark blood, saw a man in the black uniform of the SS. Everything was completely still, Prague glowed and arched above that black blood and above the black thing lying in it, no longer dangerous. I remember saying to myself, "Now, at this moment, at this spot, the war ends because he is dead and I am alive."

That was the end of that horrible, long, and now almost forgotten war. Life went on, over the corpses both dead and living; no one quite survived that war. Something terribly important and precious had died in that war, perhaps it had been killed, perhaps it had died of horror, of hunger, of revulsion—who knows. We buried it hurridly and the earth settled over it. And we turned our backs on it, because after all now the real life was beginning, and what to make out of it was up to us.

Now people were creeping out of their hiding places, out of the forests and the prisons, and they could think only "it is over, it is over." I remember a boy whose clogs had to be operated off his feet because his soles had literally grown into them. I think of Eliška, who passed through Auschwitz twice, twice escaped death, then walked all the way to Prague. She sat on the ground before the statue of St. Wenceslas, kissed the pavement, and fainted. An ambulance took her to a hospital where she died a week later—she virtually had no lungs left. Or Mr. Lustig, who spent the whole war hidden, walled in in a corner and almost lost his eyesight. But he was lucky, he survived. Then, during the Prague uprising, he walked out, for the first time in years into the daylight, and a few steps later he was shot through the head.

People returned, some said nothing and some talked constantly, as if to speak of something were to be rid of it. But it is just the other way around, things that have been said and described win a new reality, as if by giving them our words we gave them a part of ourselves, and cannot leave them behind. And so people tried to speak of death and flames, of blood and gallows, while in the background a thousand voices repeated persistently, tirelessly, "Oh, yes, we too have suffered, how often there was not even margarine to spread on our bread. . . ."

Occasionally a threadbare, barefooted returnee gathered up his courage and knocked on a friend's door to ask, "Excuse me, would you happen to have something of all the things we left in your keeping?" And people would say, "Oh no, you must be mistaken, you left nothing with us, but come in anyway. . . ." And they would seat him in a room where his rug covered the floor, would pour him herb tea in the china that used to belong to his grandmother, and the survivor would thank them, sip his tea, look at his paintings on the wall and say to himself, "It doesn't matter, does it. . . . It does not matter, as long as we are alive, it doesn't matter, does it?"

On other occasions it would not turn out so nicely. The

friends would not brew tea, would say nothing about mistakes. Some just laughed and wondered out loud, "Did you really think we took all those risks keeping it all through the war just to give it back to you?" And the survivor would laugh, too, wonder at his own stupidity and apologize, "Sorry, terribly sorry," as he backed out the door. In front of the house he would laugh again, and would be glad that it was spring and that the sun was shining on him.

Or it happened that the survivor needed a lawyer to help him replace lost identity papers, and he remembered one who used to represent prosperous Jewish businessmen. He'd go and sit in the Empire chair in a well-appointed waiting room, relishing the joy of sitting again in such luxury, watching the pretty secretaries running from door to door. Then one such pretty girl forgot to close the door behind her and the lawyer's sonorous bass flowed through the crack, "God almighty, I thought we were finally rid of them! But oh no, they are indestructible. Not even that fellow Hitler managed it; every day the vermin come back like rats. . . ." And the survivor got up quietly, creeping out the hall, but this time not laughing, and on the stairs his eyes grew dim as with the smoke of the furnaces of Auschwitz.

The friends in the country sent an invitation, "Come see us, let us fatten you up a bit, we have enough of everything." The survivor reached the village and could hardly believe his eyes. The house was twice as big as before the war, there was a refrigerator in the kitchen and a washer in the hall, Persian carpets covered the floors and original paintings on the walls, the fat sausage was served on silver holloware and draft beer from the tavern in cut crystal. The farmer stroked his whiskers and said, sounding worried, "Why deny it, the war was good for us. You know, people have to eat and if you know your business. . . . Just as long as those Communists don't come to power. . . ."

It was a long time before I could get up my courage for a trip to the village of Huť. We used to spend our vacations there, our cottage there was as much home to me as our apartment in Prague, perhaps more so for all the summertime memories it held. To go back to the place where we had been together, and to go all alone, the only one left, that was hard. Throughout the long trainride the train seemed to move far too fast; I felt stifled and sick. When I changed trains in Beroun, a horror seized me and I almost took the train back to Prague. When at last I reached Huť, I shuffled hesitantly from the station to the village. From the distance I could see the windows where my mother used to look out, alive and happy. The trees in the orchard were past bloom and no one was about. I rang the bell; a while later a grumpy, unshaven man opened the door, stared at me for a few moments and then almost screamed "Good God, you've come back! Oh, no, that's all we needed!"

I turned around and walked into the woods. I spent the three hours until the next train walking among the trees, listening to the birds.

When I returned from Huť, I spent days wandering through Prague in a daze, tripping over cobblestones torn out in the fighting. Occasionally I met old acquaintances; some turned away, others greeted me, gave me food, and asked questions. Once I met my mother's dressmaker—she cried when she saw me, led me by the hand to her flat and stitched me a dress on the spot, out of remnants saved up through the war, sobbing constantly. Each day I listened to the radio for the news about liberated prisoners, and occasionally I heard familiar names. Then once the voice on the radio announced,

"Brother Ervin Bloch has arrived in Prague and is organizing the return of other prisoners. . . ."

Ervin Bloch was my father's name. The room spun around me, I could not catch my breath. My father. . . . I saw his face before me, pale and emaciated, as I last saw him in Auschwitz with a group of people destined to die, his eyes, signaling to me, "Goodbye, take care of mother." But a few minutes later they tore my mother from me, and when I started running after her, a soldier with a submachine gun seized me and knocked me down. In the meantime pretty Dr. Mengele waved his hand and my mother was swallowed up by the thousand-headed snake winding into a building without windows. When I rose from the sand, half dazed, I could see only her arms, reaching out toward me as if she were drowning. I cried out to the soldier with the submachine gun, "What will happen to them? What will you do with them?" He grinned contemptuously and said,

"Don't make a scene; nothing will happen to them. In a few hours you'll see them again." But a girl in striped rags with a shaven head brushed against me and whispered, "Don't believe him, you'll never see them again. They'll burn them all." In that moment the whole world exploded in fire and smoke and the fire seared my brain to ashes, leaving only one cell alive. For weeks afterward that cell would automatically light up and go out like a signal lamp, and each time it lit up it showed me my mother and father, falling into flames with outstretched arms. And now my father. . . . Was it possible, could he have been saved? In the last moment, had some miracle snatched him away?

I jumped up and a moment later I was in the street, hobbling anxiously down the hill toward the radio station. There was still no transportation in the smashed city, and I had to cover quite a distance. As I approached the building that housed the radio station, I could see the street completely packed with a dense crowd trying to get to the radio people, to that center through which passed all the news about the living and the missing. I was terrified by the impenetrable wall of human backs but I knew I had to get inside.

Then one, two people look around at me and drew aside. More heads turned, and a path slowly opened before me. Someone pushed me gently forward and I flew down the path, staring straight ahead. Even the man guarding the locked door just looked at me and opened the door.

A moment later I stood in a tiny office before the man who was organizing the broadcasts. He was frightfully emaciated, his head was no more than a skull under tight skin and his eyes were half closed with fatigue. He thought for a while. "I haven't a moment free in the broadcast. Hundreds of people call in and plead to have at least the shortest message included; it is impossible, nothing more will fit. But sit and wait, perhaps I can snatch a second somewhere."

I sat through hour after hour in that office, occasionally I heard a voice on the monitor repeating my father's name, asking him to call his daughter at the radio station. But no one called. That incredibly thin, overworked man looked at me sadly every few minutes and finally said, "Don't lose all hope yet. Late at night I broadcast a news program to which all the prisoners listen. I'll mention your father once more; if he is alive, he's bound to respond. Now go home, as soon as I find out something, I'll call you."

I went back to the empty, strange apartment where I was still spending the nights, and huddled on a chair by the radio, listening to that gentle, tired voice once again calling the name of my long dead father with whom the unknown returnee had nothing in common except a name. The telephone rang two days later. "I'm sorry we did not find your father, but today someone brought a letter from a Rudolf Margolius. He escaped from Dachau, and the Americans put him in charge of the camp at Garmisch-Partenkirchen, where they are gathering the former prisoners. He is supposed to organized the people's transportation home. He heard my broadcast and sent me a report on the camp—most of all he asked about you. Your name is Heda, isn't it? Listen again tonight, I'll broadcast your answer to him."

That evening I sat by the radio once more, listening. "We thank Rudolf Margolius for the report and are happy to tell him that. . . ." Only much later I learned that Rudolf heard only the first three words. Then the electricity went off, the radio fell silent, and the mystery remained unsolved. Rudolf's friends among the Czechs spent their time betting, was it she, wasn't it? By mid-June the evacuation of the camp was completed and Rudolf returned to Prague with the last group of prisoners. But when the train halted, no one got off. All stood by the windows and doors of the train, watching Rudolf run for the phonebooth and dial the number of the radio station. When he came out again, the whole train called to him, "Was it Heda?" Rudolf smiled and nodded; only then did his comrades leap out of the cars and started on their way home.

That was some six weeks after the end of the war. People no longer were rejoicing and embracing in the streets and handing out gifts of food and clothing—they were selling them on the black market. People now were calculating and planning, covering their tracks, watching, and spying on each other. There was squabbling over property gained by collaboration, by cowardice and denunciation, or over property seized from deported Jews. Guilt and fear gave birth to hate and suspicion, which turned most of all against the real victims of the occupation—against passive and active resisters, partisans and political prisoners, or simply against people who had paid the price of persecution and suffering rather than to betray. Now, uncompromised, they seemed a threat to all those who had made profit from the war. Feared and hated, worn to shreds by the endless waiting in lines for documents, for ration cards and food, disgusted by petty conflicts with bureaucrats and greed, the victims of the war began to think seriously and fearfully about the country's future. Many of them saw clearly that only evil comes by itself, that the good has to be won in a hard struggle. They all were convinced that we had to set clear goals and join forces if apathy and greed were not to prevail. But each of them saw those goals differently.

The biggest problem for the returnees was to find housing. Partisans from the forests, widows of the executed who had for years slept somewhere on a floor, ailing survivors of concentration camps—they all stood on aching legs in endless lines at housing offices while the butchers and the grocers made deals, walking in through the back door. Most of the time these people had adequate apartments, but they had grown affluent in the war and wanted better ones, nicely furnished. So many had been abandoned by the Germans, and after all, the butchers and the grocers had kept the officials supplied all through the war with meat and flour—they felt they deserved some compensation now. In the waiting room housing officials screamed at weeping women, "What do you think this is? So damn many of you survived, where are we supposed to find housing for you all?"

People would leave, and clench their fists. I have often thought that many of our people turned to Communism less out of revulsion over the social order of their time than out of despair over those aspects of human nature that the war showed up in the worst light. Humans always find it hard to despair over themselves—they prefer to blame the system. Communist rhetoric may have offered few concrete solutions to such problems as the housing shortage, but it gave a vent to emotions that had to be vented.

In the end I did manage to find a flat, and even before

Mr. Souček, the owner of a poultry farm whom I frequently saw conferring with the Housing Office officials. To be sure, what he wanted was something more sumptious; all I asked for was a roof over my head.

One evening, shortly after the end of office hours, I marched in with a huge shopping bag containing everything I owned in the world—mostly gifts from friends. I planted myself in the office of the Director of Housing and announced that I planned to live in that office until I was assigned an apartment, since quite truthfully I had no place to go at night. The last few nights we had spent in various improvised public shelters. Before that, I had made the rounds of all our friends who were willing to shelter me until I sensed that I could not misuse their hospitality much longer. Besides, I had come to the conclusion that after all those years it was high time I slept in my own bed.

The director started storming up and down, but I did my best to ignore him. Deliberately, I unpacked a cake of soap toothbrush and glass; I spread a clean, white napkin on his desk and put a piece of bread and cheese on it, together with a bottle of milk. Then I tossed my towel and nightgown over the back of the office chair, sat down in the director's easy chair, poured a glass of milk and bit into my bread.

The director was still shouting. I finished eating and slowly took off my shoes. Next I undid a button on my blouse and started praying for something to happen. Then the second button. The director turned dark red, wiped his soaking neck with a handkerchief and shot out of the office. I put up my feet on another chair, lit a cigarette—a precious present—and waited.

A while later someone knocked on the door, and upon my invitation the door opened. The director's bald head slipped in cautiously. When he saw that my preparations for the night had not progressed, he sighed, relieved. He nodded to someone and came in together with his assistant who had explained to me time and again that he understood and would like to help, with all his heart, but that he had no apartments available. Now he was holding a sheet of paper and asked, "If we give you a deed, right here and now, so that you can move in tomorrow, will you *please* go away?"

I signed the deed, finished my milk and offered some to them. Both men declined, courteously and nervously, the director personally collected my belongings and put them in my shopping bag. I took the deed and the bag and set out to see the house where I was to live.

I have the impression that the Housing Office was arrested, soon thereafter, for taking bribes, though I am not sure.

Our new apartment was so tiny that two years later, when I was expecting my baby, Rudolf had to do the cooking—I did not fit between the wall and the kitchen stove. But there were many bookshelves, and the sun shone in all day long. Friends came and brought cups and plates and covers and pillows, and by the end of the summer that tiny cubbyhole had become a home.

The shelves filled rapidly with fat volumes on politics and economics, old and dog-eared, which Rudolf was constantly studying, and with a flood of new paperbacks, printed on shoddy paper, which I read. These books offered such clear, simple answers to the most complex questions that I kept feeling there must be a mistake somewhere. All injustice, they told me, all discrimination, misery and war come from the unwillingness of a handful of the mighty to relinquish their greed, their limitless exploitation and lust for domination. But as soon as the working people, the creators of all value, come to understand what is to be done, they will overcome the exploiters and their allies, they will reeducate them and themselves—and there will be paradise on earth. The only enemies are those who grow fat on human sweat and callouses—let us divide the riches of the world equally and get to work: each will contribute according to his ability and the society will make sure that he will not want. We will not fight each other for a bigger slice of the common loaf, we will join hands and build happiness and prosperity for everyone. The soil belongs to those who till it, the factories to those who work in them.

At first we will of course have to move firmly against those who do not want to give up their unjust privileges voluntarily—and it is only natural that the capitalist will not give up his profits without a struggle. But when we have established the new order, even he will understand and willingly join the common effort. We shall all be brothers, without distinction of language or race. Only capitalism gives birth to racism, in a socialist society all men are equal. Democracy, progressive in its beginnings, had become degenerate and its role is finished. The capitalist economy leads to economic crises, and economic crises lead to fascism and war. The bourgeoisie led the world to the edge of utter destruction: do you want another war in a few years, the final nuclear catastrophy? Isn't it time to change the world? Let's convince others, explain that we do not want to force anyone to change, that people themselves must come to see, learn from their own experience—but that we can help them understand. Let's spread our ideas, our literature, our own only correct truth. Why are there wars? Does God exist? What causes depressions? What is truth? Marxism-Leninism, the super-science, provides the only correct answers to all questions. Our brochures resolve for you definitively and in a few short pages all the problems that humankind, misled for centuries by obscurantist reactionary class ideologies, had not been able to resolve. The change you demanded is under way. Humans will change the conditions of their existence, and with them they themselves will be transformed. . . .

Friends used to come to visit us, sit on the floor since there was nowhere else to sit, and debate till dawn. There was no view that would not find a defender. I used to sit in a corner, listening. It was clear to me that I knew nothing whatever about politics, and even less about economics. But I could see that life had become politics, and politics life, that it was impossible to say, I don't care, and leave me alone.

Whenever someone defended the idea of democracy, on which I was raised, everything in me called out, yes, that is how it should be. But I would grow uncertain when I heard the objections—that Masaryk's democracy was an unrealizable illusion, that it had permitted the growth of fascism and Nazism in our country, that it had surrendered to Hitler without a shot—and that it is impossible to go back to repeat the same mistakes, and in time to see another Munich. Who sold us to Hitler? Our allies, the Western capitalists. Who offered help when everyone deserted us? The Soviet Union. Who liberated

Prague while the American army stood motionless at Pilsen, thirty undefeated miles away? The Soviet Union.

Once two men met in our apartment, both of whom we had known since childhood. Zdeněk's father had been a worker and had been unemployed for years. Shortly after the occupation the Germans arrested him and executed him somewhere in Germany. Zdeněk spent the war years with partisans in the forests. He walked awkwardly on frost-bitten feet, but he brought with him into the room that familiar self-assurance and strength of people for whom physical suffering is a challenge, a chance to measure how far they can reach, how far they can push the limits of their will, their personality, their humanity. Zdeněk was accepted into the Party somewhere in a tent in the forests, by candlelight, with a submachine gun in his hand.

The other man was Franta, one of those who had refused to help me after I had escaped from the concentration camp. He lived out the war in Prague, inconspicuously, quietly, never having done anything dishonorable, never having collaborated, never having betrayed, but also never having risked anything. Although before the war he had finished his military service as an officer, he never gave any thought to resistance. He survived the war as a hibernating animal, gained nothing and lost a little.

I thought of that conversation again and again in later years. Everything Franta had to say sounded right and reasonable, sober and democratic. But Zdeněk's arguments carried the weight of his personality, of his experiences. What he said sounded strong and convincing because he was saying it. Listening to him I felt ashamed to agree with that other man—rationalistic and cautious—who never forgot on which side his bread was buttered. I felt ashamed to take Franta's side in this confrontation of reason and courage. As usual, the discussion ended in total disagreement, but this time it was sharper, because it was not simply a confrontation of two views, but of two completely contradictory ways of thinking, of temperaments, feeling, and vision.

Much later, in the stunned daze of the 1950s, when I foolishly tried to pinpoint the fateful break, the moment at which our good will and enthusiasm started to turn to destruction, I used to think of that evening. Rudolf then listened tensely, saying little, but I could sense that he was heart and soul on Zdeněk's side—in part because he never forgave Franta for his cowardice toward me, but only in part. If Rudolf's reason then still objected, he had decided to silence it.

Rudolf was a quiet, serious man, completely unselfish. The experience of the concentration camps and the occupation had wounded him more deeply than anyone I knew. He never overcame the humiliation that he, a young, healthy man, an officer in the Czechoslovak army, let himself be herded unresisting into the concentration camp and looked on like a helpless cripple while people he loved were being slaughtered. In fact, he had often risked his life to help friends—and many of them visited us and spoke of it—but that sense of impotence and guilt never stopped torturing him. More than ever before he believed that to win happiness for all men is the chief task of each individual; but now he was beginning to doubt that this goal could be reached through the path that had failed so totally once before.

About a week after the debate between Zdeněk and Franta, Rudolf took me to visit some of his acquaintances. They had been Communists before the war and had spent the war years in Russia. Now they lived in a handsome villa, tastefully furnished in an entirely unproletarian style. Both were well-educated, much older than we were, and I felt quite at home with them. The woman spoke with me about daily cares and gave me hints on how to prepare the pork and apples that came to us in UNRRA cans to make them taste Czech. Then we asked them to tell us something about life in the Soviet Union. Almost with tears in their eyes they described the sacrifices and patriotism of the common people, their endurance and their unshakable faith in victory. They spoke of the complete equality of all the many nationalities and races in the Soviet Union, of the enthusiasm with which people carried out even the most onerous tasks for their country, about the profound sense of brotherhood and understanding among people, the Party's and the government's unceasing care for the people, and about the friendly welcome accorded to all refugees. We left, deeply moved, and two days later Rudolf brought home applications for Communist party membership.

Ten years later that woman confessed to me what they had told us that day had been almost entirely a lie. They had lived through hard times in Russia, people had been afraid to speak to them, black market and collaboration had flourished and so had anti-Semitism and corruption, and men often had died for no reason. But because most of them did not dare guess the causes of their suffering, many died blessing the Party and Stalin. . . .

ii. Uneasy Peace
As time brings out the pattern in the events of my life, I can see that our revolutionary apprenticeship had begun in the concentration camps. For one thing, there was the example of individual Communists who seemed beings of a new, higher order. Their idealism and their Party training seemed to give them a strength the rest of us did not even dream about. Somewhat like the priests in Communist concentration camps ten years later, they were like superbly trained soldiers among helpless children.

But there were other things, too. There was the sense of determination that dominated that time, the total concentration on a single goal: the end of the war. Life was not life in any ordinary sense, it was simply a thrust in that one direction. Every thought, every act was justified by the future: the present had no meaning except as something to be survived, somehow, anyhow. The intensity of that feeling was, I think, proportionate to the suffering each of us had to bear.

When we finally reached the end of the war, the release and joy soon gave way to a sense of anticlimax, to a sense of emptiness left after the end of all the intensity of expectation, of exertion of will, and perhaps even of coping with physical suffering. It was very much like the feeling that overwhelmed the new exiles after the Russian occupation in 1968: what we missed was, perhaps, not so much Prague itself as the sense of fulfillment with which the common hope and effort of the Spring had suffused us.

In the concentration camps during the war there grew up among us a strong sense of solidarity, the idea that an individual fate is in everything bound up with the fate of the group, whether that of fellow prisoners or of the whole nation—or perhaps even humanity. At the same time, many people lost their desire for material possessions. Even though we longed endlessly for the good things of life—for food, decent clothes, a home—all that became secondary. It seemed clear that our happiness, the meaning of our lives, was something else altogether and something far less tangible. I remember how some of our fellow citizens, for whom the years of the war were years of profit and accumulation, could not understand when we did not go searching after our stolen things, did not try to get compensation or refused inheritances from dead relatives. When I say "we," I don't mean just Rudolf and myself but a great many people for whom an ideal, a sense of purpose, had become more important than the tangible effects of daily life—and many of whom quite understandably ended up in the most ideologically explicit party, that of the Communists.

There was one other, rather paradoxical reality. During the years of imprisonment, the common good came to seem far more important than personal freedom. I cannot explain it and I was repelled by it from the start, but for a great many of us freedom stopped being something natural, self-evident. It became much more of a privilege man must earn rather than his birthright—something to be awarded like a medal. To be sure, there were also the perennial arguments about the weakness of democracy, which could not defend its people against Nazism, and so on and on. But I think the emotional factor was more important. You cannot live for so many years as a slave, in constant contact with fascists and fascism, without becoming twisted, without contracting something of that dry rot, against your will and often without your awareness. Usually the reasoning went something like this: if to build a new, better society it is necessary to give up freedom for a time, or to subordinate our interests to something we believe in, this is a sacrifice we are ready to make. We are in any case a lost generation, we might very well have died uselessly and senselessly in concentration camps like so many others. Since we survived, we want to dedicate what is left of our lives to the future.

This martyr complex was stronger than we realized. Those who survive often feel chosen by providence to self-sacrifice. Besides, there is inevitably a strong sense of guilt about surviving: why did I, just I, survive—why not my father, brother, friend? I have an obligation to those who died in my place, to do battle for a world in which this can never happen again.

The devil of it is that Communism appeared to many of us the one system under which this could "never happen again." Of course not the Russian Communism of the 1930s—that seemed a long-past era of cruelties from which a great transformation is born. Could we condemn democracy because of the rampage of the Jacobins after the French Revolution? Why should we condemn Communism because of the terror of the 1930s? I need not even mention such convictions as that under Communism there can be no national oppression and especially no anti-Semitism, just as I need not speak any more of the fables of glorious life in the Soviet Union, systematically spread by old Communists who had spent the war years there. Only years later they began to admit that most of them had lived there, too, in concentration camps or in miserable hovels in Siberia.

But we know all that now. Factual evidence is no longer hard to come by—it is our mental state at that time that matters and helps explain why even today so many people cannot give up their old faith. For a majority of them, the struggle for the ideal was the zenith of their lives, the most unselfish self-sacrifice, the most shining idealism, the truth bought at a high price. The ideology of 1945 was illusory, but to those who believed in it, it seemed true and pure.

I see the most destructive trait in that cult of martyrdom, that cult of self-sacrifice. It is pathological, antihuman. A good society is one in which all can live well, myself included. When a society cannot function without martyrs, it is a bad society. But in those years we had not come to know that. Martyrdom had been thrust on us: we had to give it justification.

There, too, were the endless discussions about socialist

economics. I did not understand those discussions well enough, and I still don't. But I do remember that the most urgent task at the time was to put our economy on solid ground, and that Rudolf and his friends were unwavering in their conviction that only socialist economics as they understood it could manage that task. Of course, they imagined it along lines entirely different from the autocratic mismanagement after the Communist coup—even while Rudolf was still employed in the Chamber of Industry, he concentrated on trade with the West and subsequently, as undersecretary of foreign trade, he initiated our "dollar offensive."

Today, after the fact, it is easy to judge and condemn. But I am sure that the intentions of Rudolf and people like him were pure and good. They were naive about the logic of power, but the errors they made were errors of judgment, not of character. Unfortunately, the world judges by results—intentions do not matter. Sometimes evil intentions produce the best results and good intentions shrink to the opposite.

It all depends on the overall matrix in which a man operates. If that is good, even the worst deeds can be transformed in the perspective of history into forgivable mistakes. But when a man chooses a matrix that proves to be evil, incapable of correcting its errors, in retrospect all his oversights appear almost criminal. Today few people condemn democracy because the West signed the Munich Pact, or because many capitalists supported Hitler. Few people will blame France for its collaborationists, or give up all hope for America because of its botch-up war in Vietnam. Democracy can correct its mistakes—those who committed inane errors can, a few years later, be regarded with tolerance, even compassion, rather than with disgust and hatred.

We must not forget that before the Communist coup in 1948 no one, except perhaps NKVD agents, had the least doubt that in our country we would do things our way, which would be quite different from Russian totalitarianism. What we called "our specific national road to socialism" was a presupposition even for a Gottwald, the old Stalinist who became secretary general of the Communist party of Czechoslovakia, and it is known that Stalin encouraged him in it until after the coup. In those days Tito was still a hero, the pride of socialism. When he was recast in the role of the "bloody dog," it was too late. This is why, from a Russian perspective, the accusation of "Titoism" was the one aspect of the purge trials in the 1950s that had some justification in fact. Not that men like Rudolf spied on Tito's behalf or wanted to imitate Tito, but they did consider the Soviet system unsuited for our country, and they wanted to create something quite new.

We also must not forget how very much the Party meant to people like Rudolf—which explains why it could become a vehicle for "the Soviet Model." To the new Communists Party membership was very much like membership in a religious order. It meant constant self-examination, a searching of one's thoughts, desires, inclinations. Whenever a Communist discovered some discrepancy between what the Party commanded and his personal inclinations, he was expected to explain it by his own failings —bourgeois origins, antiquated thought patterns, intellectual decadence, erroneous education. Like the Church, the Party could never be wrong: only individual members could err. When a person became a Communist, he wanted to be a *good* Communist. We believed that, while we were building upon the ruins of a system that had failed, we were still deeply marked by that system and were still burdened with a great deal of obsolete prejudice and weakness. Most of all weakness—why didn't we stand up to Hitler? Why did we let ourselves be locked up in concentration camps and prisons, why did we die on gallows and in crematoria? Because we were weak, degenerate, spoiled. If we want to achieve something, we must be willing to be transofrmed. Communism, we believed, is the eternal, perennial ideal of humanity. If we want to be reborn, we must not doubt the ideal—only ourselves. Even I, a totally unfanatical person by temperament, often despaired—how can I think if not with my own mind? It is an invidious method, as old as civilization, as old as the world. Were it not for the war and that irrepressible need for change and negation, damning all that had been including ourselves, we could have seen through it easily. But when a person despairs over the world and doubts everything, it means first of all that he doubts himself—and the Party was prepared to provide the certainty and assurance we lacked. While the democrats asked us to trust in ourselves, the Party offered us the chance to put our trust in someone and something we did not have to doubt.

Today I know that we would have done a hundred times better, would have hurt ourselves and others far less, if we had simply taken to trading on the black market or even stealing, buying up antiques and gold, or begging money from acquaintances abroad and hoarding it against hard times; or if we had simply disappeared over the border, like so many perfectly reasonable people who would not have any part of the coup and what followed. But we didn't do that because we did not believe it was right. We paid literally a bloody price for that mistake. I wish we had been wiser, more critical, less trusting. But I would rather have to live through it all once more, with all the horror, than to say now that poeple like Rudolf acted from low or dishonorable motives. That would be a lie and a sin for which there is no absolution in this world or the other.

If I was not swept up in this idealism of the Party, it was not because I was better or smarter than people like Rudolf, but because I am a woman through and through, far closer to reality, more interested in what is happening around me, in the present, among people I like, than in the foggy spheres of ideology. Rudolf could conclude from the statistics he saw—sure, they had been doctored—that people live better, that they are happier under Communism. I could see close up, with my own eyes, that it was not so. The great redeeming feature of democracy is that it makes daily reality much harder to hide. Idealists don't like to think about the everyday consequences of their proposals. Communism made daily hardships seem trite in comparison with its shining ideology. Perhaps that was the greatest part of its appeal—definitely that was what destroyed us.

After the war and again now I often meet people who are genuinely puzzled by the fascination that Communist slogans of revolution and dictatorship hold for recent victims of another revolution and another dictatorship. Sometime they ask me how a Jew could be a Communist. Rationally, there is no answer for any of it. But there are other considerations. For many people, the war was a hard test. For us, it was a complete trauma. It meant a wiping out of everything we thought of ourselves, of everything we had taken for granted about people, history, human life, and even ourselves, of everything we had learned from our teachers and our parents. Our personal experiences before the war were no help in trying to come to terms with the war, the occupation, Nazism. Masaryk's democracy convinced us that some things simply could not happen any more. And suddenly not only could they happen, they were happening—and in far worse form than we could imagine. Before the war we had half-heard in school that long ago, in the middle ages, there had been some sorts of torture and persecution; but that was hardly something to weigh down the minds of us young, future citizens of a free and democratic state. When it happened in our time, it felt like the end of the world. It seemed to us that we were living through a complete break in the evolution of mankind, through a total collapse of man as a rational being.

The sudden collapse of personal identity was probably even worse. It was suffered not only by Jews but by many others —good men, not traitors—who began to wonder just what and who they were, whether one could even speak of a Czech nation and whether that nation had the right and the ability to exist. For the Jews it was incomparably worse, especially for those who, like my family and Rudolf's, had for generations thought of themselves as Czechs. Until Hitler took over our country, it simply never occured to me that there could be some basic difference between me as a Jew and any other Czech. And then, suddenly, there was a difference. Rudolf once said to me, "When I used to read *Ivanhoe* and *The Three Musketeers*, I always imagined myself, like all the boys did, living in that age, fighting, fencing, doing brave deeds. Now it dawns on me, had I lived then, I would have been rotting in some ghetto." Suddenly, we were no longer Czechs, no longer citizens or students. We stopped being anything at all. Our value dropped lower than that of cattle; cattle were at least worth feeding. Finally, in Auschwitz, we became no more than troublesome trash to be burned en masse in an incinerator.

So much has been written about the physical suffering of people in the concentration camps, but I don't know whether anyone ever succeeded in describing what happened in the minds of the inmates. I think for us in Bohemia the destruction of personal identity cut even deeper than in, say, the Nordic countries where people showed the Jews far greater sympathy and so proved to them that they still could count as one of them, as belonging. There the Jews could think of themselves as the particularly persecuted members of their nation, rather like hostages or prisoners of war.

The Communists were different, too, and that included the Jews who were Communists. They could feel that they suffered for an idea, for something they had chosen, not for what they were. They knew what to expect from the fascists, the collapse of the old order simply confirmed their convictions. Their world did not turn inside out like ours, but moved quite logically in the direction in which they fully expected the bourgeoisie to lead it.

Living in a democracy requires first of all a faith in man, confidence in oneself. Jews have often hated themselves for what they have suffered; for being the perennial focus of evil and hate. How much more difficult it would have been for the Germans without them. How many people joined the Nazis simply to pour out all their frustrations on the Jews or to pinch a small share of Jewish property! The Jews, by their very existence, helped the Nazis to power more than anyone else. It was quite natural that after the experience of the occupation most people found it impossible simply to return to the place where the war had caught them, as if nothing had happened. They wanted change—radical, fundamental change. Communism was constantly being proclaimed as the complete opposite of Nazism, as the movement that would restore precisely the values Nazism had destroyed: most of all, the dignity and solidarity of all humans. It came to seem that only another revolution could undo what the first one had committed.

Let me tell you one more story. A few months after the war was over, I took a trip to my father's birthplace, a forsaken little village near Benesov. It was a long trip, first by train, then on the bus. There was time to remember.

Once I had gone there with my parents in the winter. I was quite small then, the mountains and the countryside were covered with snow but my grandmother's cottage was warm with the fire of fresh-smelling wood. A spotted puppy played with me, newly-hatched chicks peeped in the brood bin under the bed, and grandmother welcomed us with cakes and huge walnuts. My father took me for a walk in the fields and showed me where he used to mind the geese. When we were coming back, it was dusk. The fishpond was freezing over and grandmother waited for us on the threshold, tears in her eyes, because while we were out father's sister at the farm nearby had given birth to a baby girl. Grandmother said she was beautiful and that she would be called Martha after my mother. When little Martha grew only a few years older, she died in a concentration camp. Just as her parents and her brothers and sisters—and grandmother.

After the war I did not go back to my uncle's farm; I did not know the people who had taken it over. My grandmother's cottage was neglected, everything seemed shrunken and tired. A gentle old neighbor unlocked it for me. She walked with me through the cottage, and told me, "This is where your grandmother put down her coffee just before the Germans came for her, and here's where she sat down to catch her breath. And I said to her, I said, 'Mrs. Bloch, don't be afraid. . . .' "

Can you understand it? Can you comprehend it? I know there was nothing anyone could do, but they were taking away an eighty-six-year-old grandmother to a horrible death—and the village where she had lived all her life, where everyone had loved her, could say nothing more than "Mrs. Bloch, don't be afraid. . . ."

iii. The Party
I hesitated for a long time before I made up my mind to sign the application for Party membership. I knew that I would find the mindless party discipline hard to bear. I had a horror of the meeting mania and I had little interest in taking an active part in political life. I wanted to work and to study, to have a baby—to catch up on everything the war years had taken away. I have always had a hard time

marching in closed ranks, and after our experience with Nazism I found the enthusiasm of crowds shouting slogans chilling. Right from the start I took a dislike to the word "masses" with which the pamphlets bristled. Whenever I read or heard it, I had visions of endless flocks of sheep, one like the next, a waving sea of bent backs and bent heads, the monotonous grinding of chewing mouths. I hated the hysterical veneration of Stalin, the bombastic phrases of political speeches, and the country-fair finery of medals and decorations covering the pot bellies of Soviet officers.

But I admitted that all of that was superficial, something to suit Russian tastes, nurtured by the Czars. In Czechoslovakia it would all be different. We would not be building socialism in a backward country under conditions of imperialist intervention and capitalist encirclement, but at peace, in an industrially mature country with an intelligent, educated population. We would leap over a whole epoch. I simply wrote myself off as a hopeless individualist, product of my bourgeois education, and humbly resolved to change. Rudolf used to laugh at me—"I never thought you would be one of those who are neither hot nor cold. If you stand aside now, you will reproach yourself for the rest of your life." That was the first mistake.

And then—"After all, if you find that you don't get along with the Party, you can always resign." That was the second mistake.

The truth of the matter is that we had almost incredible illusions about the Soviet Union. We let ourselves become persuaded that in the Soviet Union there was complete social justice and freedom, flowing from the unconditional agreement of all citizens with the regime, and that these ideal conditions have given rise to the most advanced science and, perhaps with a few exceptions, to the most advanced industry. Once in the movies I saw a report from some factory in the Soviet Union. I no longer remember what it produced, but I remember that at the end of the assembly line, which was being shown as one of the peaks of modern technology, there sat a girl who glued labels on each bottle by hand. At that moment the whole cinema whispered in amazement, because everyone knew that, in our factories, this kind of work had been done by machines for decades. But such details, and many far more serious phenomena of Soviet public life, we dismissed with a wave of the hand as minor Russian idiosyncracies that did not concern us. Only years later I realized that precisely those details to which we gave no thought were really the only facts about the Soviet Union we actually knew firsthand.

We were less naive about the past. The period of collectivization, of the liquidation of the kulaks and of opposition in general, the trials of the 1930's—though we knew relatively little about all this, it did scare us all a bit. The veterans of the Spanish Civil War had their unpleasant experiences, for instance with people like André Marty. But we were all confident we could learn from Russian "mistakes" and could achieve the goal by different means. I remember at the time I was very much impressed because the Russians had abolished capital punishment; I thought it a convincing proof of complete social consolidation. The slogan, "the Soviet Union—our model" (which the people of Prague changed handily into "Soviet Inane—our model") did not appear until after the coup, and it shocked us then. I don't know what the people at the top thought of it—Gottwald, Slánský, and the others. I am writing about *us*, and at that time we did believe that in our country things would be different.

Nor were we alone in our illusions. The Soviet experiment had aroused tremendous hope in the 1920's, and though there were signs of Soviet reality even then, they appeared insignificant against the background of the depression, the rise of fascism, and the beginnings of war. Western intellectuals, far more concerned with the abstract idea of revolution than with human lives, continued to write the Soviet Union's praises: Heinrich Mann extolled the humanism of the Soviets in 1937, while the purge trials were in progress; Sartre eulogized Communism in 1952, the year of the Slánský trial.

So it finally happened: one evening I was sitting in a meeting of the local Party organization and met all those who to this day style themselves "comrades." I rather liked that form of address. I liked to think that there is a place where people from all countries, of all tongues and races, can meet and call each other "comrade," recognizing immediately that, though they have never met before, can't even understand each other's language, they are alike and share something they have chosen consciously and freely.

The first meeting depressed me. Among those present I noticed my old acquaintance from the Housing Office, Mr. Souček, together with another man about whom the street rumored that the Germans had locked him up for black marketeering but who now presented himself as a former political prisoner, almost a national martyr, and was capitalizing on his "struggle against fascism." Most of those present were at least twice my age, and I was relieved when a youth with a flowing beard arrived to lecture us on The Foundations of Marxism.

The speech was a collection of bombastic phrases, spiced with a few underhanded attacks on Masaryk which aroused me. I felt quite disturbed by the time he had finished. But then an older, worn man, a bricklayer by trade, got up to speak. "This is all very nice," he said, "but let me tell you something about real life." Then he talked of years of drudgery and poverty, alternating with years of unemployment and misery, and in the end he spoke of what he expected from the future. He spoke slowly, searching for words, but his ideas seemed clear and straightforward. On the way home I was saying to myself, "One man like that is worth a hundred Mr. Součeks and his kin" and, "Yes, yes, I am on the right side. Life is never simple, what is good is never completely good and little of what is bad is nothing but bad. I must not let myself become discouraged."

But that is how I started, slowly and to my surprise, to discover that the Party does not consist simply of class-conscious, proletarian types, antifascists, and idealistic intellectuals. I think I won't be far wrong in saying that such people were a vanishing minority. Much later the official spokesmen of the Party declared that the Party had been infiltrated . . . but by whom, really? There were collaborators who calculated that their dubious wartime past could best be masked by loud proclamations of faith in progress and socialism, there were black marketeers and confidence men who hoped that with a Party card they could protect their earnings, there were incompetent, corrupt bureaucrats and endless lists of the offended and the humiliated who through incompetence or just plain laziness never had accomplished anything and who knew that the Party offered a chance to turn their shortcomings into assets. They sensed clearly that in a Party in which such rigid, mindless discipline prevailed, mediocrity and total absence of all independent judgement would prove high virtues.

For such people, a totalitarian regime is ideal. The state and the Communist party think for them, care for them, and give them ample opportunity to revenge themselves on those whom they had envied all their lives. In such a society there is a constant demand for petty informers and spies, and there is the chance to snatch a bit of power and glory for all who could not succeed in life through intelligence, initiative, or honesty. Devotion to the Party, obsequiousness and obedience become adequate substitutes.

Others joined, too. The Party card became an essential part of equipment for all the greediest who soon started fighting each other over jobs as administrators of nationalized farms and factories, over the property taken from Germans and emigrants. Several years later I happened to visit a comrade who had just returned from two years in the border district. His apartment looked like a museum: I don't think I have ever seen so many magnificent antiques and paintings in private ownership. "When I left for the border district," the man told me, "I owned nothing but the suitcase in my hand. And now look!"

The most respected Party members were the prewar "revolutionaries by trade," people who had never done a bit of useful work but also never missed a meeting or a strike and knew how to speak to the people in words and tones that would in time bear them to the highest positions in the Party and the government. It was not long before the chief backbone of the Party organization became the concierges. For years to come, they ruled with an iron hand, not only in individual houses but on whole streets. Their lives became one intoxicating orgy of spying and denunciations, at times even outright blackmail. Woe to anyone who offended one of these self-righteous guardians of the new order. Even the highest Party functionaries were careful never to drop cigarette ashes on the stairway or to miss an opportunity to slip comrade concierge—who also was usually a Party cell leader—some small present. Their importance in the years of Zápotocký's presidency came out in what one of them said to me in those days: "I think Comrade President must have been a concierge when he was young; he has so much sympathy for us." No, my dear lady, I thought, Comrade President never lowered himself to anything more demanding than playing an accordion. When he was young, being a concierge was hard, honest work.

Yes, the Party was right—many dark elements did infiltrate its ranks. But later we often wondered whether these dark elements were not the true core of the Party, and whether it was not the honest, idealistic workers and intellectuals who were the outsiders and the infiltrators.

Yet even many of those honest idealists underwent a rapid tranformation as soon as the Party seized power and started handing out jobs. Lord Acton wrote that power corrupts, but I think that what corrupted our people was not so much power as fear. As soon as a man gains power, he also becomes afraid of losing it. And to lose power in a Communist society does not mean to step down the social ladder on one's original place, but to fall that much deeper for having risen up. The more power grows, the more threatening does its loss become, and the greater the fear. Power sustained by fear is an infinitely cruel and dangerous combination.

I think back to this time frequently when I hear people extoll the beauty of simple human life. I don't know how many times, then and later, I used to say to myself, "all I want is just an entirely ordinary life." But that life precisely is not ordinary. In order to be able to live peacefully, contentedly, to work, raise children, plan a life and find joy in it, man must choose not only the right partner for life, the right occupation, the right virtues, but most of all he must have a very solid social foundation on which to build such a life. He must live in a society with which he can agree, at least in principle, and which he can trust.

During the war all we hoped was that we could return to such a life. In our escape from the concentration camp or on that last trip home in cattle cars we were not led by visions of future struggles but of a heel of bread. Yet we soon realized that we could not build a contented private life in a disrupted, corrupt society any more than you can build a house on a freshly plowed field. You have to lay a foundation first. I think this is the difference between what we call an ordinary life and the ball of manure that the two bugs roll back and forth in Karel Čapek's *The Insect Play*—that can be rolled on any manure pile. After all, even today in Czechoslovakia millions of people live an "ordinary life"—but at what a price!

The tragedy of our frame of mind at the time was the disappointment, the bitterness of the discovery that after all we had been through we could not simply live—that even this was too much to ask. It was this frame of mind that drove so many of us to total negation, to the longing for a *radical*, one-blow change that would make this ordinary life possible, then and there, or at least for the future. Instead of trying to repair the damage we wanted to tear it all down. We did not reject ordinary life because we wanted to struggle, but we felt that we had to struggle because even ordinary life with clear conscience was denied to us. It may have been folly, but we thought then that the good ordinary life was precisely what we were fighting for.

But after saying all this I have to admit that in the first postwar years I did not pay much attention to public matters. Everything seemed in order, and I had my hands full just finding my way back to everyday life. I spent months waiting in offices for the few pieces of paper that proved who I am and what I am. The Germans had destroyed most of the archives; you needed three documents for each new one, and to get those three you had to produce at least five others, and to get those five—it was an endless progression. Nor was it easier with other basic things—household equipment, clothing, food.

At the same time I was trying to find out what had become of the rest of my family, though always with the same results. Shot in Minsk. Died in Maidanek. Died in Mauthausen. Deported to Auschwitz. Unaccounted for. Missing. Missing.

I walked through Prague as through a mine field, at every step the ground seemed to open up under my feet. This is where I used to go shopping with my mother. This sweetshop was where father used to take me secretly for ice cream on Sunday mornings so that mother would not know. This is where I first saw the Swastika flag. Through this street our transport walked to the railway station—people paused on the sidewalks and took off their hats; the SS shouted at them, *Bewegung*! Move on or we'll take you along!

I could not bring myself to listen to the people who told me to forget, not to turn back—this, they said, was the only way back to life. I wanted to preserve it all in my memory, hide nothing from myself, pretty up nothing, see things as they were and are and still live with them, bear them. I wanted to live because I was alive, not simply because by some chance I was not dead.

A year after the war I found work in a small, high-quality publishing house as an art editor. I drew, designed book covers, assembled illustrations and reproductions, negotiated with authors and artists—in short, did a thousand things I thoroughly enjoyed. The publisher was an older man who taught me more about literature and art than I could have learned at the university. We spent endless hours in museums and libraries and sometimes simply wandering through Prague where he knew every stone, the story of every building, statue, or picture. I had plenty of time for it, because Rudolf was up to his ears in work, used to come home late and then sit even later over his books. He had been trained as a lawyer, but now he started studying economics and with great conscientiousness and diligence tried to catch up on all he had lost during the war. I grew accustomed to going to sleep in our tiny apartment with the desk lamp shining on a stack of books on the table. To this day, when I think of Rudolf, I usually see him sitting there quietly, with the dim light outlining his head.

We were both so taken up with our interests that we paid little attention to what was happening around us. I remember only that wherever one turned in those days—at home, in taverns, in the streets—wherever two people met a debate would start, or even a quarrel, Czech style. I remember the first election, too, when someone wrote in white paint on a fence near us, "Vote Communist or Social Democratic!" It seemed a rather funny slogan. I voted for the Social Democrats, because my father used to vote for them and Rudolf's father had been a

Social Democratic Party official. I was proud to carry on a family tradition. The Communist party emerged strongest in the Parliament even without my vote.

I wanted to register at the university, too, but when the time came, I was expecting a baby and the doctor would shake his head in concern: "Save your strength, you are still so weak—for goodness' sake, people, why are you young ones in such a hurry with everything?" In the end, I did have to spend the final months of my pregnancy in bed. And then one Monday evening Rudolf, all flustered, drove me to a sanatorium. Until the Thursday morning when the baby was finally born he ran about the apartment, uncombed, unshaved, then into the streets, then into the halls of the sanitorium, scattering behind him a trail of rose petals from a faded bouquet that did not stand up too well under the waiting.

If you were to ask me about the most beautiful moment of my life, I could tell you, to the minute—it was the moment when the nurse brought in a tiny baby, its hair brushed to a peak, a baby with long eyelashes and eyebrows that looked painted on that soft tiny face, and said, "What a pretty boy you have." The whole world glowed and sang and the bare room filled with the light of paradise and I could see my father and mother and grandmother around my bed, for the first time smiling. I held that tiny head to my breast and said to myself, as so many times before, yet quite differently, life, life. . . .

Not long after that I again took up my work, but now I would draw at home so that I would not have to leave my child. I had withdrawn completely into a private world. The world around us was changing, but I hardly noticed it. Rudolf used to come back from his office at the Chamber of Industry even later at night, regretful that he could not spend more time with his son, but I had a feeling that he was pleased with his work. When I look back now, this seems to have been the most peaceful, most contented time of our life. And yet, objectively, that was the last moment we could have collected our few belongings, packed them in a bundle and run as fast as we could, run before the light from the East that would change, ever more rapidly, into a conflagration.

Once or twice a week Mrs. Mach would come and take

my son for a walk. I used those half-days to take finished drawings to the publishing house, bring home new work, and look around to see what was new. One day in February of 1948, I was in a particularly good mood. I put on my nicest coat and a new hat and trotted happily through Prague. Near the center of town the streets were blocked by masses of people, all marching toward the Old Town Square. Another demonstration, I thought sourly—how can it keep anyone amused in this cold? The intersection at the foot of St. Wenceslas Square was completely blocked by workers from the ČKD factories. They made way for me and shouted light-hearted compliments after me as only the men in Prague can. I smiled at them and pushed my way to Narodní Avenue.

In the publishing house the old man was standing by the window, looking into the packed street. He did not turn around to greet me. He said quietly, "This is a day to remember. Today our democracy dies." I stood next to him, my heart suddenly a block of ice. Out in the street the voice of Klement Gottwald began thundering from the loudspeakers.

-*III*-
Bitter Harvest

i. The Revolution

I went for a walk today; it was still cold but there is a promise of spring in the air, and spring has always been a time to remember.

Springtimes in Huť, before the war, when people emerged from their houses into the gardens, aired out striped featherbeds and started turning the damp soil of their gardens. Our neighbor, Grandfather Pleticha, never seemed to go back inside; whenever I looked out into his garden, I would see him standing there in an old short jacket, his hands in his pockets, a cloth cap and the weathered face of an old Czech puppet like the ones Matěj Kopecký used to carve. I almost expected him to sink roots and start budding. From the corner window I used to see a slope covered with trees, bare and black—then one morning I would look out and a green wind seemed to have blown through the forest. A few days later, the cobwebs of bare branches would be hidden in a flood of bright green leaves. People now would stand outside their houses, warm themselves in the sunshine, and year after year they would say to each other, "Isn't it just beautiful?" as if they have never seen it before.

76

Then there were the springtimes in the Lodz ghetto. There not a blade of grass would grow, not a single bird fly—the stench of quicklime used for disinfection repelled or killed all living things. But even in the Lodz ghetto the wind would sometimes bring the smell of soil, of life. Far away somewhere—really only just beyond the fence of the ghetto—there were fields where the Germans grew wheat for the inmates' bread.

Our last spring in Lodz my father volunteered to work in those fields. I was concerned for him. One day, I no longer remember by what subterfuge, I procured a free afternoon and a pass to go after him. The sun was shining and I saw him walking slowly, bent under the strain, behind the plow. I realized how terribly he had aged, how pale and withered he had become with hunger and humiliation. We stood for a moment together in the sunshine, then my father took off his cap and said shyly, "Now when it is spring my heart feels so heavy. . . ." Only many years later I understood why he had chosen this work, far more strenuous than what he had done before. Each day he had to cover a long distance before reaching the fields, and then from dawn to dusk dragged himself behind the plow in heavy clogs sticky with hunks of clay. But there he was alone, with what he loved most—the freshly turned earth, the open sky, the clean breeze. On the eve of his death he had returned to the things from which he had come.

And springtimes in Prague—who could forget them? Forsythias on the Letná plain; Strahov; the chestnuts on Žofín; the gulls on Jirásek bridge. There is no city like Prague. You have to wander to the end of the earth to appreciate the magic that is not simply the beauty of the buildings, of the towers and the bridges, though it is that, too. They rise up from the ground in such a natural harmony as if nature had created them, growing out of the slopes and riverbanks like trees and flowers. But what is unique about Prague is the relation between the city and its people. Prague is not an eternal, uncaring backdrop, which stands there through good and ill, ignoring happiness and suffering alike. Prague lives in the lives of her people and shares in them, and they repay her with love that we usually reserve for humans. Prague is not an aggregate of buildings where people are born, work, and die. She is alive, sad and brave, and when she smiles with spring her smile glistens like a tear.

The spring of 1948 began inauspiciously, with the death of Jan Masaryk. Jan Masaryk, much as his father had been and in his own right, was a symbol of humanism, and his presence in the new government had been a token that our road to socialism might be different, after all. We did not know whether his death, less than a month after the coup, had been suicide or murder. There were many conjectures. Pavel Kavan, a good friend of ours who worked at the Ministry of Foreign Affairs was probably the last person to see Jan Masaryk alive—except possibly for some midnight visitors who might have come later. Kavan insisted that Masaryk seemed his usual self that night, neither nervous nor depressed. Incidentally, Kavan was arrested in 1952 and sentenced to twenty-five years, imprisonment. He was rehabilitated four years later with broken health and died some two years afterward.

Another acquaintance of ours, Stanislav Marek, insisted with equal vehemence that Jan Masaryk was subject to severe depressions and that no one who really knew him was surprised by his suicide. Marek had been Masaryk's friend for years: at the time of the death, he was police president. A year or two later he paid for the strain of his post with a heart attack, retired, and died a few years later.

None of us knew what to believe, but whether Masaryk committed suicide or was murdered, it was clear that the Communist party's "Victorious February" was the cause. What Masaryk stood for was incompatible with what was taking place all around us. Our people did not forget him. Twenty years later, during the Czechoslovak Spring of 1968 one of the first things the students did was to march to his grave in Lány, which is always covered with flowers.

One evening in the late spring of 1948, some three or four months after the coup, Rudolf told me over dinner that he had been offered the position of chief in the cabinet of the Minister of Foreign Trade. The thought frightened me. By that time we all realized that the Communist coup had been more than another ripple on the continuous stream of our political life.

It was a fundamental transformation that was to have tremendous consequences for our country. It was a revolution that some welcomed with joy, others with bitterness. Many of our acquaintances escaped abroad, others stayed on and lived in fear; everything around us was tumbling or being torn down. The basic change of which we had heard for so long had come, but it was not at all clear that it would prove to be a change for the better.

I wanted Rudolf to stand aside and wait, in case the development took a direction that he could not support. What if all those glowing ideals were to fail in practice? As an ordinary Party member he might still be able to express dissent, protest, or might resign—but by then I was sufficiently familiar with Communist practice to realize that highly placed functionaries had little margin for dissent. "Who is not with us is against us"—either you belong to the Party body and soul, or you are a traitor.

Fortunately, Rudolf himself said he did not want to take the job. "I am not suited for it," he said. "I am contented with what I am doing now, and there is much more I need to learn. I have turned down the offer." Still, he was surprised he had been chosen for the job—a young, inexperienced man, who had only recently joined the Party and had never held a political office or performed a Party function.

Two days later we were expecting Ota and Milena for supper and afterward planned to go to the theater. Rudolf came in breathless at the last minute. He told me his refusal had been rejected; he had received an official Party order to accept the job at the Ministry. His Party superiors explained that they had followed his work in the Chamber of Industry in detail, that they considered his professional qualifications outstanding, and that his knowledge of foreign languages would prove useful. The Party needed him, and the Party had decided.

Now the choice was simple, to accept the job or to resign from the Party and turn his back on everything he believed in. I started to protest, but Rudolf said, "How very much like us! As long as we read it on paper, think of it in theory, we can be ever so enthusiastic. But when the time comes to act, we lose our nerve. I don't know whether I am doing the right thing, but don't ask me to turn away now and have to reproach myself all my life for being a coward. You can't achieve anything without taking risks of making mistakes. I am convinced we can build a better society, a more just society, and in the end even a freer society. I have to accept responsibility for that conviction. I know, you are afraid that we'll repeat the Soviet terror. But study it carefully, you'll understand that in our country the conditions are different. It all depends on getting rational, honest men into the key positions. Then we will not waste out resources and energy, and won't do injustice to anyone."

I remember arguing that as a cabinet chief Rudolf would be no more than a minister's errand boy. "You'll do what they decide without you. Experts like you will have no say in policy. Can't you see that it is always the second or the third man down the line who bears the responsibility, and that it is the first one who gets the credit when something works out well?"

"But I am not interested in recognition," Rudolf told me, "I realize very well that I am acceptable only in the interim. No matter how hard I try, I am still a man of the old order. In a year or two, when enough young workers have finished their studies at the university I'll be glad to turn over the job to one of them and go back to my books. You see, my only real qualification for the job is that I am not interested in making a career, in securing a position, in getting advantages. I'll work honestly."

I suddenly was overcome by the tension of the last few weeks, the sense of insecurity and helplessness, and I began to weep. Then the bell rang and Ota and Milena came in. Rudolf explained to them what had happened and Milena clasped her hands—"Good grief, I've known you since first grade, I've lived through every kind of horror with you, but the first time I see you cry is when your husband is getting a chance to make a career. You're out of your mind."

In the end we did go to the theater and for the moment forgot about our anxieties. We did not even speak of them when we came home. For a long time we lay in bed, each listening to the other's breathing, knowing the other, too, was awake. Finally Rudolf said, "I know the next few years won't be easy. But after that, if we do not fail, everyone will live well and happy. And that is worth a try." I felt his fingers touch my lips gently. "Please," he said, "smile at least a little bit."

When I think back to the period following the coup what stands out most clearly is my sense of bewilderment and groping; it was doubly oppressive because the darkness not only was all around me but within me as well. It seems that once you decide to believe something your faith becomes more precious than truth, more real than reality.

The day when the newspapers printed the news of Rudolf's nomination to his new post in the Ministry my world began to change. That week I stopped at my hairdresser's, quite as usual. The hairdresser was a fine fellow; he and all the people in his shop had always treated me with the casual friendliness one finds in Prague. Usually one of the apprentices played with my baby when my hair was drying, and sometimes even wheeled him out into the street in his carriage.

This time they did not welcome me with the usual light banter. Instead, the entire shop stood respectively at attention, the hairdresser himself helped me off with my coat and then started dancing around me, offering me every kind of rinse and paste about which he used to say "You should be glad you don't need that junk." I stared at them in disbelief—"What has happened to you?" "Nothing," he answered. "But something has happened to you. We can't treat a highly placed person like you as if we had played marbles with her all our lives. . . ."

That was the first symptom. I had to get used to it: for everyone, except for a handful of our oldest friends, I ceased to be a human being. I had become an object of envy, hate, suspicion, or obsequious deference. In all the years that Rudolf held his post at the Ministry, I did not succeed in making a single friend among the Comrades. Once ideology takes the front seat, human relations cannot survive. When every deed, every thought, every moment of one's life has to be dedicated to "building socialism," under constant supervision, there is no room for something as private as a feeling of friendship. Feelings, anyway, are tricky things, hard to control, hard to channel; they lead people away from work and revolutionary dedication. In short, they are a suspicious, shady business, something one better avoids altogether. The only thing we can afford safely and happily is to love the party and her representatives, and feel comradely solidarity and confidence in the struggle for socialism.

But be careful, use caution: you have to examine each comrade thoroughly before you can trust him. Only the Party is worthy of limitless devotion. I remember an older actress, an outstanding artist, who declared that anyone whose eyes do not grow moist upon hearing Lenin's name is not worthy of standing on the stage of the National Theater. . . .

Sometime early in 1949, one of Rudolf's colleagues came to visit us and the conversation turned to these matters. That man said, "Rudolf, you know how much I like you, you know you are my friend, but if I ever suspected you of any deviation, I would turn against you without hesitation and do everything in my power to make sure you paid for it." A few months later he started coming to our apartment, terrified, pale, nervous, telling us of a black police Tatra limousine that followed his every step and begging us to let him sit and relax with us for a few moments. He was one of the first Party members who were arrested. I felt sorry for him, but as he had always seemed rather mysterious and capable of anything, I was prepared to believe he had been involved in some nefarious dealings.

About two months after the coup an older woman whom I did not know called at our apartment. She said she had heard we wanted to move—that was true, our tiny apartment had been bursting at the seams ever since my son was born. She offered me an apartment in her house in the Letná, district, left vacant by people who had escaped abroad. When I went to see it, it turned out to be none too spacious and quite expensive. The rooms were strewn with belongings left behind by the former tenants. In the kitchen I found their housemaid, a fat, slow girl who was helping the landlady clear the apartment. She was sitting over a cup of coffee, and as I came in, whispered to me, "Lady, don't take this place, there's a curse on it. First some Jews lived here, they all died in a concentration camp. Then some Germans who just barely got away, the people here like as not would have beat them to death. And the people

I worked for, they ran off with a bundle on their back. No one ever leaves here ordinary like."

Still, the apartment was convenient, and I liked it. Besides, Rudolf's position brought new social obligations with it, and we needed a place where three people would not be a crowd. I have little taste for formal entertaining, but I was willing to put up with it for Rudolf's sake. The thought of the dinners and receptions we had to attend still depresses me. The men, most of them as completely involved in their work as Rudolf, used those occasions as working conferences and left the wives to amuse themselves as best they could. The wives fell into two categories: the proletarian cadres and women with a bourgeois past like mine. The first, proud of their proletarian origins, bore themselves with utmost confidence, loud and hearty, knowing that whatever they said or did would be justified by their proletarian background. The second group was perennially terrified lest they say something that was not dedicated enough, something "intellectualistic," or politically inappropriate, which could hurt their husbands. More than once, when we had exhausted the safe topic of children, we would sit or stand for hours in cramped silence, with a smile that made our faces ache, nodding to the jabber of the comrades with proletarian origins. I remember once standing for a half hour in a corner with the wife of one of our leading economists. Finally she could stand it no longer and babbled, "Have you seen anything interesting at the theater lately?" She had hardly spoken before she became terrified of her words and added hurridly, "If you'll forgive me such a bourgeois question." Yet she was an intelligent, educated woman who later did some excellent work in literature. Soon our lack of class-consciousness became so obvious that the Party arranged a special series of lectures on Marxism to which many comrades' wives brought knitting or darning as evidence of their positive attitude to manual labor.

Perhaps the most startling aspect of that time was the ostentatious luxury of official receptions—where the tables were heaped with the choicest delicacies while ordinary people were still living on rations—and the nouveau-riche snobbery among just those who made most of their proletarian origins and mentality and ruled in the name of the working class. At one occasion, one older comrade reprimanded me severely because I was wearing merely a simple, full-length dress to a reception for Ambassador Zorin instead of a full formal costume. At the time, clothes were still rationed. Later, when Rudolf and I bought our first car—a secondhand one—and drove it to a reception, Rudolf received an official rebuke both for driving a secondhand car and for driving it himself: the new elite considered nothing appropriate short of a chauffeur-driven limousine.

I found myself in a crossfire. On the one hand, I was aware of the critical glare of the neighbors on our street who carefully noted and examined my every step. Once, at a meeting of the local party organization, the comrades actually discussed the style of my clothes, making the point that they considered them insufficiently proletarian. On the other hand, there were the members of the equally watchful new elite, who were drowning in luxuries and bad taste supported by special ration cards, which Rudolf consistently refused. To them I appeared far too undignified. I resolved the problem, to my own damage, I suppose, by ignoring both sides.

In contrast with our old place, our new apartment was on a street of nice and rather expensive apartments. During the war, most of them had been taken over by the Germans, and later fell to a strange assortment of the newly rich who had joined the Party for entirely private reasons. Few workers lived on this street, but many tradesmen and shopkeepers who hoped that they could keep their shops if they posed as hard-core Bolsheviks and so glowed with constant enthusiasm. Almost at every meeting one would rise and declare in a voice choked with emotion, "Comrades, I do love our party so. . . ." and sit down again.

Once just before the May Day celebration someone inquired timidly whether it was not wasteful to use up countless miles of good cloth and lumber for May Day decorations when they could surely be put to much better use in our postwar economy. This brought the owner of a local dairy shop to his feet, thundering in righteous indignation: "What's this? What traitor dares say that something is wasted for the Party? I tell you comrades, the more the better, let's make even bigger and better decorations, the devil take the cost; make the capitalists jealous." It did not help him—several months later his shop, too, was nationalized.

The chairman of the local organization was a strange, short man with a long horse face. He had a tawdry wife who also, in some indefinite way, reminded me of a horse. Those two were endowed with a pathological, venomous curiosity, and day and night searched out every bit of gossip about the most intimate affairs of the people in the street, Communists and non-Communists alike. The opportunity of spying on the private lives of others was, I think, what made many people join the local Party organizations. Gossip had become a virtue: a Communist, after all, not only had a right but the duty to know everything that went on around him. I knew a number of people, both men and women, who spent the best hours of their day standing on corners or looking out of their windows to make sure nothing escaped their notice.

But, at the time, all these things did not upset me too much. It was unpleasant, but it seemed trite rather than ominous. I had a few illusions about people, and I was determined not to let myself be soured by details. For me, Rudolf's conviction that we were on the right path and would overcome all obstacles outweighed all else.

Occasionally people came to us to complain of some injustice or to ask us for help. For the most part these were older people, tradesmen whose shops had been confiscated but who, having formerly been self-employed, were not eligible for social security. Now they looked in vain for jobs or old-age pensions. Frequently, Rudolf was able to help them. Others came, who wanted to leave the country; but then there was no help for them. Of all the injustices and inanities of those years closing the frontiers probably was the worst. Why not let people go if they did not want to stay? Why keep them against their will? One comrade from the Minisrty of Foreign Affairs explained it to me: "It is simply a temporary measure; the Republic cannot afford such a loss of labor. Many people want to leave without real reason, they do not understand our situation and have become victims of an entirely unjustified panic. Once they see they have nothing to fear, they'll be glad they stayed. Then we will open the frontiers again and everyone will be able to travel wherever he wants to go."

There also were many people, especially among the young, to whom it seemed that 1948 was the year of the realization of great hopes. There was more than enough work for all. Even housewives began to take employment, some out of necessity—to earn a second income—some for the satisfaction of taking part in public life. We all worked furiously, even on holidays and Sundays; and many people spent their evenings studying. People earned enough, often more than they needed, and bought up everything in sight. In addition we were organizing tax-supported medical care, old-age pensions, vacations for workers. Nationalization and collectivization caused a great deal of bad blood, but we were told this was to be expected: it was a difficult step but necessary for the future growth of our economy. Looking out of a train at the countryside divided into those incredibly tiny strips of private fields, I had to agree that private agriculture had no future. At the time, none of us had dreamed that the ruthless, crude procedure did so much damage that it would be ten, fifteen, even twenty years before the nationalized enterprises and agricultural collectives could begin to function effectively.

Sometime in 1950, an acquaintance of ours from the country came to visit us in Prague. We called him Karlíček. Before the coup, he had owned a relatively large farm not far from Prague. He was a superb farmer and a good man whom the people in his village liked and welcomed as a friend when he occasionally came to see the farm of which he had been so proud deteriorate after the collectivization. He arrived at our apartment, upset and furious.

He practically shouted at Rudolf, "In my time, when a cow gave less than ten liters, I sold it for meat because she ate up more than she yielded. Today they make a show out of awarding a medal to a cow that is yielding four liters! You idiots!" About that time Prague wits began to define socialism as a system designed to resolve successfully all the problems that would never arise under any other system.

Rudolf, however, now threw himself into his work with so much enthusiasm and optimism that he carried me with him. The people with whom he worked seemed as intelligent and diligent as he, and as far as I could judge, their task—commercial relations with the West—was showing promising signs of development. I myself was especially pleased with the help Czechoslovakia was giving to the new State of Israel. Rudolf was instrumental in that program. I knew little about it concretely: at the time, all government projects were secret and usually top secret, and so after a while I stopped asking about them altogether. Rudolf's world, symbolized by his briefcase that no one dared to touch, closed more and more before me.

He now worked late almost every night, and was often called to the Ministry even on Sundays, while I spent the afternoon alone in the park wheeling our baby in his carriage, envying the happy family clusters around me. Before, we had not passed up a single good play, and both of us, especially Rudolf, a gifted violinist, loved music. Now whenever I bought theater or concert tickets, Rudolf almost always called at the last minute to say that he could not come. Our child was growing up hardly knowing his father.

Once I managed to convince Rudolf to drive up to the mountains for a weekend. We both were devoted skiers. There is nothing more beautiful than our mountains in the winter, but that Saturday the weather was against us; a few miles out of Prague we ran into a snowstorm and when we reached the foothills, it was snowing so hard that we could not tell whether we were still on the road or somewhere in an open field. We moved at a snail's pace, looking out of a half-open door, trying to guess where we were. Suddenly Rudolf turned to me and said with amazement, "Would you believe it, for almost a half hour I have not thought of foreign trade?"

Today I wonder whether that insane overloading of work was not intentional. Not one of those who assumed responsible positions had a moment to verify how his efforts were reflected in the people's daily life. They met no one but each other, in conferences, meetings, and councils; they judged the situation only from official releases and reports, which were, to begin with, quite unrealistic. Precisely by their concentration on a narrow segment they inevitably lost perspective and all true sense for the real needs and wishes of the people. And even if occasionally they happened to speak with those who did not belong to their circle, few dared to complain. In Rudolf's case, I don't think they were afraid: they all knew he was incapable of hurting a fly. But his fanatic conviction that what he was doing was right disarmed and silenced everyone and left Rudolf isolated.

Gradually I became Rudolf's only link with the ordinary world. Throughout our marriage, except for one fierce fight two weeks after our wedding, occasioned by my muffing a serve at volleyball, I don't think we ever had any of those personal quarrels that usually occur in even the best of marriages. But now we wasted most of our precious moments together in bitter, vain debates about politics—vain, because Rudolf considered his statistics far more reliable than my experience and complaints, which he dismissed as narrow and prejudiced. People are doing fine, there is no starvation, no unemployment—yes, it's true we may botch something here and there, but in time that will all be smoothed over; just wait a few years and you'll see.

Perhaps the first thing that jarred Rudolf as much as me was really quite minor. One night the wife of the grocer where before the war my mother used to shop came to our apartment, terrified and in tears. She told us that the police had broken into her home late at night, turned everything upside down and taken her husband away without telling her where or why.

The grocer, a kind, jolly man, dreadfully fat, was a known black marketeer; so it did not seem altogether impossible that he had been arrested for good and sufficient reason. But why in such gangster fashion? Rudolf promised to do all he could and the poor woman left, somewhat relieved. The following day we found out that a great many shopkeepers and tradesmen had been dragged away the same night, and for a time no one knew what had become of them or with what they had been charged. Many of them waited many months before they were finally tried by the so-called People's Tribunals whose decisions were based not on law but on "sound class feeling" meting out punishments arbitrarily left and right.

I think this gave Rudolf his first glimpse of the utter precariousness of law and justice in our country. By that time it was late in 1949, and the Soviet Union had become our binding model, Yugoslavia had been declared a preserve of traitors and spies, and all the ministries were being reorganized along much more centralized lines. Rudolf's job at the Ministry of Foreign

Trade had been abolished and he was placed in charge of the Western trade section with the title of Undersecretary. Officially, the "class war" was supposed to be intensified, but we were assured that fortunately the Party was alert and aware. The movie theaters showed films about saboteurs and spies striving to disrupt the unity of the working class, the bookstores were stocked with books about the Great Conspiracy against the Party and Comrade Stalin. We were told about the incredible cleverness of the enemy who could mask himself even before his fellow workers, even before his own family. By then no one was saying any more that anyone who means well will have the opportunity to grow and participate in building socialism. The Party gave up persuasion; instead, it took up cadre evaluation. People sat late into the night over questionnaires that searched their minds and ancestry to the third and fourth generation. What a man could do and how well he did his work had become irrelevant. The things that now mattered were his class awareness, class origin, attitude to the "pop-dem" order, and most of all his attitude to the Soviet Union.

The rule of thumb was not at all complex: every man is a product of his class, education, environment. A man whose father operated a penny-candy store or a peanut stand is a product of the private-enterprise mentality and cannot be trusted, whatever he may do. The effect was sometimes comic: I knew a man who had a tiny yard-goods store in a small village and just barely fed his family. His shop was nationalized, and as a member of the bourgeoisie he was assigned to a factory for reeducation. But of course from that moment on his children could proudly write "worker" in the questionnaires' category of "occupation of father," and so were able to secure positions and salaries of which their exploiter father never had dreamed. On the other hand, the son of Party ideologue and Minister Ladislav Štoll was at first refused admission to the university and was advised to go to work in the mines since, as the son of a government official, he was not of worker or peasant origin.

Insecurity and fear were settling in and bearing down on us. That summer Rudolf was getting ready to go to London at the head of a delegation that was to negotiate a trade agreement with England. Under our conditions, that was an extremely difficult, dangerous task. To reach an agreement, the arrangements would have to be mutually advantageous, but in our country any concession to which Rudolf would agree could later be held against him as intentional sabotage of national interests or at least incompetence.

As the time drew near, I noticed that Rudolf was more concerned and thoughtful than ever, until one evening when he came home in an altogether different mood: he told me that the government had assured him of a completely free hand, and that the Party would consider it a success if he reached any agreement at all. If I remember correctly, Rudolf came back from England twice for consultations, but though I was glad to see him, he had little to say. His thoughts were miles away. When the treaty was finally signed and Rudolf returned, Klement Gottwald invited him to his private apartment. Deeply moved, Gottwald embraced him and congratulated him on a superb achievement, greater than anyone had expected. The treaty signed for the British by Harold Wilson, later Labour-government prime minister, was considered an important contribution to the development of our trade with the West. Rudolf who had come home tired and sleepless, now finally relaxed.

The fall that year was beautiful and warm, and Rudolf was so exhausted that he finally agreed to take a week's vacation. We loaded the car and set out for a random drive through Bohemia. It was not a success. The beauty of the calm, restful landscape intensified our sense of tension. For hours we sat side by side in silence, but not as we had in the past, when we could sit silently because we were happy and at peace together. Now we were afraid to speak and reveal our anxiety. We had put the top down and drove through the deserted, tree-lined highways among freshly plowed fields. I clearly remember one part of the road where rich old trees vaulted over us, glittering with rays of sunlight. I tilted back my head, the wind hit my face and suddenly I felt utterly certain of impending disaster, felt an anxiety as if death itself awaited us at the end of the tunnel of trees. To this day my heart skips a beat whenever I look up in a car and in place of the sky see trees overhead, arching their branches in a gesture of despair.

On the third day we happened upon a village where my old friend Martin, a partisan who had helped hide me during the last months of the war, was spending his vacation in a cottage by a lake. We spent the night there. The sound of water splashing regularly under our windows made me feel I was falling asleep on a ship. In the morning Rudolf went for a walk in the woods and Martin invited me for a boat ride. He rowed to the middle of the lake, shipped his oars and said earnestly,

"Now listen, and listen well: you must do anything to get your husband to leave his job. If you can think of no other way, cause some kind of scandal so that he'll be fired. If he stays, he won't last much longer and he'll come to a hard end. When I speak with him I cannot comprehend how someone as intelligent as he can be so utterly blind. The more and better he works, the worse for him. Everything he achieves will turn against him. We are on the Russian track now, and the stops will be the same. Very soon they'll start looking for scapegoats, especially among people who defend specific Czechoslovak interests. Your husband is made for the role."

The whole scene: the two of us alone in the middle of the lake where no one could overhear; the urgency in Martin's voice; it all overwhelmed me with the atmosphere of the years in the underground. Martin was no longer chatting on a summer afternoon, he was speaking with grim authority, as a partisan commander. I understood.

"Martin, and what about you? Are you looking out for yourself? For God's sake, don't start anything; this is not Nazi Germany—you don't stand a chance."

ii. Faith and Doubt
The men who, like Rudolf, staked their lives on their convictions did not do it casually. Theirs was a faith that men do not give up readily. The steady deterioration of the situation in Czechoslovakia after the coup was stubbornly explained by our people's inability to master

the intensifying internal contradictions, which were in turn explained by international tension. As late as 1950 I heard people say, "The Soviets should interfere. If Stalin knew what is going on here he'd put things in order." And the wife of one of the prewar Communists who had been arrested came to me for advice, wondering if she should turn to the Soviet Embassy for help and ask the Soviet Ambassador to intercede in behalf of her husband.

Those were the years of the Cold War. The iron curtain had cut us off from the world. Our newspapers printed every word that Vyshinsky spoke in the United Nations, but never mentioned any replies. All we learned about the West was that there were strikes and that Communists were being persecuted. I remember the one bit of foreign news I heard on the radio. I had been listening to the news and picked out the dateline, Holland. It was the first mention of a Western country in months. I listened intently. The news item reported was that the Soviet Folk Dance collective had performed successfully in Holland. From the few authors who were being translated—such writers as Stefan Heym, Howard Fast, and Jack Lindsay—we could only conclude that the Party was right, that the West finally found itself in the terminal stage of moral and economic disintegration. We seldom listened to foreign broadcasts, in part because of fear, in part because the jamming was so bad that it was hard to hear. Frequently someone would make out some news item only in part, would pass it on with further distortions and people would respond with a wave of the hand, You see how they lie?

We had concluded that war was around the corner, and that police regimes had hardened all over the world, not only in our country. We all knew that our regime had many enemies in our own country and that the black market was flourishing, so that when the arrests and trials began, many people believed the accused must be guilty of something. Few people suspected at this stage that there was something badly out of joint with our system of justice. After all, the acused almost invariably confessed. . . .

I remember the amazement with which I read reports from the trial of a group of priests. They testified like instructors of Marxist ideology and formulated their confessions in such pure Party jargon that I could hardly believe it. One of our comrades offered the stock explanation: the interrogations are conducted so that the investigators seek to convince, to reeducate the accused, to explain the goals and principles of the Party and to lead them to become aware of how and in what ways they were guilty. The force of our arguments, of our truth is so great, he insisted, that in the end it convinces even our enemies.

All through 1950 and 1951 the officially proclaimed class struggle was supposed to be intensifying, and most of us still half believed that it was an inevitable evil. Every regime defends itself against its enemies and subversives—look at America, we used to think, things are no better there. Only when someone was arrested whom we knew well and of whose innocence we were convinced did we start to open our eyes.

Then the reaction came in three stages. The first response was invariably that it must be some kind of mistake, the man will be interrogated and released, some explanation will be found.

The second response was still disbelief: I know this man, he cannot be a traitor. Something shady is afoot, there must be some conspiracy, directed from the West. They want to weaken the Party, and so they are intentionally throwing suspicion on its best people. But in the end it will come out, the truth will emerge.

The third response was a stunned, fearful silence. Only few people began to realize dimly that we ourselves were really becoming victims of a conspiracy, but that this conspiracy was not directed from the West.

Once, years later, when the first cautious rehabilitations took place and a few of the former prisoners began to appear in public, I met my friend Pavel Eisler, who had never joined the Party even though he belonged among its earliest enthusiasts and until 1951 worked in the Office of the President of the Republic. He was so agitated that he could hardly speak; for a few moments we just stood there in the street staring at each other. Then he told me, "I've just ridden on the same streetcar with a man from out office who had been arrested in 1950. At the time I was amazed, but I thought to myself, who would have guessed it, he seemed so nice and he was a traitor all along. They had recently released him, after six years. He had been completely innocent. Now he looks twenty years older, his hair is grey, his teeth are all gone. And when they were taking him away, I had just nodded my head thoughtfully! Imagine, I did not even feel sorry for him. My God, what fools we have been." Just so, what fools we had been. . . .

But, at the time it would have been hard to be wise. The more the theaters repeated Gorki's statement, "Man—that has a proud ring to it," the less did men come to mean in society. The better and happier our life appeared in the pages of out journals, the worse and sadder became our reality. The stores were besieged by endless lines of would-be customers, but there were shortages of practically everything. Every few months, there were rumors of a new currency reform, and people would buy up everything in the stores, frequently useless, defective items. The unceasing ideological barrage and the chaos in the economy took all pleasure out of honest work. Most workers looked around for some additional means of earning money, frequently semilegal at best, and came to their regular jobs to rest up. The nationalized economy moved steadily downhill.

Our lives, permeated by fear, had become a deadening round of hopeless drudgery. Suspicion and distrust had prevailed to the point at which no one trusted anyone. We were told that the omnipresent enemy was no longer merely outside the Party, but had infiltrated the Party as well. Everyone suspected everyone else, no one dared speak openly. Our whole world began to disintegrate. By 1951, even Rudolf's optimism was long gone, replaced by stubborn, self-punishing toil.

In the meantime the small publishing house where I had worked was dissolved, and I had found a position as an art editor in a newly organized publishing house for scientific literature. For the first time I found myself working in a socialistic enterprise. The editors all were young men and women, almost without exception Party members, and their enthusiasm for their work knew no bounds. Almost all of them were studying on the side, and spending Sundays and vacations with labor brigades. They had every day planned down to the minute to find time for it all. But none of them had any inkling about managing a publishing house. In spite of all their good will and diligence they caused such confusion that within two years the venture failed completely and had to be disbanded.

In the beginning, their diligence, idealism, and childlike faith in the infallibility and actually the *holiness* of the Party overwhelmed me. I could not understand how young people could completely give up all private life, and discipline themselves so as to identify day by day with the prescribed modes of thought. No matter what happened, none of them ever doubted that whatever the Party did, it did well. Not one of them dreamed of complaining for a moment about the endless Party meetings and conferences. The arbitrary commands of comrades from the Central Committee, who supervised our publications, were followed enthusiastically to the letter and the names of those comrades were always spoken with respect. In this exemplary, class-conscious "comradely collective" I first overheard the rebuke that, at the time, was routinely administered to less earnest comrades: "What, you had a date? Aren't you ashamed to waste time dating when there is a war on in Korea?"

I can think of only two people who did not fit the pattern. One of them was the editor in chief, a young man named Jiri Stano, noted for less than penetrating intellect and for ephemeral diligence. His activity remained limited to inviting his favorites among the editors in his Ostrava dialect to join him for a swig from the bottle he kept in his desk. Later he was relieved from this position to apply his talents to loftier duties. Today he is one of the pillars of the Russian occupation version of the old Party daily, *Rudé Pravo*. There his articles suggest not only that he has not changed, but that he had perfected the talents he exhibited in our publishing house.

The other exception was Pavel Kovály, who seemed to be far more interested in skiing and canoeing than in Party activities. He soon became my trusted ally. He developed admirable ingenuity for getting us out of Party meetings, often walked home with me and became acquainted with Rudolf. Whenever there was a free moment, he came to our apartment for conversation or for chess with Rudolf.

About that time the movies were showing a film Comrade Stano described feelingly as a crowning achievement of socialist realism, a masterful reflection of Soviet reality. The title of the film was *Cossacks from the Kuban*. It was a most realistic description of happy life on a collective farm where strong young women and tall young men turned hey and harvested wheat to the accompaniment of a four-part chorus of socialist work songs while comradely relations blossomed like roses. One of the women editors, in a fit of temporary insanity, declared that it looked to her rather like an ordinary class-B operetta. The collective was stunned. The erring comrade was ordered to carry out self-criticism and with the eager assistance of the entire office staff corrected her erroneous views—and went on correcting them for some ten more meetings. But for the eventual total exhaustion of all concerned, she might still have been correcting them in 1968.

My colleague Bořivoj, the other staff artist with whom I shared a room officially designated as "the studio," was an exceptionally nice, friendly young man who, among other things, was a member of the Folk Song and Dance Collective with which he took part in various tours, including visits to the Soviet Union. He overflowed with energy, though somewhat surprisingly all his activity accomplished very little. Still, he was most helpful to me, procured all my drawing supplies, ran errands, prepared wall displays, looked after raising the level of my political awareness and generally kept me entertained. He liked to recount his experiences in Russia, the friendly hospitality of the people, the ancient, lovingly maintained trains, the God-forsaken railway stops in the steppe where the flowerbeds were full of red blooms.

We got along fine until the day when he arrived at the office eagerly with a cardboard map case from which he produced a print and asked my opinion. The print showed a mass of pinkish clouds, which could have represented sunrise or sunset equally well. Against that blooming background stood a pale violet tractor, and in the forefront, dominating the picture, stood Josef Vissarionovich, executed in such painstaking detail that the viewer felt like moving aside so that Little Father Stalin could step out of the picture and thunder at the audience. The effect was so overwhelming that I groaned, "Good grief, what unbelievable kitsch!"

A few seconds later I became aware that my colleague did

not respond. I looked up and discovered that his face had assumed the same hues as the clouds on the lithograph. He was gasping for breath, speechless. Finally he controlled himself enough to roar at me: "How dare you say that about a brilliant work of a leading Soviet artist? Is that your attitude to the Soviet Union?? Do you want war??? You war-monger, you . . .!!!!" With that he shot out of the room straight into the office of the editor in chief. I could hear him ranting that he could not go on sharing an office with such a benighted hussy and demanding that "something be done about it."

A great deal might have been done about it; the times did not allow for flagging enthusiasm, much less open doubt. That nothing much was done was in part thanks to Rudolf's position, in part to the editor in chief who had replaced Stano and who, in spite of twenty years in the Party, was a rather sensible woman.

Our new masters went on exhibit annually at the gala performance of Smetana's opera *Libuše* at the National Theater. One year, when Rudolf was working at the Ministry, we received an invitation. We sat down in the orchestra; Comrade President and Comrades Ministers with their wives occupied the boxes.

In the presidential box Klement Gottwald practically disappeared behind a huge bundle of silver fox from which only the chubby face of Lady Marta and her plump hands, sparkling with jewels, peeked out. Then came Dolanský, cunningly leering at the audience. Then Široký's cruel, death-mask face with its piercing black eyes set deep under his brows. Minister of Defense Čepička, powdered and arrogant, appeared in a comic-opera uniform about which someone whispered that it must be the uniform of an admiral of the Vltava excursion steamers. Then Mrs. Čepička—daughter of the "workers' president," wife of a workers-and-peasants' minister—draped in gold lamé and chains of jewels, next to her Kopecký's bald pate, rocking like the head of a giant rewt. Plojhar, the hypocritical ex-priest, his face bloated with alcohol. Bacílek's sadistic chin clinched like a fist. . . .

I felt chills running down my spine. I leaned over to Rudolf and whispered in horror, "Are you blind? Can't you see what they are?"

A short time later we had a similar experience. The occasion was another gala, this time a reception for several hundred guests at the Prague Castle. The refreshments were exquisite, a costumed group of folk musicians from Moravské Slovácko provided the entertainment. Marta Gottwald doddered along in a kelly-green robe with a train, strutting between two files of bent backs. The intellectuals among the invited seized the rare opportunity and besieged the buffet.

I stood in one of the salons with a group of acquaintances when Klement Gottwald stumbled through the door, leaning on the speaker of the National Assembly, Comrade John, who was half carrying him. The President of the Republic was blind drunk. He picked a path across the room in my direction. Rocking back and forth, he spoke with difficulty, "Whatsh this? Ya ain't drinkin', why ain't ya drinkin'?"

The group around me signaled frantically for a waiter, and one leaped toward us with a tray of wineglasses. I took a glass, so did the President, and we both drank. Then the President waved his empty glass and stared at it for a moment. His bloodshot eyes turned to me and he repeated, exactly as before, "Whatsh this? Ya ain't drinkin', why ain't ya drinkin'?"

The speaker of the National Assembly regained his presence first. He managed a laugh, muttered some conciliatory remarks, then started to shift Comrade President from the room. I stood there with the glass in my hand and felt my knees shaking: that bloated, purple face, the dull, drunken eyes drowning in fat, the incoherent blather—that is our President. I glimpsed Rudolf in the opposite corner and looked at him in supplication. We went straight home. I spent the rest of the night sitting on the edge of the bathtub, with a towel around my head. My mind echoed to the voices of our Communist Youth, shouting in time, "We are the new generation, we are Gottwald's generation. . . . " And I could see the tall, gracious figure of President Masaryk who had walked in the rooms of that castle once long ago, in the days of our innocence.

The episode proved rather a shock for Rudolf, too. For some time we had heard rumors that Gottwald took to drink because the Russians did not keep their promises. Supposedly he was drowning in beer the bitter realization of where he had led his country. The emphasis during our "Victorious February" had been very much on "putting things in the right hands"—now more and more they seemed to be slipping into the wrong hands.

By 1951 the atmosphere in Prague had almost reverted to the conditions of the war. People hardly dared whisper to each other; almost every week there were new arrests. Thursdays and Fridays were the worst days: the Central Committee of the Communist party met on Thursdays. If the doorbell rang on those evenings, people turned pale. The non-Party members had something of a momentary reprieve now: with the growing influence of Soviet advisors, the methods did not change, but they concentrated increasingly on Party members. There were more and more suicides, some mysterious, some quite clear. One rather prominent official, visited by two comrades in civilian clothes, did not even hear them out. He went out another door, pulled a revolver from his drawer and shot himself. Later the rumor had it that they had not come to make an arrest, just to ask a few questions. Or perhaps they had dropped in just for a glass of beer—who knows?

I was becoming desperate. I wanted to force Rudolf at any cost to leave his job, convince him that he could prevent nothing, improve nothing, that he could only destroy himself. I insisted that no one with any self-respect could have anything to do with what was taking place. Rudolf, pale and troubled, insisted on his position: if all decent people leave now, it will be even worse.

I did not want to give up. I kept arguing with him, begging him; for months we did not exchange a personal word. I reproached myself for torturing him, but I could not help myself. My constant question was, what if they arrest you, too?

"That cannot happen," was the invariable answer. "Even if I do not believe that the people who are being arrested are aware of being guilty of anything, still they must have made serious mistakes. It is not possible that they could arrest someone for no reason at all. You have no idea how easy it is in this atmosphere to make a mistake or to overlook something—and that can always be interpreted as sabotage. This is why I am convinced that when they finish the investigations and find there had been no wrong intent, they will release them again. And I have my things in perfect order, I watch everything so closely that no major mistake can slip by."

"Rudolf, I beg you. . . ."

"I beg *you*. You are my wife; have some confidence in me."

Late in the spring of 1951 Rudolf became seriously ill. The doctor diagnosed it as complete nervous exhaustion and ordered rest. With his help, I managed to persuade Rudolf to request release from his job. I felt so relieved that I planned to resign from my job too, and to drop my studies at the university so that we could move to the country. But it did not last. Rudolf's resignation was not accepted: he was merely given a few days' leave, and then everything returned to the old condition.

One Saturday afternoon Pavel Eisler came to our apartment, all out of breath.

"Listen," he told us, "Eda Goldstücker has disappeared. He simply cannot be found, and no one knows anything about him."

Eduard Goldstücker, was one of Rudolf's and Pavel Eisler's closest friend, had returned a few days earlier from his post as Czechoslovak ambassador to Israel. Our relations with Israel had deteriorated markedly, and we all knew that this put Goldstücker in an awkward position. "Haven't you heard anything about him?"

We had not heard and did not want to guess. But the horror touched us all. We learned a few days later Eda had been arrested. Rudolf did not say a word, but for several nights I would hear him walking back and forth, back and forth through the apartment while I lay sleepless in bed and stared helplessly into the darkness. Why do people's best intentions turn against them? What did we do wrong? Why hadn't we foreseen the consequences of our decisions?

"Rudolf," I asked once, timidly, "isn't it strange that there are so many Jews among those who've been arrested?"

"For God's sake," Rudolf reacted nervously, "are you going to think that the Communists are anti-Semites? What utter rot! That shows you still don't understand anything. You need to do much more reading."

Sometime in that fall of 1951, I believe it was in November, Secretary General of the Party Rudolf Slánský was arrested. Rudolf had always disliked him intensely, insisted that Slánský was an extremist and a dogmatist, pathologically eager for recognition and power, suspicious and ruthless. He avoided him as much as possible, and I know that he had no personal or professional contact with him to speak of. When Slánský was arrested, we like many others, thought that it would bring about a radical improvement—that Slánský had been the man behind the wave of terror. But just the opposite happened; the secret police, now known as "State Security" intensified its rampage.

Late one Saturday night Rudolf and I sat in a nook in our living room, by lamplight, and I seemed to sense that something of our old mutual confidence was returning. We spoke more calmly than we had in a year, and managed to find words that had the same meaning for both of us. Our anxieties were converging, as our hopes had converged in the past, and I dared speak openly, without fear that I would hurt or anger him.

"I cannot believe," I told him, "that something good could turn into its very opposite like this, just because of a few mistakes or personal failures. If the whole system were sound and good, it would provide ways of compensating from human failure. If it can work only when it is led by geniuses among people who are a hundred percent pure and omniscient, then it is a bad system. It might work in heaven, but in this world it is a vicious fantasy. Look what has become of all those idealists who asked nothing but to work for the good of others. Half of them in jail, the other half shuddering every time the doorbell rings. It is all a fraud, a trap for the trusting."

Rudolf got up, crossed the room pacing back and forth a few times, then stood with his back to me by the window, pushed aside the curtain and looked out at the darkness outside.

"Heda, you know how much my work means to me. I've given it everything that is good in me. When the appointment came, I thought life was giving me an opportunity to act, to make up for our passivity in the past. I know I neglected you: I have been a bad husband and a bad father. I have given up everything I loved. But there is one thing I cannot give up. I cannot give up the conviction that my ideal is essentially good and right, just as I simply cannot understand why it failed as it has. I have to believe that this failure is just a passing crisis. Don't you see, if you were right, if it all really were a fraud, then all I have done would make me an accomplice in a monstrous crime. If I let myself believe that, Heda, I could not go on living . . . and I would not want to."

This left little to be said. We did not speak of it again. The year 1951, the fourth since the coup, was drawing to a close.

Early in 1952 we attended yet another reception, I no longer remember where it was held. As we got into the car, I said to Rudolf, "Look at that man at the corner. He's been there every time we've left the house in the last few days."

Rudolf laughed. "He's probably after one of the girls in the shop across the street. What's come over you? You need a rest; take a vacation, take the boy to the country."

At that reception I received the special attention of Comrade Minister Široký, the chairman of the Cabinet. He took me by the arm, held my hand and spent a long time strolling with me. He had never paid attention to me before. Comrade Morozov from the Soviet Trade Mission also was especially cordial on that occasion. As usual, vodka flowed in streams and we toasted people who would have served mankind best if they had forgotten to be born.

On January 10, after work, I stopped at the bank to get money for material for a new suit for Rudolf. When I got to the store I found it crammed with people fighting for every conceivable piece of merchandise. Behind me a line formed rapidly. I walked out disgusted, and noticed that the same scene was being repeated in every store. Prague looked again like an agitated ant-hill. People hurried through the streets and lines formed on the sidewalks in front of every store. Evidently there was another rumor of a currency reform. At times those rumors originated at the Ministry of Domestic Trade. Whenever the warehouses were filled with defective, inferior merchandise, it was enough to hint that the government was planning another currency reform in which all savings would lose their worth or be confiscated, as before, and people would buy up everything they could lay their hands on, no matter how inferior.

I caught a streetcar home. Old Mrs. Machová was there, playing with my son. The lad was already attending nursery school and I was glad that many friends came to visit him, since the atmosphere of our home was not exactly relaxed.

After supper, when we had put him to bed, Mrs. Machová and I started complaining about the situation. We were in the thick of it when Rudolf came home. We attacked him together: "This is unbearable, so many years after the war and it is almost worse than during the occupation. How much longer can we go on like this?" And Mrs. Machová added, "It's all because people just don't expect anything good from the government any more. We don't have a government to serve the people, just to pester them and squash them. Whenever the government or the Central Committee meet, people shudder and wonder what nasty trick they will come up with next."

Mrs. Machová was one of those in whose name the Communist party made revolution. She was the daughter of a landless peasant and the wife of a worker, and had worked hard herself all her life. She had only a grade-school education, but she was probably the sharpest and wisest woman I have ever met. Rudolf had endless respect for her: he knew that her voice was the voice of the working class about which everyone spoke and which everyone ignored. Weakly and unhappily, he tried to pacify us and explain, but I was fast losing the last shreds of my patience. After Mrs. Machová left, Rudolf tried to embrace me and kiss me, for reconciliation and good night. I turned aside and pushed him away. For the first time in our life together we went to bed without reconciliation, without a word.

We did not speak to each other the following morning either, but that was not unusual, since I started work at seven, Rudolf an hour later. All morning I was troubled by my harshness of the evening before, and resolved to make it up that very day. For the first time I became aware of how much the constant fear and tension had exhausted and transformed me. I hardly recognized myself. I knew I couldn't go on this way, that I had to pull myself together or I would soon not be fit to live with. I had to get over my fears and premonitions. I had survived worse without turning into a bitter, repulsive shrew; I was determined not to give in to my moods now.

That afternoon I took my son for a long walk, bought fresh flowers for our apartment—flowershops were the only shops where there were no lines—and that evening I started to plan a new life. I would do exercises daily, starting today. I would go out among people, to the theaters and concerts, I would spend more time with my child. I telephoned Rudolf at the office to ask when he would come home. He told me he had mountains of work but that he would hurry. I put Dvořák's "Humoresque" on the phonograph together with some other records, dug out *The Good Soldier Schweik* from the library, and resolved to spend a calm, pleasant evening.

At ten o'clock I called Rudolf again. "I'm not finished yet, it will probably still take a while. Go to sleep, I'll come home as soon as I can."

Conscientiously I spent a half hour doing exercises, a quarter hour in the tub, and tried to convince myself that I was feeling light and easy. Everything depends on one's attitude, and I resolved that I would look at everything in perspective. No more depressions. But I could not sleep, and about half an hour before midnight I got up and took two aspirins.

The bell rang at one o'clock. Mařenka, the girl who lived in with us since I had started to work, and helped with the housework, came into the bedroom, all dishevelled and sleepy-eyed, and stuttered, "There are five thugs here and they have Dr. Margolius' briefcase."

The world tilted and I felt myself falling, bound hand and foot, somewhere down, down, deep, where there is no bottom. Then I snapped awake. So it happened. I had known it must happen, and now it happened. It happened again, it happened.

It was a strange moment. I accepted horror and misfortune as an old companion who left me for a time and now returned. Suddenly, the old familiar feeling came back, the stiffness that helps us when there is no more hope from anyone except ourselves, when *it has happened*, when there is no more avoiding it. It is something that is hidden deep in us, so deep we are not even aware of it, but it comes to the rescue whenever misfortune bares its fangs and attacks.

I got up calmly, put on slippers and brushed my hair. The only thing unusual was putting on Rudolf's robe instead of my own—it was far too long for me but it wrapped me all around.

I went out to the living room. The five men were there, one of them holding the fateful briefcase. They greeted me with exaggerated courtesy and announced that my husband had been arrested and they had been authorized to carry out a house search. I told them to go ahead and started to return to the bedroom. They stopped me, again most courteously, and told me that the law required my presence at the search to make sure all was in order.

I sat in a chair, lit a cigarette, and watched the comrades spread out through the apartment. The search was thorough: they moved systematically from room to room, opened and checked everything, shook the pages of every one of several hundred books, inspected and read every piece of paper. They looked under rugs, among the dishes, felt every seam of our clothes, examined shoes and toiletries. Some things they set aside. They found everything foreign especially interesting. A few days earlier someone had brought us a few packages of Albanian cigarettes. Each package included a slip with a slogan—since it ended in an exclamation point, I think it meant something like "Long live the working class!" My visitors carefully collected them and put them on their pile. One of the policemen who appeared to be in charge read through my private correspondence, added a few appreciative remarks about its literary quality and confiscated one or two letters. He paid special attention to an old diary in which I noted things about my son, mostly weights and measures. Those numbers must have appeared to him as a particularly ingenious code: when he put the book on his pile, he gave me an especially devastating look. I stayed in my chair, wrapped in Rudolf's robe, and tried not to chain smoke.

When they started to barge into the child's room I protested. What if the boy wakes up and sees five strange men digging through his toys? The shock could have serious consequences.

I offered them my word of honor that there was nothing in the room except the child'd things. They insisted that they must search the whole apartment, but promised to move as quietly as possible. They kept their promise—they went through the room and all its contents with such expertise that the boy did not wake up.

Mařenka's room came next. She had gone back to bed, and when one of the men opened her door, she came out with such vehement unwillingness and peppery commentary that the policeman emerged red all over. God bless her, I've often felt grateful to her: but of course as an exploited proletarian, she could get by with it with relative ease.

The last room was the one where I had my desk with all our most important papers and valuables. Among other things, there was a special file of correspondence with friends abroad, especially in England. At Rudolf's request I kept all their letters together, with carbons of my replies, so that we could prove there was nothing illicit.

But now everything had become illicit, even the simplest sentence could be interpreted as a secret code. Simply the fact of corresponding with someone in the West could damage Rudolf considerably. Dejectedly I awaited the triumphant outburst when this booty would be discovered. The man who opened the compartment was the one who had been most crude throughout the proceedings. All the others had treated me with ostentatious courtesy, only he kept staring at me with undisguised hatred and making coarse, insulting remarks, until even the man in charge rebuked him with a sharp look. I watched him pick up the dangerous file, and I braced myself for the shouting. I could hardly believe my eyes when he did not bat an eyelash, closed the file rapidly and pushed it back in, far behind other odds and ends stored there.

In the meantime the man in charge dug through the drawer containing our household cash and two savings account passbooks. He announced he would have to confiscate everything, but set aside one bill which he put back in the drawer. I was a thousand-crown note in the old currency—worth perhaps twenty dollars. I pointed out that the confiscated money included my last month's salary, and that both passbooks were in my name. The man in command answered courteously that he had to follow instructions and the I could later request release of any personal property. He also confiscated all of Rudolf's documents, his camera, car keys and garage keys, and some other trivia. Then he turned to search my handbag. Before he could reach it, his crude colleague grabbed it, made some snide remark while taking it aside, near a lamp, and started digging through it. Then I remembered the ten thousand-crown bills I had withdrawn from the bank for Rudolf's suit. They were still there. The man rummaged through the bag, pulled out my compact and change purse, muttered another biting remark, examined a new calendar in which I had not yet written anything and contemptuously tossed it on the pile of confiscated items. Then he snapped the bag shut.

By that time it was almost six in the morning. The policemen wrote up a protocol for me to sign and left. I wandered from room to room and tried to get my mind back in working order. Poor Mařenka was making coffee in the kitchen, sobbing quietly all the while. I don't think she had much love for me, but she adored Rudolf.

The first need was to pull myself together, act with assurance and confidence, so that everyone could see I was convinced of Rudolf's innocence. I could not think of him now—how he was, what they were doing to him—I had to concentrate on helping him. I decided first of all, to go to the publishing house where I worked, to tell them what had happened, and then to visit all our influential friends. Only then did I realize with a start how few influential comrades I knew well enough to turn to for help. I decided to phone Minister of Foreign Trade Gregor first of all. Rudolf was his immediate subordinate, could do nothing without his authorization and signature. Gregor knew every move Rudolf had made—he must speak up in his behalf. The other undersecretary, Jonáš, always treated us like his dearest friends, almost relatives, embraced me whenever we met. I would phone both of them as soon as they came to their offices. I shook off Rudolf's robe, dressed, and poured a cup of Mařenka's black coffee down my parched throat.

Even so I got to my office late. I went straight to Jura Zajonc, who was then our editor in chief. He was a well-meaning, sharp lad, from a miner's family, and a bedrock Communist, but I had long suspected him of having a mind of his own. I did not feel easy walking into his office but was grateful that it was he I had to speak to. He listened, pondered, then said, "We have to hope that some explanation will come up. I don't know your husband, but I know you. For the moment I see no reason why you could nor keep on working here."

"Do I have to tell the whole office?" I asked.

"Right now don't tell anyone anything, perhaps your husband will come home in a few days."

Had I been capable of it that day, I would have smiled at him. If Jura speaks like that, why can't it happen? Perhaps they will discover that they have arrested a completely innocent man. Rudolf had been so confident that no one could reproach him, nor even for an oversight. . . .

I went into my office and dialed the first number:

"Could I speak with Comrade Minister?"

"Who is calling?"

"Mrs. Margolius."

"Comrade Minister is not in."

I dialed the second number.

"Could I speak with Comrade Undersecretary?"

"Who is calling?"

"Mrs. Margolius."

"Comrade Undersecretary is not in." Perhaps they really aren't in. Perhaps they all are in a conference. I'll call later.

I decided to go see Borek, an Undersecretary at the Ministry of Foreign Affairs. He was Rudolf's distant relative and fond of him. Borek was an older man, a deserving Party member who had been a Communist newspaperman before the war and knew everyone who mattered. Later, in 1952, he was to behave badly, testifying in the trials against his collegues from the Ministry. Not long after that, he was to die rather mysteriously. His death occasioned numerous conjectures—even his wife was not altogether convinced it was a natural death.

I called Borek and from the tone of his voice guessed he

had not heard of Rudolf's arrest. I asked to see him right away. He seemed surprised but told me to come ahead.

When I told Borek that Rudolf had been arrested, he turned deathly pale. He tried to pull himself together quickly, but repeated over and over, "So even he, even he. . . ." I did not know exactly what he meant. We talked a little longer, and I begged him earnestly to use his influence and help. He promised solemnly that he would.

I hurried back to my office. I realized that I would have to work now even harder, more conscientiously, to give them no excuse to fire me. I stayed in my office all afternoon. I knew I looked worn and wanted to avoid questions. Every hour I called the Ministry, but none of Rudolf's colleagues could be reached, least of all Minister Gregor. In the end I had to admit that this effort was in vain. They would not talk to me, and if I managed to catch one of them, it would be no use. They all were trembling with fear and careful not to create the suspicion that they sympathized with Rudolf. They would not move a finger.

After work I stopped by a phone booth and called Pavel Eisler. What should I say about Pavel? The best and finest friend I've ever had. He was an economist, after the war he had worked at the U.N. with Gunnar Myrdal and then had returned to Prague. At first his competence and experience won him recognition, but now for several months he had been working in a factory as an unskilled laborer, earned almost nothing and expected to be arrested any moment. None of us could understand why it never happened, but most probably Eisler was protected by the fact that his wife Jean was the daughter of an influential Englishman, a personal friend of Prime Minister Churchill, who could cause a good bit of trouble if his son-in-law were arrested. Yet, I knew that Pavel himself was a in a precarious position and did not dare contact him directly lest I make his life even more difficult. When he answered the phone, I said as quietly as possible, "Pavel, my husband went to visit Eda. I feel depressed; I'd like to talk with you but I don't know if you can spare the time."

There was a moment of terrified silence, then Pavel's voice

came shouting over the wire, "Heda, you dunce, of course we have to talk. Come, come right away."

"I'd rather come in the evening."

"Fine, then come in the evening."

I took my usual tram home. Mrs. Machová, who had an unfailing sense that brought her to us whenever we needed her most, was sitting in the kitchen, chatting with Mařenka. Only then did I learn that Rudolf's arrest had been staged like the climax in a spy film. The whole street had been lit up by headlights of police cars manned with secret police and covering strategic points. When Rudolf's car had stopped, other police cars blocked the street. As Rudolf got out, the agents surrounded him, disarmed him by taking away his briefcase and announced that he was under arrest. The people who lived on our street were properly impressed by this alert, fearless maneuver of our State Security.

I braced myself to face my small son. As casually as I could, I told him that Father had gone on another business trip. The boy was used to that; he just nodded and went back to play.

I put him to bed as early as I could and set out to the Eislers. Then it occured to me that the Security was probably on my back, too. I looked around the traffic island at the tram stop. There were several people but no one paid attention to me. The tram arrived, but I remained standing while several people got on. Only when the tram started moving again I jumped on. Out of the corner of my eye I saw the young man who had stood there, reading a newspaper, look up and jump on. Oh. I got off at the next stop. The young man did, too, and went into a phone booth. I jumped onto the next tram, heading to Libeň rather than to Smíchov where the Eislers lived. The young man was still on the telephone. At the next stop I changed cars again, taking a tram in the opposite direction. I repeated this procedure a few more times, until I concluded that if I had not managed to shake my companions, at least I had given them some exercise. Not that it mattered much; as I learned later, Eisler's house was under surveillance anyway. State Security knew of everyone who visited him. Eisler was always willing to listen and give advice, though he could help no more than anyone else. His apartment became the meeting place of the wives and children of many of the arrested, until the cynical agents nicknamed him "protector of widows and orphans."

I sat with him that day long into the night, discussing what to do. Pavel advised me to do everything but expect nothing. "Do not leave them in peace. Visit everyone you can think of, write everywhere, telephone, don't let them silence you. Even if they refuse to answer, call every day. If they don't answer letters, write again. Be like a bad conscience. But cross the streets with care so that you don't just happen to get run over by some shiny black Tatra limousine." He helped me draft a letter I wanted to mail to Gottwald and the Central Committee. I was afraid that in my innocence I could write something that would count against Rudolf. We also agreed that I must find a lawyer who would not be afraid to represent him.

Then Pavel asked me, "Did you watch the people who searched your place?"

"I think I did . . . why?"

"I would not be a bit surprised if they had installed some listening device in your apartment."

"They couldn't have. . . ." I started to say but then I stopped. I remembered one seemingly unimportant episode. We had two telephones, one ordinary one, and a "hot line" phone that was linked to various offices. That one was installed when Rudolf was appointed to the ministry. The man who installed the telephone, a friendly older workman, pulled me aside as he was leaving and said "I would not want that phone in my house for anything." I laughed and did not think of it again. Now it dawned on me that the man probably wanted to warn me that the phone was bugged. That phone had been in the bedroom, the one room separated from the rest of the apartment where I usually moved with my friends when we wanted to share complaints about the regime, in peace, without having to whisper. Now I realized that the regime had spied on us from the very beginning, in fact from the time when it entrusted Rudolf with an important job.

Late that night, when I finally got to bed, I dared for the first time to think of Rudolf—what he was thinking, what they were doing to him. I lay motionless and the darkness drove through my heart like a black spike. I tried to hope that people were no longer physically tortured at interrogations, that they were decently treated. But even so, it would be so terribly hard. . . . I kept hearing his words, "I would not want to, I could not go on living."

If he could only hold out, not give in, resist. Perhaps they will just interrogate him, after all, and then let him go—that, too, had been known to happen. I heard the elevator start in the hall below. I caught my breath; he's coming. Now the elevator will stop at our floor, I'll hear the key in the lock and the door will open. . . . But the elevator passed our floor without stopping.

The following afternoon I went to Ludvík Frejka's office. I knew him only slightly, but he always seemed kind and reminded me vaguely of an uncle of mine. Now he received me as an elderly relative would, sitting hunched behind his desk, listening. He had heard about Rudolf's arrest, and gave the impression of knowing a great deal, none of it good. He sighed.

"My dear girl, you have no idea how highly I think of Rudolf and how much I'd like to help you. Some time ago I might have been able to do a few things. Then I was still a deserving old Communist. Today I am just a stinking kike. I cannot help you—or myself." A few weeks later he, too, was arrested.

At Pavel Kavan's it was the same story. Next I went to see Bohumil Sucharda, who was then an undersecretary in the Ministry of Finance. I knew that he could do nothing for Rudolf, but I was grateful to him for courageously receiving me in his office and for speaking of Rudolf in a friendly, confident tone.

Other doors remained closed. Of all the highly placed comrades the only one who came to visit me in our apartment was Ota Klička. At the time he was our ambassador in, I believe, Finland. One day he showed up and told me, "I've known Rudolf since our school years. I will never believe he has done anything dishonorable. I would stake my life on him. It's all nonsense."

By then I had become something of a leper, avoided by anyone who valued his life. Even the most casual encounter with me could place anyone under suspicion. I could bear the isolation better than most who were similarly afflicted. The war years had given me good training, and I had never expected much from people. Why should anyone risk his job, perhaps even freedom and safety of his family, for my sake? It is quite natural that people should think first of those for whom they bear direct responsibility. If all men were heroes, courage would lose value. I watched without bitterness as people suddenly crossed the street or, if they noticed me too late, at least turned the other way. And to the few who, in spite of everything, decided to admit knowing me I used to tell myself, don't stop, don't speak, there's no point to it.

A few friends, mostly people I had known for years, stood by me despite all my protests. They believed in Rudolf, and never thought of condemning him, even though most of them were not Party members. Almost all of them had lost their original jobs and were living from day to day in worries and deprivation. And so far, the parents of my son's friends still allowed their children to play with him, so that at least in that first year he did not suffer from loneliness. State Security knew of everyone I met, and interrogated some of my friends rather rudely, including the family of the erstwhile publisher for whom I had worked before the coup.

Once, some months later, I was coming home from work past the house of a friend, a pediatrician, Dr. Procházková. She had a reputation for being always ready to help those in need. Suddenly my loneliness overwhelmed me and I longed to visit her at least for a few minutes, even though all through the months I had never done anything so careless. I took the elevator to her floor and rang the bell. My friend opened the door, her face white as a sheet, and said sharply, "No, I don't have the keys to the laundry room. Try across the hall." I shot back in the coarsest voice I could muster, "All right, all right; I'll try there," and ran down the stairs. Later I found out that a moment earlier State Security had broken into her apartment and found her with Magda Husáková, the wife of Gustav Husák, the present-day first secretary of the Czechoslovak Communist party, who had been arrested much earlier than Rudolf. Had they caught me there, too, they would probably have concluded that we were preparing some conspiracy and arrested all of us on the spot. As it was, they just turned the apartment inside out and left, and that merely was part of everyday life in the Czechoslovakia of 1952.

After Pavel Kavan was arrested I joined forces with his wife, an Englishwoman who had two sons roughly my son's age. She and I helped each other for years to come, as best we could, and more that once shared our last ten crowns, or a last bit of food for the children. The only good side of our life then was that it forged such human relations, friendships of a kind that may not even be possible among free, untroubled people.

Several days after Rudolf's arrest, I found a lawyer who was supposed to have high-level connections and took on political cases. Dr. Bartos received me with much flourish, addressed me as "my Lady," and promised to defend Rudolf. I admitted to him that I did not have a penny, but told him that the Security had confiscated two savings passbooks. That money was mine. It was not a great deal, but if he could get it released, I would be able to pay him.

About two weeks later I received the first, brief letter from Rudolf. Though I read it carefully over and over again, I could not figure out anything from it other than that it said he was well and that he did not want me to worry.

I had not yet got over the initial shock and was still trying to avoid thinking or despairing. I carried out all my duties like a robot: office in the morning, in the afternoon vain attempts to contact some influential person, in the evening composing and writing innumerable letters in which I swore to my husband's innocence, offered my testimony and that of our friends, argued, denied, at times almost threatened. Then came the nights, worse than the days, nights I spent lying awake for hours, repeating aloud to the deaf darkness, "Rudolf, hold out, hold out, don't give in."

My position at the publishing house was becoming more difficult each day. No one spoke an unnecessary word to me, conversations stopped and faces froze whenever I appeared. This awkward interlude did not last long, because soon afterward the editor-in-chief called me in and told me that he had received instructions from above to fire me immediately. I had expected as much, but until it happened I had not wanted to burden my mind with this worry. I knew, if I were not to break, I had to deal with problems one at a time as they came up and could not afford to think even a day ahead. But now the chips were down.

To be without a job did not mean simply having no way to feed my child. The worst of it was that it provided the police with a pretext for arresting me for parasitism. In Czechoslovakia, as in all of Eastern Europe, being unemployed not only is hard luck, it is also a crime. But in a country where all jobs had become government jobs, who would employ an outcast like me? For a few days I lived in utter horror until help came, again from friends. At the urgent plea from Ota and Milena, the manager of a machine shop, which was already employing several people with doubtful cadre profiles, consented to give me a job. The wages were miniscule; they did not even cover my rent, but at least I was legally employed.

My first concern was to rid myself of that damnable rent. I found a small, inexpensive apartment and was ready to move when I was notified that I would need permission from the Ministry of Foreign Trade to give up our old apartment. The Ministry declared that the apartment did not belong to me, but to the Ministry, and that I could not move until my husband's case had been "resolved." I replied that I could not understand how an apartment that I myself had found, rented, and for which I paid the rent could belong to the Ministry, and I repeated my request. The correspondence dragged on for a year, without results but with reason. It was a fine apartment, and with the critical housing shortage, the comrades at the ministry did not want to miss out on it. If I moved, the apartment would be gone. If they could keep me there, then once my husband was convicted they could simply throw me out into the street.

The evening after I got the job in the machine shop I held a conference with Mařenka. I explained to her that I could no longer pay her, but that she could go on living with us and that I would try to get enough food for all of us. In return I asked her to help with my child. I was to work two shifts, one week from six in the morning to two in the afternoon, the next week from two in the afternoon till ten at night. I asked Mařenka to take my child to nursery school when I worked the morning shift—pick him up, give him supper, and put him to bed when I worked the afternoon shift. She agreed, and a few days later found a good job in a bakery, which she enjoyed. Frequently, in the worst times, she would bring my child a roll or a cookie. She arranged shifts to complement mine, so that my son was never left alone.

The months that followed were like a spell-bound merry-go-round. I have an innate incompetence for everything mechanical. Between every machine and me there exists some primordial, almost mythical contradiction. I've always thought that any machine can tell from far off that I do not understand it and am afraid of it—and so it breaks down and resists out of sheer self-preservation. I tried desperately, but I never achieved even average productivity and no machine broke down as often as mine. On the shop wall there was the "ladder" on which the names of all the workers were listed in order of productivity. I was always last but one—the last place belonged permanently to a dear, chubby blonde who visibly was mentally retarded. Frequently I stayed in the shop at the end of the evening shift long after the others had left, to make up what I had not accomplished during working hours; but still my overall production never improved.

In the tension in which I lived the devilish din of the machines gave me excruciating headaches and echoed in my mind for hours after I had left work. My finances were a worse headache still. I was feeding three people, my son, Mařenka, and myself, and paying an utterly disproportionate rent. In addition I was sending some money to Rudolf each month, in case he was allowed to buy extra food or cigarettes or small necessities, but also to let him know that we were all right and to keep him from worrying about us.

There simply was no alternative but to find some additional income. Fortunately, at first I was able to find, under assumed names or anonymously, at least enough work to keep my head above water. I drew illustrations for children's magazines, copied technical drawings, did any graphic work I could find. Altogether I worked my eight hours every day on the job and at least six more at home—and usually walked to and from work because I did not have the money for the tram fare. At night I wrote my persistent litanies to all the imaginable Ministries, to the Central Committee of the Party, to the Office of the Prime Minister, to all the leading officials. I never received a reply, except from the Office of the President of the Republic, which informed me officially that my husband's case "would be investigated."

Sometimes I slept only three or four hours a night, but I made it an iron rule never to work on Sunday afternoons. Every week I saved up enough money for tram fare so that I could take my son for a walk. In the spring we used to take the tram to the last stop in the wooded valley of the Šárka, where we played in the grass and whittled boats to float on the brook.

All through those weeks I dreamed the same dream, night after night. I would be sitting in some public room, in a café, in a restaurant, in a concert hall. Suddenly a door would open, Rudolf would come in and stop. I would sit as if nailed to the spot and could not move, while he stood motionless in the door, looking at me, never moving a step closer.

Once a month I would receive a letter from Rudolf, and would be allowed to write an answer. Those letters had to be strictly personal, not a word about where he was or what was happening to him. We both knew that a single careless reference would keep the letter from being delivered. From what Rudolf wrote I could see that he had fixed his mind completely on the past. He wrote a great deal about our child, and I could see how much he regretted that he had not spent more time with him. His letters revived a hundred small memories I had forgotten long ago.

"Remember," he wrote, "how we first met each other?" I remembered. It had been a beautiful sunny day in the spring.

I must have been about twelve then. I ran across the street to the shop to buy a bag of marbles. A young man with glasses walked in the opposite direction. He looked at me intently and smiled. I was puzzled that an adult should pay attention to me, and peeked over my shoulder after him. He was standing there, still watching me. That evening Rudolf went out with a group of friends, including my cousin who was then very much interested in him. While they were dancing Rudolf told her, "Today I met a little girl that I will wait for. When she grows up, I'll marry her." And that is what he did. We met again a year later, over tea at my cousin's. As soon as I walked in, Rudolf came up to me and introduced himself. From that time on, he became my grown-up friend. He helped me with school work, put in a good word with my parents when I got in trouble, took me to lectures and to the theater, and patiently waited for me to grow up. The relationship between us had that special strength of a love flowing from trust and mutual understanding. In spite of everything that separated us for a time, we knew we belonged to each other and that it could not be otherwise.

Now it was a great consolation that Rudolf could find so many happy memories in our difficult past. Several times he mentioned a forest spring where we used to sit motionless for hours and wait for the young deer to come to drink. It was many years later before I got up the courage to go to that village again and look for the spring. It was dry and filled in. Only a shallow depression among the roots marked the spot, full of old leaves.

In my letters I tried to describe our everyday life as happily as I could. Every night I made notes so that I'd forget nothing, and I tried to give the impression that the child and I were getting along well. In each letter I mentioned some episode, usually from wartime, which demanded determination, confidence, and courage. I believe Rudolf understood what I was trying to tell him—that just those traits could help him, and those alone—and that as I stood by him then, I was with him now. We both lied in those letters, we lied in all we did not say, but we were together in uncovering the one truth that really matters.

I never sent those letters by mail. Each month I carried them to a special section at the Police Headquarters in Bartolomějská Street, I believe it was the Fourth Section. I don't know what I expected from those very unpleasant visits, but I told myself that it was an opportunity to penetrate at least to the most superficial level of power, that there was some hope of finding something out, of meeting someone who might be willing to slightly ease Rudolf's fate. I had to pass several guards who interrogated me in detail. Most of them were uniformed police matrons who never missed an opportunity to hurt and humiliate me. Coming into that building was like a descent into a lions' den. I arranged with Mrs. Machová that I would call her when I came out again—if I did not call, she would go immediately to my apartment and take my son away. From the start I had a detailed plan to keep my child from the police in case I were arrested. As under the Germans, children of prisoners were placed in institutions where they were subjected to every possible humiliation and raised to hate and despise their parents.

The Security agent who took my letters always treated me with appropriate crudity, but in the end there grew up a strange relation between us, which reminded me of stories from the First World War, when, between salvoes, soldiers from opposing trenches shouted back and forth in a completely human way—and a few minutes later they took up their rifles and started shooting at each other. I think my persistence amused that man. From his comments I got the impression, probably false, that he would himself see Rudolf, and I fixed my mind on the thought that he was really a courier, the one link between us.

During that time I had been trying to find some devious route to helping Rudolf. I was convinced that there must be cracks even in the Security apparatus, if only I could find them. Once late at night a strange older woman in a kerchief came to my apartment, and when she had made sure we were alone, told me, "You do not know me, and I will not tell you who I am or who sends me. I came to warn you not to attempt anything; you can only cause harm. One man who knows your husband and knows he is innocent has informed himself about his case and wants to help him. But for the time being nothing can be done. He asked me to tell you this: your husband's material is marked with a capital S."

That was all. The woman left without saying anything else. What was that S? I puzzled over it in vain, and the next day I let everything go and went to see Pavel Eisler right after work. Pavel knew a thousand times more about Rudolf's doings and might be able to solve this riddle. But he could not. For several weeks we pondered, guessed, speculated, went over all of Rudolf's acquaintances, over everything he had been involved in, even the most far-fetched possibilities. None of us ever suspected that that "S" meant the Slánský case.

iii. On Trial
Ordinary life in Prague, from which I was almost completely excluded, was acquiring an increasingly negative character. People no longer aspired toward positive goals. They now were only concerned *not* to do anything that might have bad consequences, *not* to be seen anywhere, *not* to speak to anyone, *not* to attract attention in any way. The great joy was that something did *not* happen: when you were not fired, when you were not investigated or followed, when your apartment was not searched, when you were not arrested. Some fifty thousand people had already been arrested in our small country, and still others were disappearing daily. A Prague anecdote of that era had one of the perennial Western leftists complaining about the monotony of life in the West and extolling the joys of socialism. A Czech replies, "Yes, a thousand joys every day. I get up at five, go buy bread for breakfast, and there is no line—what a joy! I make my coffee, and they don't turn off the water or the power—what a joy! Then I make a dash for the streetcar, and don't get crowded off, and don't come late to work, what a joy!" He goes on through our daily routine—no purge at work, no "No eggs" sign at the store, and finally he concludes, "At eleven at night the doorbell rings; two men in

trenchcoats ask, 'Does Comrade Novák live here?' And I can answer, 'No, he lives one flight up'—and *that* is a joy!"

I still had no idea where Rudolf was being kept. In one letter he mentioned occasionally hearing a nightingale at night. That told me that he was not in Prague, but it was months before I found out about the horrible prison in Ruzyn, right near the new International Airport—a prison that fully deserves a place alongside the most notorious Nazi torture chambers.

Beside the stifling fear for Rudolf and the growing worry over my son's future I was most troubled by the impossibility of earning a living wage. No matter how much I worked I could not cover our minimal needs. Our landlady got into the habit of coming to our apartment when I was away, and later even while I was asleep, and carried off anything that could be sold, as insurance—just in case I could not pay her murderous rent. This drove me into such a state that I started selling my belongings, foolishly, for a fraction of their value, so that I would not o⁻ ' . anything.

Occasionally now my son would ask when Father would finally come back, but I managed to put him off one way or another. I read to him what Rudolf always added just for him in his letters, and since he wondered why Father wrote so seldom, at times I wrote a letter from Father myself.

The summer came and my child, pale, thin, and nervous in spite of all my efforts, desperately needed to get out into the fresh air. Of all Rudolf's relatives only one had survived the war, his cousin Marie, who was then living in Bratislava. Her husband lost a good job because he was related to Rudolf, and now they were feeding five mouths on a tiny income. I knew how badly off they were and did not want to ask them for help, but Marie wrote to me herself that she was taking the children to their grandmother in the country and invited my son along. That was a stroke of luck I had not even dreamed of. I promised to send whatever money I could scrape together, and sent the child off.

When he was gone I redoubled my efforts to find additional work but it was becoming increasingly difficult. By then I was more dangerous than the plague, and the fear of those around me locked me into strict quarantine. About that time I was notified that Rudolf had been expelled from the Party. That was a bad sign—the interrogations apparently had taken a turn for the worse. His expulsion was publicized in the local Party organization as well, and so my own situation deteriorated considerably. Up till then, the people who lived on our street simply avoided and ignored me. Now a tide of petty, malicious hatred rose up around me. Some women, especially, would stop and stare at me full of hate, whispering remarks and frequently some comrade concierge would spit after I had passed, making sure I could see her. It was fortunate that my son was away and not exposed to all of that. In his absence I saved by living on bread and milk, which I bought on my way home from work. To walk into a shop in our neighborhood had become a severe test of self-control.

Prague burned with summer heat, and my isolation now had become complete. My friends had left for their vacations, my child and Mařenka were away, and the one-sided conversations I carried on each night with Rudolf choked me up with fatigue and despair.

The first time my long-silent doorbell rang, it announced a man and a woman who introduced themselves as inspectors of the Local National Committee, come to secure the property of Dr. Rudolf Margolius. I led them into the apartment in a daze. Confiscation of property—that normally did not come until after the conviction. Did this mean that Rudolf had been tried, and I knew nothing about it? What was the sentence, what did they do with him, where was he? Then the room grew dark, the red rug swung up and hit me on the head.

I woke up in a puddle of cold water, with the grotesque, indistinct faces of my visitors bending over me. They helped me drag myself to the bedroom, brought towels from the bathroom, covered me with a robe and retreated to the next room for a conference. I kept trying to speak up but nothing would come. My teeth chattered like a typewriter. The two returned and bent over me. I managed to grab the woman's hand and to draw her near. "What happened to him?"

She stared at me, uncomprehending; then she understood.

"Oh, nothing," she said casually. "How silly, getting so scared." They explained to me that Rudolf had not been tried, that they had come only to take inventory of his property, just in case his sentence was going to entail the confiscation of his property, so that nothing would disappear from the apartment and the State would not suffer loss. Simply a preliminary measure, they assured me. They knew nothing about my husband's case.

They then proceeded to impress upon me what a highly responsible and official act they were about to perform, that I must be present and most attentive so that I would not complain later that things had not been done with scrupulous regard for the letter of the law. But since they realized that the state of my health today did not allow for proper concentration, they would take only a rough inventory and would return the following morning, giving me a certificate so that I could take the day off from work.

I remained lying down after they left, staring at the ceiling. That evening the bell rang again—as I had half expected, it was Mrs. Machová. She quickly grasped the situation. "Damned thieving rascals," she said, "they know what a pinch you're in, and they're afraid you might sell some of your furniture. Then they'd have nothing to steal. You should have sold everything long ago."

She was right, of course. But I had kept wanting to preserve something of a home to which Rudolf could return. Now I watched her as she went into the storeroom, took out our biggest suitcase and put in two rugs, not big but quite valuable, which my mother had hidden with her ten years earlier before our deportation to the concentration camp.

"One pack of thieves did not get 'em," she mumbled, "and I should leave 'em for the second? I'll see about that!"

"Don't do it," I begged her. "You can't carry it out, the whole street is watching me. If someone denounces you, they'll arrest you, too."

"Don't worry, I know I'd better not go out with it. I'll

wait here until they're all asleep; then I'll hide it in the cellar. And don't tell that scum tomorrow that there is a cellar."

Grumbling ceaselessly she moved the remaining rugs so that the disappearance of the two would not be conspicuous. Then she dragged two old, worn scatter rugs from the store room—"In case they counted pieces, they'll get the right count." In the corners of the suitcase she stored a few small things she knew Rudolf and I were fond of—a carved baroque candelabrum, a terracotta statuette, two or three pieces of old glass.

The following day I pulled myself sufficiently together to be able to assist the comrades in carrying out their official duties. Their harvest was not rich. In the few years since our return from the concentration camps we did not accumulate any treasures. Perhaps to make up for it, the comrades sealed up everything except my clothes, the child's crib, and a picture of my grandmother, even though under Czechoslovak law all property of a man and wife is held in common and half of it belongs to the wife. Comrade Inspectress, though she was getting on in years, brightened her work with obscene comments and jokes addressed to her colleague, who was older still.

I commented that they were fortunate that the police—entirely illegally—had confiscated my car keys and garage keys when they arrested Rudolf: but for that I should have sold the car long ago. I made a point of saying that because I knew that Security agents had been using the car all along, driving in it all around Prague. And as long as the National Committee was confiscating, why shouldn't they confiscate the Security's new car? The eyes of Comrade Inspectress lit up, she drew me aside and whispered, "I'll see to it that they release the car to you if you'll sell it to me cheap." It was a rare pleasure to give her back one of her devastating looks and say far too loud, "Comrade, how could you?? That would'nt be honorable!"

My boy returned from the country suntanned and refreshed, and it seemed to me that he had grown in those few weeks. He was not eager to go back to nursery school, and Mrs. Honziková, the mother of his best friend in the apartment house, invited him several times to spend the day. Her husband, a former bank employee, had been transferred into a factory long ago, and her attitude tended to be, "What else can they do to us? Compared to the constant worry about feeding three children on what they pay him, jail would be a vacation." She laughed about it: she was young, pretty, and took life with its joys and sorrows happily and carelessly as a bird in the sky. Her attitude again proved to me that what used to be called a "clearly defined world view" and "ideological loyalty" imprisons and restricts men more than anything else. In every crisis the people who proved most capable of coping were those who had no more than the elementary ideological commitment to love of life. Not only did they seem instinctively able to find ways of protecting themselves from danger, but most of them were also willing to help others without ulterior motives or heroic posturing.

The shop where I worked was located in a basement. The walls were heavy masonry, the stone floor oozed a damp cold, almost as much in the summer as in the winter. Early in September the weather was still beautiful and warm, but the girls at the machines were already wrapped in sweaters and scarves. No one shivered with cold as much as I did. In the end my compassionate fellow workers took up a collection and bought me warm checkered carpet slippers, the kind the grandmothers in the villages used to wear. But neither those nor a heavy old sweater helped; I was still freezing.

Once at the end of the evening shift, when I was alone in the shop trying to catch up on my production schedule, I suddenly felt a flash of blinding, searing pain. I huddled in a chair and with clenched teeth tried to last through the cramp. It passed in time, but from that moment on, some lively tiny rodent settled inside me, a small mouse that gnawed at me, at first not too harshly, but persistently. The following Sunday I stayed in bed, but I felt no better the next day. There was little I could do; I had to bear it somehow and hoped it would go away. I could not afford to be sick. Medical care was free and a fraction of my pay would continue even if I were ill, but I could not make ends meet without my bits of moonlighting.

In October the weather turned chilly. I began to suffer constant chills and could barely force myself to walk. In mid-October the shop started buzzing with excited discussion about our working conditions, and we reached the conclusion that we would write about our complaints in the shop magazine. I was charged with writing the piece. Two days later the director of the enterprise called me in and asked me to spend a few days each month working for the magazine. He told me he could not transfer me into the editorial office—surely you understand—and could not add anything to my pay, but it would free me from the drudgery as the machine for a few days each month and let me sit in a clean, warm office.

That was the first stroke of luck in many months, but by that time I could barely think of anything other than keeping the persistent pain under control. But it was not the last surprise. I had barely managed to get home when the phone rang. It was my lawyer.

"There's been a miracle. Listen, I still cannot believe it, it is against all laws of nature, but it happened. They returned your savings books. You can pick them up tonight, if you like."

To this day I do not know how it happened. Perhaps the lawyer was able to pull a few strings, after all. Perhaps my listing the car stolen by the Security had set the National Committee against the State Security and got someone upset. I don't know, and at the time I was not overly interested. I was ready to believe in miracles: it was neither the first nor the last in my life. Completely exhausted and beside myself with pain I could only understand that my financial problems were staved off for some time and that I could finally afford to stop working for a few weeks and get medical help.

I knew I had to get into a hospital, but that was no simple matter. Medicine had been no less bureaucratized than everything else. The only doctor I was permitted to see was the shop physician, who in turn had the right to recommend me further either to a clinic or to a hospital. But the hospitals were crowded and no one was sent there without a foot in the grave. There was continuous warfare between hospitals and outpatient clinics because the overworked, desperately underpaid doctors at the clinics would either send the hospitals patients they could have cured by home care, or patients who were so critically sick that there was little help for them.

Our shop physician was an old woman, herself chronically ill and so preoccupied with her own symptoms and pains that she could not bear thinking of the illness of others. Each patient coming to her office had to announce succinctly and clearly what his problem was and to suggest what medication he needed. Then she would willingly give him a prescription for anything he suggested. But anyone who was unable to give his own diagnosis and determine the means of cure had no hope of help.

The situation, I concluded, required a radical solution. Right in the office door I announced that I had appendicitis, undressed without waiting for instructions, and lay down on the examining table. When the doctor laid her icy fingertips on what was probably the only part of my body without pain I roared like a wounded bison. The poor old woman panicked, but not enough to send me to a hospital. She referred me instead to the surgical outpatient clinic nearest my home.

There I found myself in the hands of still another pride of the medical profession, a young blonde woman with an oversized bun and unfeeling calculating eyes. She felt my stomach and took my temperature, without interrupting her discussion with the nurse about some personal conflict with the clinic's director. She noted that I had a fever, about 102°, and remarked that it was probably appendicitis but that before she could send me to the hospital I would have to go home for a day, eat nothing, and come back the next morning.

When I took my temperature the next day, it was 104°. I was feeling far worse and the pain was becoming more than I could bear. I called the doctor, told her I was worse and could not make it to the clinic on my own. She pondered that a while, then announced that she would turn my case over to the General Practice Clinic and someone would call on me. She had apparently reached the conclusion that if someone had to tangle with a hospital about my admission, it should be some other doctor.

That afternoon an older woman doctor from the clinic came, sat as far from the bed as possible and told me there was no point in examining me—it was an intestinal flu that was going around. "I'll give you a prescription for some pills; get a bottle of brandy and drink it mixed half and half with hot tea, a full cup three times a day."

Although the fever had started affecting my mind, her instructions still seemed a bit strange. I objected weakly that

I had had the pains for some six weeks by then and that it did not seem like a flu, but the doctor cut me off impatiently, saying that the flu is a lingering illness and I should not flatter myself that I was some kind of special case.

Marenka went out for a bottle of brandy and the prescription, and I started the cure. In the middle of the night I suddenly woke up. The room swam in a flourescent blue fog. I raised my arm and saw drops of sweat emerge from my pores, condense and flow down over my skin. My head was spinning. I sensed that I had to get to the bathroom and douse myself with cold water or I would faint. That was my last clear thought.

In the morning Marenka found me at the other end of the apartment, contorted on the floor and stiff with cold, a large lump on my head where I had hit the cold radiator while falling.

This scared Marenka. She ran helter-skelter to the clinic. There she shouted to everyone that she was afraid to stay in the apartment, that I might die there and she would be stuck with me. The woman doctor told her morosely that those pampered ladies were a pain in the neck, but consented to give her authorization for hospital admission, commenting, "Just wait, they'll chase her back fast enough."

I managed to put through a call to Bratislava. Marie offered to come and fetch my son the next day, and Mrs. Honzíková, who had helped look after him ever since I had become ill, took him in the meantime to her apartment and promised to care for him. I did not want him to see me carried out on a stretcher.

Two hospital orderlies with a stretcher arrived that afternoon. They stared at me, unbelieving. One of them said, "Dear girl, why didn't you send for us sooner?" By that time I had great trouble breathing, and when Dr. Hůlek at Bulovka Hospital examined me, I could answer only one syllable at a time in a whisper. He examined me thoroughly and the list of my ills filled a long column, beginning with nephritis and ending with pelveoperitonitis. Perhaps the only thing missing was appendicitis.

"Are you quite sure they prescribed alcohol for this?" Dr. Hůlek asked me several times. "The worst part of it is that you are so horribly run down—for goodness sake, how did you manage to get this way? Have you ever seen people coming back from concentration camps?"

I nodded, yes, I had seen a few.

"You are not one bit better. I'm almost afraid to give you a shot. I cannot start a radical cure until you've recovered a bit. Give the nurse here your telephone number, tell her to call your husband and your parents. She will tell them what food to bring you. What we can feed you here at the hospital won't do a thing for you."

There was nothing left to do; I gathered my last remaining strength and told him in a broken whisper how I got to be so horribly run down. In spite of that, Dr. Hůlek took exemplary care of me. But during the first weeks I got no better, and I was plagued by the thought of my child, who had no one to look after him. Father behind bars, mother in a hospital—what if I were to die? Who would care for him?

I was one of the most critical cases on the ward, and all the doctors took particular care of me, especially Dr. Wiklická, who, whenever she was on duty, would prescribe some special strengthening medicines for me and never spared some caustic observation about Dr. Hůlek's healing methods.

Early in November I got another letter from Rudolf. It was the most optimistic one he had written, and the first in which he mentioned the future. "It will take some time before I can come home, but we shall be together again. . . ." Apparently the interrogations were over and perhaps the results were not as bad as they might be. I answered him in the usual happy tone. I did not mention being sick, but I wrote that our son was visiting in Bratislava and so this time could not add his usual drawing.

Marie wrote from Bratislava, "Don't worry about little Ivan, he looks well and is happy, has learned many songs and is singing all day long." I was beginning to believe that I was getting better when, without warning, a few days later, that flash of agonizing pain struck me again. This time it stabbed me in the side and burst all through my body like a sparkler. I could not move my arm to reach for the bell, I could not even cry out. It was several minutes before the girl in the next bed looked up from her book and noticed me. She sounded the alarm, and soon white coats surrounded my bed and a morphine syringe jabbed into my arm.

Several hours later, when I opened my eyes, I thought I was still asleep because I saw over me once again the face of the inspector from the National Committee, blurred like the time I came to on the floor of our apartment. But I was not dreaming. Two men sat at the edge of my bed. One of them, the man from the National Committee whom I remembered, kept repeating my name. I nodded to let him know I heard. They told me they had been ordered to bring Rudolf a shirt, a sweater and a suit and asked for the keys to my apartment. I nodded at the drawer of the bed table. The man pulled out my handbag and found a bundle of keys. I managed to speak as he was leaving. Through the veil of morphine I asked him, stupidly,

"Is he coming home?"

The Inspector shook his head in silence, and stood still for a moment looking at me. I closed my eyes.

In the middle of the night I woke again. I sat up in bed and said out loud into the quiet of the ward, "Trial."

Of course—why would they send for a fresh suit and shirt if they were sending him home? It could mean only one thing—a trial.

The night nurse came in with a flashlight. "Tut, tut—we must get our sleep now, mustn't we?"

November 20. That morning, as usual, the old news-vendor woman brought around the papers in the hospital. The large print on the front page swam before my eyes. An odd silence settled on the ward. The Trial for the Anti-State Conspiracy of Rudolf Slánský. For God's sake, what conspiracy? Those poor people. . . but at least this could not include Rudolf, he had nothing to do with Slánský. Then I saw the list of the accused—fourteen names, eleven marked "of Jewish origin." And then the words, like salvoes at daybreak: sabotage, espionage, high treason. One of the names was Rudolf Margolius. Rudolf Margolius, of Jewish origin.

With uncanny clarity I heard the woman in the next bed

whisper to her neighbor, "Read this, it's *Der Stürmer* all over again." And from the hall I heard the lame newsvendor: "Read this, read it and see how those swine sold us out to the imperialists, that trash, they should all get a public hanging."

Dr Hůlek appeared in the door with a hypodermic needle. "Lie still, try not to think." I don't know what kind of a shot it was but this time it did not put me to sleep. A while later I staggered out of the room into the washroom and stood there vomiting until a nurse found me and took me back to bed. I think until that day the women in the ward did not know who I was. Now it must have all been clear. If only they would not talk about it. If only I could be alone.

Day after day the newspapers carried detailed testimony of the accused who not only made no attempt at a defense but on the contrary kept introducing one accusation against themselves after another. "Is that all, or have you betrayed your country and sold out our people to the enemy in other ways?"—"No, there is more. In my boundless hatred for the popular democratic order I also committed the crime of. . . ."

There was much else, often worse than the trial itself. There was the letter from Lisa London, the wife of one of the three accused who survived. Writing about her husband, a man with whom she had lived for sixteen years, with whom she had raised children, with whom she had fought in the French resistance against the Germans, she wrote with obviously sincere sorrow and despair, "I have lived with a traitor. . . ."

Another letter came from a child, the sixteen-year-old Thomas Frejka: "I demand for my father the highest punishment, a death sentence. . . and I want this letter read to him." I am not sure those were the words, but this was their meaning. It would be hard to say whether those words were more tragic for the father, who carried them to his death, or for the child who would have to live with them.

Each day there were also a few commentaries from various "intellectuals." Not all these writers were incompetent scribblers like Ivan Skála, the poet whose sole claim to immortality is the unsurpassed crudity of his outbursts against the victims. His article about Rudolf concluded, "A dog's death to a dog!" Other, respected, acknowledged authors like Karel Konrad, Ivan

Obracht, and Jarmila Glazarova also volunteered venomous comments.

The women in my ward maintained a stony silence. At night I used to creep out and huddle on a bench in the hall. In time the nurses grew accustomed to it and stopped chasing me back to bed. At times one of them would bring a blanket and throw it over me. Even the whole silent hospital boiled over with hate and fury—I could hardly imagine what it was like outside. Then one night I heard a nurse speaking with someone in an office behind a half-closed door. "Back home, in my village, when a thief stole a goose, he would deny it to the last minute, even if they caught him with the goose in his hands. And all he had to worry about was a few days in the hoose-gow. Here these people are confessing even to things no one is asking them about. God knows what they had done to those poor people. To me, it sounds fishy!"

The following day, the fifth day of the trial, it was Rudolf's turn to testify. I could not stand the tension in the hospital, and that morning pleaded with Dr. Hůlek to send me home. He would not hear of it. "I know how you feel but I cannot take the responsibility. You are still on our critical list. It is absolutely out of the question, I can't let you go home."

The trial was broadcast over the radio. I waited for the nurse whom I had heard speak the day before, and after long pleading managed to persuade her to let me listen to the proceedings in her private room. She came for me with a wheelchair that evening and took me to her cubicle.

Until that evening I kept a spark of hope alive. Rudolf was the only recent Party member among the accused, had never associated with Slánský, and did not fit into that group of old Party officials in any way. Then, for the first time in almost a year, I heard his voice. As soon as he began to speak I knew things were bad. He spoke in such a strange, tense monotone that my first thought was that he must be drugged. Then I realized he was repeating something he had memorized. Occasionally he stumbled, trying to remember his lines, then started up again like a machine. And the things he was saying—first about his parents, then about himself, finally about his work—one lie after another, such utter nonsense. He said he joined the

Party in order to betray it, that in his office he devoted his time to nothing but espionage and sabotage, that he enriched himself and took bribes, that in the pay of the imperialists he had conspired on a grand scale against the Republic and the people. Then came the unfortunate treaty with England, on which Gottwald himself had congratulated him. This had now become the high point of his sabotage that was to deal the fatal blow to our economy. At one point he even mentioned that he had engaged in espionage for the imperialists in London during the war. But Rudolf had spent the entire war in German concentration camps! The next day the transcript in the Party newspaper included that sentence, but later, when the testimony was published in book form, it had been edited out. Someone had noticed.

How could they force him to give such testimony? How could they force my Rudolf, who had not told a lie in all the years I knew him, to lie about all he had done, to defame his poor parents, murdered in Auschwitz? What had he suffered before they had broken him, crushed him like that? What had they done to him? Toward the end of the testimony I could no longer take it in. The nurse wheeled me back to the ward without a word.

The next morning Dr. Hůlek had me brought to his office. He looked agonized. "Please forgive me, but I have received orders to turn you out immediately. It is horrible, you desperately need hospital care, but it simply isn't in my power to keep you here. I have to obey."

"Don't worry about it, doctor, I'll be better off at home. Can you have an ambulance take me there?"

"I am very sorry but. . . ."

Later I found out what had happened. In the hospital, as in all institutions and enterprises, the Party ordered mass meetings of all the employees at which a resolution was read demanding the death penalty for all the accused. Then a vote was called for. Dr. Hůlek alone did not raise his hand. The comrades noted it down and got after him. Most wehement among them was Dr. Wiklická, the physician who had been so solicitous before she realized who I was. She attacked dr. Hůlek publicly, accused him of keeping me in the hospital to protect me from the righteous wrath of the people and so actually helping the enemy of the

Party and of the working class. This was a dangerous accusation. Even the chief surgeon became afraid and took her side. Poor Hůlek, a simple staff physician and father of three children, had little choice.

I returned to the ward and slowly started to get my things together. In a few minutes I was completely soaked with sweat and collapsed on my bed, exhausted. I had no idea how to get home. The ambulance brought me to the hospital, just in a robe under a blanket. I had neither clothes nor stockings nor shoes nor a coat. Outside it was already freezing. My usual savior, Mrs. Machová, was herself badly ill in another hospital. And in any case, I would not have dared call her; she had a husband, a family. . . . Finally I thought of the former secretary of my first publisher, an older, single woman who had always been kind to me. She was now retired, had no family, and therefore was not so vulnerable. I called her cautiously and begged her to come for me in a taxi and lend me an old coat and a pair of shoes.

The trip home exhausted me again. Crawling on all fours, I took forever to negotiate the few steps from the door to the elevator. But when I finally lay down, I felt better. I did not have to pretend any more, I did not have to control myself. At last I was alone, and could prepare for what was to come.

The trial was over; now the sentences were to be pronounced. On the twenty-seventh of November I got up, pulled on Rudolf's robe and staggered into the deserted nursery. I lay down on little Ivan's cot and turned on the radio. By that time I had stopped taking in my surroundings, myself, even the pain that had returned in full force. Finally a voice came out of the radio, flooding the room from floor to ceiling, forcing out the last ray of light, the last breath of air.

"In the trial of the anti-State conspiracy. . . Rudolf Slánský, death penalty. . . Vlado Clementis, death penalty. . . Ludvík Frejka, death penalty. . . death penalty. . . death penalty. . . Rudolf Margolius, death penalty. . . ."

I don't know how long I lay there, motionless, without a thought, without even a sense of pain, in total emptiness.

In Bratislava, cousin Marie sat in the kitchen with her old

mother, listening to the radio. Her children, Ivan, and several of their neighborhood friends were playing noisily at the other end of the apartment. A different voice came from her radio, but the horrible words were the same. Marie's old, ailing mother cried out. None of the children noticed, only Rudolf's son came to the door and asked anxiously, "What happened?" Marie told him, "Nothing, nothing. Grandmother was not feeling well; she is all right now. Go and play." Ivan looked at her seriously. "Oh, good. I was scared. I thought someone died."

The doorbell rang and rang, but I lay there motionless. I heard the sound quite clearly, but I could not understand what it meant. It was as if my mind could not cope with it, could not comprehend what my senses went on registering. It must have taken me a long time to slide down from the cot and crawl to the door.

I reached up to the knob and opened the door. Pavel Eisler stood over me. He bent down, picked me up and carried me to a bed. Then the bell rang again. It was Rudolf's closest friend, Jan Hanuš. I had always thought that between him and Rudolf there was a kinship that could not be explained simply as friendship. They were like two houses, built in different styles but of the same stone. Jan sat at the foot of my bed and spoke quietly. I did not understand his words, only the soothing tone of his voice and the expression on his beautiful, kind face.

The phone by the bed rang. It was Rudolf's lawyer.

"Mr. Bartoš," I gasped, "how is it possible. . ."

"What do you expect, your husband confessed."

Rudolf, my Rudolf. . .

I remember almost nothing of the week that followed the sentencing. In my bedroom it was always night. Only now and again a face would emerge out of the darkness, I would hear a few words in the silence. . . . The hand of Dr. Procházková who came alone and at great risk, with a hypodermic syringe that would erase it all for a few hours. . . . Two cadre referents from the shop where I worked, "You're fired, effective immediately". . . . Karlíček's anxious face and then his voice from the next room, "That woman is on her last legs. What will become of the child?" . . . and once, unexpectedly, a man in Army uniform: Pavel Kovály, who had gone AWOL to come to see me. . . .

On the evening of the second of December two men came to my bedroom. I recognized one of them as the Security agent who used to take my letters to Rudolf from me. "You have a last opportunity to speak with your husband, but if you are too sick, stay in bed; we'll just go back."

I started screaming and pleading with them to wait, that I'd be ready in a few moments. They looked at me, then at each other. One of them said, "Fine," and they sat down to wait in the next room. I tried to hurry, but things fell out of my hands as if I had lost the capacity for purposeful movement. When I finished dressing, I was shaking so hard that I fell back on my bed. The Security agents came in, held me up by both arms and step by step led me to the car outside the house. The car started—I looked out the window and saw Prague covered with snow—and empty streets. The ride seemed long. Finally we stopped at a side entrance of the Court at Pankrác, the two agents helped me out of the car and, holding me up, led me down a long corridor to a tiny cubicle. There they ordered me to wait. Through the shabby grey partition I could hear voices, a woman speaking impatiently, harshly, as if she were quarreling with someone. "I don't want to speak with him; he is a traitor. He deceived us all, even me. I have nothing to say to him. . . ."

"Mrs. Frejková," a man's voice pleaded, probably the voice of the Security agent who had brought her there, "Mrs. Frejková, be human—that man will die tomorrow."

Then the door flew open and the two agents picked me up again and led me to the next room, divided in half by a double barrier of wire mesh. The room was empty. Then, on the other side, behind the wire, two policemen in uniform appeared, leading Rudolf between them. I jumped to the wire mesh and gripped the wires with all my might. I saw Rudolf's face before me, crosshatched by wire as by so many scars. Then in a moment the black web seemed to dissolve and I looked straight into his eyes. There was neither despair nor fear in them, only a strange, distant calm, the calm a man finds only at the very depth of suffering.

He looked at me for a long time before he spoke. "I was so afraid you would not come."

I could not speak a word. Rudolf, Rudolf, have you gone so far from me that you could have thought I would not come? He looked at me again in silence. I could not help being conscious of how thin, haggard, and worn by illness and pain I had become. He said, "You are so beautiful."

Then he asked about little Ivan, and I started to tell him all I could think of. About that nice, merry lad who was singing all the time. In a while we were smiling at each other.

"I spoke at length with Minister Bacilek today," Rudolf said. "He promised that they would look after you and the child, that you will get a good job, that they will help you out. Listen, this is important: I want you to change the boy's name. He must not suffer on my account. Don't protest, don't say anything, just do it—it is my last wish."

He was silent for a moment, then he said,

"Come, let's smoke a cigarette together."

A security agent leaped to my side with a cigarette and a lighter. "You know," Rudolf said, "lately I shared a cell with a man who loves music as much as I do. We tried to remember together, and by now we can whistle all of Dvořák's cello concerto by heart."

For a while longer we smoked in silence, looking at each other. "Don't question the trial," Rudolf said suddenly. "Please. Think of Ivan, not of me."

"No, don't say anything. I understand, I understand it all. Don't worry about me or about the boy. I'll bring him up, I'll make a good man of him."

"Heda, forget about me. Find him a new father, don't stay alone. . ."

"I know I have to look after the child, but believe me, I'd rather go where you are going. . . it would be easier. . . . I will take care of Ivan, but I am still with you, you must know I am with you. . . ."

"Did you notice," Rudolf said, "that all the important things in my life happened either on the third or the thirteenth day of the month? Tomorrow is the third, and I am three times thirteen years old."

"Three times thirteen hard years. But you had a woman who loved you and will always believe in you. . . ."

I turned to the Security agent next to me. "I've brought my husband photographs of our child. Can you give them to him?"

"That is prohibited."

"Won't you at least let us shake hands?"

"That is prohibited."

I pushed a finger through the wire mesh as far as I could, to touch Rudolf's hand, but I could not reach. Rudolf smiled.

We spoke a while longer, though with increasing awareness of the fleeting minutes. One of the uniformed policemen on Rudolf's side looked at his watch. Rudolf nodded. "One more thing I wanted to tell you," he said hurriedly. "Recently I read a fine book here. It was called *Men of Clear Conscience*."

I don't know whether he said anything else, I no longer registered anything except that these were the last moments, the last. . . . Rudolf backed toward the door, and as he passed through it, the expression in his eyes changed and what appeared in them for that brief moment was something I shall bear within me as long as I live.

As soon as the door closed after him, my knees gave way. I hung there by my fingers on the wire mesh, and one of the Security agents bent toward me to catch me. As soon as he touched me, something in me revolted. I jerked myself free and marched upright through the corridors to the car. When we arrived at our house, I walked again alone, upright, all the way to my apartment.

Then came the night. All that night I kept seeing before me a gigantic hammer, nailing a splatter of blood to a stone wall with regular strokes, hammering, hammering . . .

Toward morning I fell asleep for a few minutes. Exactly at the moment, I learned later, when Rudolf died, without a word.

It has been twenty years since Rudolf died, but that night still isn't over. It remains as the screen on which I project my present. All my happiness and all my misfortunes are something I measure against that night, as the height of mountains and depth of ravines is measured against sea level.

I asked myself more than once, what if Rudolf had died of some lingering illness, what if he had suffered excruciating pain for months and months, with both of us knowing, as we knew then, that he must die? Would it have been any easier? I think it would. We can all bear the pain that comes from being people of flesh and blood, transients, doomed to pass on. We cannot come to terms with suffering that man intentionally in cold blood inflicts on his fellow man.

After Rudolf's execution I spent several weeks lying in my bed as in a coffin. Sometime in those weeks I received notice that I had been expelled from the Party—I thought of Rudolf's words, ". . . you can always resign. . . ." Prague's streets boiled over with hate and fury against the victims. The rumor about me had it that someone had carried me and my child off to the West, or that I was in jail, or that I had committed suicide. There was at least this much truth in the last rumor—there was not much life left in me. Once a doctor from the clinic stopped in to see me. He looked me over perfunctorily, nervous and eager to leave as soon as possible. "It's difficult," he told me, "you just don't fight against your illness; you have no will to live."

That was not true. I knew I must live, that I must look after my child, but I had no strength left and got worse day by day. Finally one night the landlady came into my apartment —perhaps she was beginning to regret her heartlessness—and brought in a doctor I did not know, a Dr. Urbánek. He examined me thoroughly and said, "I am going to prescribe a rather high-risk cure for you; it is the only thing that might still work. If that does not help, you simply have to get yourself admitted to a hospital. Otherwise. . . ."

He wrote out a series of prescriptions and then cautiously, secretively, stole out again. Later I learned that he was given a disciplinary transfer to a small town far in the country. I hope it was not punishment for having saved my life. Mařenka spent several days crisscrossing Prague from one pharmaceutical dispensary to another before she could get all the prescriptions filled, but once I started taking the medicines, the illness began to yield, even though slowly; it would be a year before I was well again.

When I started to walk again, I decided not to go outside except in deep mourning. I could not afford new clothes, but we found an old black coat in the closet and a pair of black shoes. Mařenka and I dyed the rest.

I could feel dozens of poisonous stares as I shuffled along the sidewalk, stopping every few steps to lean against a wall and catch my breath. I was prepared for the possibility that someone might attack me, that a stone would come flying from somewhere; it had happened to some of the children and wives of the condemned. But surprisingly, I began to sense that the street, for the first time, seemed to waver. Years later a woman told me, "You know, it is not that people are so vicious, they just don't think. Persecuting public enemies is almost a tradition. But people have a different set of fixed reactions to a widow in mourning, especially when she looks as woebegone as you did then. And once it began to dawn on people that if you hadn't been completely certain of your husband's innocence you would not have dared provoke trouble by wearing mourning, they started to wonder about the whole thing."

To be sure, no one dared associate with me, but I could watch people's reactions at the clinic, where they grudgingly consented to give me at least perfunctory attention and occasionally even a prescription. One of the saddest signs of those times was the revival of anti-Semitism, which in Bohemia usually remains hidden and emerges only when it is prodded from above. I remember a conversation I overheard at the clinic. As is usual in doctors' waiting rooms, two old women were discussing their complaints. "I was *so* sick, you can't imagine how many doctors I'd been to, and none of them could help me until this one here. He fixed me up in a few weeks—you wouldn't believe how he took care of me; if it wasn't for him, I'd be six feet under." — "You don't say. What kind of a doctor was it?" — "Oh, just some little kike. . . ."

In January Marie brought Ivan back to me. She had guessed quite accurately that now we needed each other more than anything else. The children of the Bratislava Party comrades received rigorous instructions not to play with the son of a traitor and the lad was becoming lonely. But he looked healthy, spoke with a soft Slovak intonation, and to me seemed dearer than ever. He was startled when he saw me, but said nothing and went to greet his toys. A while later he returned:

"Mother, why are you wearing black clothes? They are ugly, they make you look sad."

I sat him down beside me and told him as gently as I could that his father had died. He listened, terrified, but did not weep. Then he asked, "Where is he buried? I will plant a flower on his grave for him."

I told him that his father died far away, in another country. "When you grow up, we will go see it."

He went to his room, rummaged about for a while, then he came back. "Don't worry, mother," he said. "I am big now, I will look after you."

As soon as I could stay up long enough to cross a few streets I went to the local police station. I presented my citizen's identity card and asked to have the entry changed from "married" to "widowed." A chubby young policeman looked at me, then at my card, then said, "Fine, let's have the death certificate."

The official death certificate was precisely what I wanted.

"I have not received any."

"Then at least show me the notification of the verdict."

"I did not receive one, either. I learned about the trial and the verdict only from the radio and the papers, like everyone else."

"But that is impossible! The law entitles you. . . ." By then his superior stood beside him and nudged him with his elbow. The young policeman stopped.

"Go over to the National Committee," the older man said, "and ask them to make out a death certificate for you."

I walked a few blocks to the Local National Committee office. "Certainly," the official there said, "please show me the coroner's report."

"I did not receive one."

"But we cannot make out a death certificate without it."

"Then what should I do?"

The official looked embarassed. "Know what? Why don't you go to the Central National Committee."

By that time I had learned to recognize bureaucrats and human beings at first glance. The man behind the desk at the Central National Committee was a human being. I sat down by his desk and explained the situation.

"I know about that already," he replied. "A death certificate cannot be issued without a coroner's report, and no coroner's report has been filed on any of the condemned."

My heart jumped. "Do you think they might be alive?"

The man shrugged his shoulders. "Today, anything is possible. Don't take any more trips, save your strength. Make out a written request for me—that will give me an excuse for inquiring into it. Call me in a week."

Weeks and months went by, but the answer to my question was always the same—"Nothing so far."

Why would they not make out a death certificate? Could it be all a farce—could Rudolf be still alive? Could they all be just tucked away somewhere, could it be that once the trial had served its purpose the Party had decided to spare the lives of innocent men? Friends warned me against hoping, but still, perhaps. . . .

I received a death certificate two years later. It is a unique document:

Date of death:	December 3, 1952
Date of certificate:	January 5, 1955
Occupation of deceased:	Ministerial Undersecretary
Cause of death:	Suffocation by hanging
Place of burial:	_____.

Almost twenty years later I learned that after the execution the bodies of the victims were cremated and the ashes turned over to two members of State Security for disposal. The driver of the official limousine joked, "This is the first time I've carried fourteen people in this car—the three of us and those eleven in the sack."

A few miles out of Prague the car skidded on the icy road. The State Security men got out and scattered the ashes under the wheels.

-IV-

The
Shoots
of
Hope

i. Stagnant Water With the new year of 1953 began
the tug-of-war over my apartment. The Ministry sent an appealing young comrade whose name I have forgotten and a rather
overweight middle-aged spinster, Comrade Vokurková. Comrade
Vokurková—the name means "Pickle"—looked over the apartment without much interest, but paid scrupulous attention to
me. She had apparently concluded that she must infuse me with
some of her hard Bolshevik combativeness and revolutionary
verve—and that this healthy spirit would restore my ailing body.
She stood in the middle of the kitchen in all her overwhelming
presence and proceeded to deliver a rousing speech:

"The only thing that can keep you alive is hate. Your husband was a traitor and a rat and you ought to hate him for
that. Keep saying to youself, I hate him, I hate him, I hate
him—just wait and see how it will pick you up. Women think
that love moves mountains, but remember that hate is much
stronger."

I started shaking all over. The young man took my arm
and led me to a back room. "For goodness' sake," he told me

there, "don't listen to that hag, she is a sour old maid. You
were always a thorn in her side, even though she never spoke
a word with you. Don't believe what she says. All of us at
the Ministry are convinced that your husband was innocent.
I know that Section Chief Hrubiš has been interrogated because
of him, and was as brave as can be; testified unqualifiedly in
his favor."

On that occasion I also learned that higher authorities had
decided to move me out of Prague to a village nearby, where
I would be assigned "a whole house" for my own use.

Mrs. Machová, herself still weak from her recent illness,
offered to go with me to see it. It was a long trip, in freezing
weather and snow. When we finally arrived, we discovered that
the information had been slightly inaccurate—the house was
anything but "whole." It turned out to be a tumble-down shack,
condemned long ago. There was no electricity; the plaster had
fallen off the soaking walls. There was no water—I would have
to carry it up a quarter mile slope from the neighbors—"if they
let you," the hearty old secretary of the Local National Committee
added with a touch of warning. Nor was there any possibility
of employment anywhere within reach. It was clear that the
child and I could not survive there more than two months
—perhaps we were not supposed to. There are many ways
to commit murder.

In the train on the way home Mrs. Machová came up with
a solution. "You can beat it only if the Local National Committee
gives you a certificate that the Five-Year Plan calls for razing
the shack—the Plan is holy, they won't let anything interfere.
You know what, write to the secretary of the Local National
Committee that you want to negotiate it with him but that you
are ill; ask him to come to Prague. We'll write out the certificate
ahead of time, then buy a bottle of booze and keep pouring
for him until he signs. Then you can mail it to the Ministry.
It's no lie, it's all true and I've noticed that they aren't too eager
to have you in the village anyway."

That is what happened. The Secretary came, drank, signed.
I think he was cordially delighted to be rid of me. The Ministry
made a sour face, but announced that they would assign me
other quarters.

Then came the Comrades Inspectors from the Local National Committee and announced that they had come to take away the confiscated property. They advised me to request release of personal necessities. The request was granted, and I was able to keep a bed, a table with two chairs, cups, plates and cutlery for two persons, and some pots and pans from the kitchen.

The confiscation of our personal effects went ahead without a hitch except for one detail. I had told my child that we would have to move to a small apartment and that I had decided to sell everything we would not need. He agreed, but pleaded with me not to "sell" the radio which I had bought as a present for our last common Christmas before Rudolf's arrest. Little Ivan had become very fond of it, and would spend hours playing with all the buttons he could push and turn.

I started negotiating with one of the Inspectors. I had bought the radio myself, with my own earnings, and could prove it. I was not protesting the illegal confiscation of all my other things, but I wanted to keep the radio. Comrade Inspector pondered it, then said he was not authorized to make the decision, and called the procurator who was the highest authorized person available. The procurator declared, "Sure, sure, legally she has a right to keep it, but if she wants to claim it, let her sue us! Just let her try, she'll see how we deal with people like her."

When the Inspector repeated it to me, the answer of a man who was the guardian of law and order in our country, he turned deep red.

About that time I also noticed that the doctor at the clinic, who examined me weekly and had to make out a certificate that I was still not able to work, was becoming more and more nervous. Apparently he, too, had received orders not to coddle me, but he also knew my physical condition. I in turn knew that once he declared me capable of work, the Labor Office would waste no time in getting after me. But who would employ me now?

Then by chance I stumbled across a peculiar enterprise. It was located in a small basement room, full of scrap wool and cotton threads. There an older man held court, always dressed in an overcoat and a hat. This, too, was a state enterprise—all private businesses had been liquidated. The manager handed out to his employees tiny hand looms and armfuls of wool, which they took home and wove into scarves. Most of them were pensioners or handicapped, who used this work to earn some pocket money to supplement their pensions. The work would not yield more, even if I worked twenty-four hours a day. But it was employment, and shielded me against Labor Office investigations and a possible criminal charge of parasitism.

While I was weaving scarves mankind suffered a grievous loss that supposedly shook it to its foundations, though it re-covered rather quickly—Little Father Stalin, the inspired leader of all peoples, had died. I, too, mourned quite sincerely, that this tragic event had not happened at least half a year earlier. Shortly after Stalin's death the press carried an announcement that the conviction of fifteen Jewish doctors, recently condemned to death in the Soviet Union, had been reversed. The announce-ment observed laconically that their confessions had been obtained by illegal means.

As soon as I read this news, I sat down and wrote to the Central Committee of the Party, swearing that my husband was as innocent as the doctors, and that he undoubtedly had confessed under similar, illegal pressure, and I requested a review of his trial. Once again, there was no answer.

Perhaps a month later Comrade Gottwald, ever obedient, followed the great Stalin to eternity. He died quietly from an aneurisma aortae caused by advanced syphilis. It was said that the circumstances of his death had been quite moving, though on a somewhat smaller scale than Stalin's—after all, we are a smaller country.

We got our second "workers' President," Comrade Zápotocký; but all that changed was that the new President, instead of getting drunk quietly and usually alone over his beer, as Gottwald had done, played cards publicly and noisily with soldiers of the Palace guard.

The Party also got a new General Secretary, Antonín Novot-ný, a man of the future, who had won the respect and trust of the Party primarily by unmasking the Anti-State Conspiracy of Rudolf Slánský. That had been a most difficult task, as he once complained to his closest friends, "Gottwald just wouldn't and wouldn't believe it. You have no idea how much work it took before I managed to convince him that they are traitors."

But all of this was happening somewhere in a sphere high above us. What concerned me more immediately was that the Ministry finally assigned me new living quarters. It must have taken a lot of searching, because in all of Prague there could have been at most a handful of such hovels. It was a single room, with an old brick oven in one corner. The floor boards had been broken out and the door and one window were so warped that whenever the wind blew outside, papers and anything light in the room would fly about even with the door and window closed. In this more than a hundred-year-old tenement, the only modern convenience was the bare electric bulb in the room and a broken cold-water faucet in the hall that served all the tenants on the floor. No other sign of progress had pierced the old building.

I put a coal scuttle in one corner of the room, a box for our potatoes and other food in the other corner, and stretched clothes lines across the ceiling. For doing laundry I had an old bassinette that also doubled as our bathroom. Pavel Kovály showed up with a tiny cannon stove he had managed to scrounge somewhere together with lengths of pipe. He fitted the pipes ingeniously all around the room so that not a bit of heat would be wasted. Unfortunately, the stove only gave off heat when it was full of glowing coals. As soon as the fire would die down, the room would turn again into an icebox. Ivánek and I always ran down the incredibly neglected staircase with our eyes closed so that we would not have to see the huge cockroaches, almost the size of mice, that crawled all over the walls.

Before we could move in, I had to go to the landlord and sign a lease. The landlord, an ancient invalid in a wheelchair, stared long at my application.

"Your name is Margolius?" he asked me. "You wouldn't happen to be related to the one they hanged?"

Silently I pleaded, Rudolf, forgive me but I can take no more. Out loud I said, "No."

"Well, aren't you lucky," the landlord said, nodding his white-haired head.

Ivánek kept his word. He helped me in every way, and

because I continued intermittently to be ill for another year, he would do all the housework whenever I could not get up. Many times, while I could hear the voices of the children playing outside, he would be washing dishes or scrubbing the floor. At the age of six, he was more responsible and mature than many an adult. He never asked for anything; quite the contrary, he kept insisting he was just fine and lacked nothing. Only one evening he said wistfully, "All the children bring such beautiful red apples to school. . . ." But that was at a time when even a few of those apples were an unreachable dream. Today he is living his fifth year in London. He is studying architecture, with brilliant success. Before long he will be a citizen of Great Britain, the oldest democracy in the world. Rudolf, can you see?

In the spring of 1953 the long-awaited currency reform finally took place. The currency was exchanged at the rate of fifty old crowns to one new crown—and the tiny remnant of my savings shrank to almost nothing. At that point I panicked: I became desperate to keep my present job, bad as it was, at all costs. Then I had an idea—I would sign up for the whole summer to work on one of the state farms, which were constantly appealing for volunteers. That would give me high marks on my job, and my child would be out in the fresh air all summer. I hoped I could manage the work somehow. My former neighbor Mrs. Honzíková offered me a room at her mother's in a village where there was a large state farm. I went to see the manager of the enterprise where I worked. He glowed when he heard the news: "I'll report it higher up right away. You know, all our workers are doddering old men or handicapped, you will be our one volunteer, the pride of the enterprise. Now they'll think better of you; you won't have to worry about keeping your job next year."

The first six weeks on the farm, while we were just turning hey or weeding carrots, everything went fine. But then came the harvest with backbreaking hard labor. My illness returned, and I had to go back to Prague. A new woman doctor at the clinic examined me and was furious: "Give me the name of the doctor who certified you fit for field work," she demanded.

"I will sue that man!" It took me quite a while to calm her down. Then I went to my job. But this time the manager did not hand me an armful of wool as before. He hesitated for a while, cleared his throat, turned away and said, "You see, two weeks ago I got orders from higher up that I must fire you. I was supposed to write to you that, but, you know, I felt sorry for you. . . ."

As soon as I had sufficiently recovered, I started looking for work again, but I knew it was hopeless. Some cadre employment officials, who would not dream of hiring me for the enterprise where they worked, played games at my expense. They would sit me down at a desk, aim a sharp light in my face and start asking cunning questions. In my strained determination to look innocent I must have looked as if I had just murdered everyone on my street—but for God's sake, what does an innocent person look like? I lasted about a week. Then the cadre employment official of a dental clinic where I was applying for a job as a charwoman told me, "Unthinkable—we have high political standards here." At that point I decided, enough. I will not put up with any more of this. This is all I can take.

My friends helped out as best they could. Occasionally someone would bring me a short translation, some proofreading, or an order for an illustration. Pavel Kovály, who had finished his tour of duty with the Army and was back at the publishing house where I used to work, had the cheek to tell the editor in chief that he had learned to draw in the service and occasionally would bring me an order for a book cover design and then proudly sign it himself.

But it all added up to desperately little, and I began to wonder seriously whether I was as indispensable to Ivan as I thought. As long as I was alive, I condemned him automatically to endless deprivation and troubles. If I died, Marie or Mrs. Machová would take care of him, and he could grow up under tolerable conditions, in a decent apartment, in a family. I kept brooding about it day after day until I once was delayed longer than usual on yet another of my forays to find work. When I finally opened the door, Ivan ran up to me, all upset:

"Where were you so long, mother? I was so afraid something had happened to you."

It seemed like an opportunity to start preparing him, and so I first calmed him down and assured him that nothing would happen to me, that I was being quite careful.

"But even if something should happen to me," I said, laughing, "you'd move in with Aunt Marie and everything would really be so much better there than it is here."

Ivan stared at me, amazed, with Rudolf's eyes:

"But then I wouldn't have my own mother!"

I took him in my arms, ashamed as never before in my life.

Eventually an inspector from the Labor Office came. She sat down at the table, pulled out a file and a questionnaire, and said, "I've come to investigate how you are supporting yourself since you have been without a job since August."

That infuriated me, and I exploded,

"I just don't feel like working. I have a rich lover and he is keeping me."

The inspector looked at me sadly. "Listen, I understand your situation. Don't think I like doing this. But I have to file some report on you. I'd like to protect you. Please be reasonable."

I pulled out a file with a few drawings, more than three years old, and showed them to her. "Write there that I work as a free-lance artist. Here you have some of my work."

We survived the first winter in our hovel more or less intact. The winter of 1955 was worse. There was ice in the water pitcher each morning, my health took a turn for the worse, and Ivánek, too, started being sick. One day Pavel Kovály came to visit and found the boy lying on one bed, me on the other. Both of us had influenza and high fever. The room was as cold as the street, some pieces of paper swirled around the floor, blown about by the north wind. I had not had the strength to get up and build a fire in the stove, much less to walk several blocks to the phone booth and call a doctor. Pavel took a blanket, wrapped up Ivan and took him to Mrs. Machová. Then he came back, wrapped me in a second blanket and carried me to his mother's.

Several weeks later Pavel and I were married. It was all

odd wedding. This time, for a change, the groom had the flu and shook with fever throughout the ceremony. I could barely control my excitement, and the few friends who dared to come cried. Pavel Eisler was my witness and, of course, dear Mrs. Machová was with us, too. After the ceremony we all searched our pockets, collected what we found, and we all went to Cafe Pelikan for coffee and cake.

Not surprisingly, marrying me cost Pavel Kovály his job, and in the months that followed he helped to build socialism in the underground, literally, as a heating-plumber's mate. That was a time when it mattered little how well a man worked only whether he could cheat and fix up reports. Pavel, who was not much good at that, often earned almost nothing. We all moved into two tiny rooms with his mother, and were glad when Pavel found a job in a large bakery and sometimes he managed to smuggle out a roll, under his shirt, for Ivánek.

But 1956, the year of great revelations and small changes, was drawing near.

After 1956, the gates of prisons and concentration camps did begin to creek open, quietly. Men and women emerged, emaciated, shattered, blinking cautiously at the sharp light of day. Their journey from prison led to broken homes, to ill, exhausted wives, and to children who no longer knew them. The people they encountered avoided them, not as much out of fear any more as out of confusion and shame. Most of the released prisoners came back with broken health, and some died shortly after their return. For almost all of them it took months to find housing and work. State Security continued to watch over them, solicitous lest they hurt themselves by recounting their experiences too vividly.

I recall my first meeting with Eda Goldstuecker following his release. It was at Pavel Eisler's. Eda was so thin and shrunken that he looked like a boy. He gazed at us and everything around him with hungry fascination, as if he were constantly comparing all he saw with what he had missed for years and only remembered—and now was full of amazement to see how much richer and more beautiful reality is than even the most accurate memory.

Among the released were Artur London, Eugen Löbl, and

Vavro Hajdu, who had been sentenced to life imprisonment in the Slánský Conspiracy Trial. They were rehabilitated by fiat, without a word of explanation. Because they were alive, they were declared innocent. The dead remained traitors, even though the accusations against the whole group had linked the deeds of each accused with those of all the others, so that if one were innocent, none could be guilty. Despite that, as late as 1957 a special commission headed by Rudolf Barák "reexamined" the trials and concluded that they had been carried out fairly, in strict conformity with the law, and had served the needs of the Party.

Others, too, were released, some were cautiously, quietly rehabilitated, others amnestied, but tens of thousands remained behind bars for years to come.

It took the Party only a few months to regain its footing after Khrushchev's revelations, and hurriedly the screws were tightened once more. But those months were enough to open most people's eyes. Millions expected that the Party would finally speak out. We wanted to know the truth, and most of all we wanted to hear the truth spoken. But in 1956 the truth was still whatever served the needs of the Party, and the Party by that time meant Comrade Novotny and his handful of faithful, bound together inseparably by common crimes and common guilt. The revelations did not come forth: the country, which had just begun to recover from the paralysis of unspoken fear, sank into a morass of unspoken guilt and shame.

Our society became sharply polarized between those who had wielded a power that had become self-sufficient, independent of popular will—and all other mortals. This rift penetrated the whole society. Even the thoughts and actions of most individuals reflected a similar split into a public and a private sector, and the two often had nothing in common. People would devote their days to doing their jobs and fulfilling their Party obligations; then they would go home, remove their masks and live privately for a few hours. Lying and play-acting had become a mode of existence, inertia and apathy the content of life. Even small children grew up aware that what was said at home must not be repeated in school, that the best course is to take no interest in anything, to become involved in nothing.

My personal situation gradually improved. Thanks to the help of friends, Pavel managed to squeeze into an appointment at the Academy of Science, and I managed to get my first major translation assignment. Rather symbolically, it happened to be Arnold Zweig's *Der Streit um den Sergeanten Grischa (The Case of Sergeant Grischa)*, a novel about an innocent man crushed in the machinery of power. After that I devoted almost all my time to translations. At first they appeared under the name of my husband, Pavel Kovály, then under Pavel and Heda Kovály. Finally, after 1963, I was permitted to publish under my own name—simply as Heda Kovály. We still did not have an apartment of our own, life was still anything but easy, but we had work. And slowly, gradually, people stopped avoiding us.

The Party continued to avoid the issue of the trials for seven more years. It could afford to ignore internal discontent, but in the long-run it could not resist the growing pressure from abroad. In Hungary, in Bulgaria, in Poland, the victims of staged trials had been rehabilitated long ago; only in our country not a whisper had disturbed the calm surface of the official propaganda. Finally, in the spring of 1963, the Party decided, willy-nilly, to admit that the Soviet Union, just as in everything else, had been its model for its executions and tortures of the innocent. The Central Committee prepared a document entitled "A Communication," intended solely for Party members, which one day was read behind locked doors at plenary meetings of all the Party organizations. "A Communication" admitted that the people convicted in the trials had been innocent, that their confessions had been extorted by illegal means, that the interrogations included a whole range of crude pressure—drugs and physical and psychological torture. The document also announced that most of those who had been convicted, including Rudolf, were now fully rehabilitated, both in their civil and Party standing.

Only strictly selected Party officials were permitted to handle the text; the Party members to whom it was read were strictly forbidden to speak of it. Despite that prohibition, I heard almost every word of that document the very next day. For me it meant first of all that the time had come to face up to the most difficult task: to tell my son Ivan about the trial. For years he had known only that his father had died. My friends had insisted all along that I tell him everything. One must not lie to children: when he finds out, he will turn against you, he will never forgive you. Still, I had decided to risk it. I would rather have him hate me when he grew up than to have him grow up hating his whole world, living with such monstrous, incomprehensible injustice and bearing the mark of an outcast. There had always been the risk that someone else might tell him, hint at it, but the isolation in which we lived protected him, and when he started school, it was already under a different name.

Now the truth had to come out. It was shortly before Easter, and the lad had a few days' vacation; that would give him time to pull himself together before facing school again. One evening I sat with him at the table, choking, with a heavy heart. But he was almost an adult now—he could take it. I told him everything as honestly as I knew how. He listened in silence, not looking at me, asking nothing, his head sinking lower and lower over the table. I could see that I was tearing his whole world to shreds, but I could spare him nothing, I could not protect him from anything.

The next few days were hard. Then he came to me himself and said, "Father really died for his convictions, didn't he?" and started asking questions. A load fell off my mind. The worst was over.

In mid-April I received a summons to report to the Central Committee of the Communist party. I wondered all that night how to act. I knew that by then they could not arrest me, no matter what I said, but I decided to maintain a dignified bearing and an icy calm.

It did not turn out that way. The cowardice, the hypocrisy, the dishonesty, the shabbiness with which Party officials tried to gloss over the whole horrible past, wanting to wipe it from memory with a few half-hearted admissions, drove me into a fury. Hundreds of people had been murdered in the 1950's, innocent people were compelled to confess imaginary crimes "for the good of the Party"—and now those who had forced them to it with the crudest torture and the lowest subterfuges again invoked "the good of the Party," so that they would not have to admit their responsibility. The Party had ordered the victims to give up their lives; now it was ordering the hangmen to stop at nothing to keep a secure hold on their privileged positions.

It is remarkable how terrified such "men of action" are of words. No act is too horrible, no act too shameful to them, no act makes them recoil or disturbs their peaceful sleep as long as no one speaks of it, no one calls it by its right name, no one puts it into words. Just because of that, words are the only weapon of the defenseless.

The entrance of the Central Committee building swam before my eyes as I walked in. After a short wait I was ushered into an office where two completely insignificant Party bureaucrats waited for me. I remember the name of only one of them, it was Jerman, who had published a pamphlet in the 1950s, analyzing and uncovering the infinite malice of the criminals clustered around Slánský. Apparently he had been selected to deal with the survivors because he was such an expert on the trials.

I started out by asking, "With whom can I speak? Take me to see the Secretary General of the Central Committee."

"The Party has assigned us to go over the whole matter with you and communicate any reminders you may have to the proper authorities," Comrade Jerman countered pompously.

"I'm not here to gossip with office help," I responded irritably. "I believe the case of Rudolf Margolius is important enough to deserve the attention of the highest representatives of the Party."

"Don't worry, Comrade Secretary will hear every word you will say here."

That, I felt sure, was true. I knew there had to be a tape recorder somewhere, taking down every word in the room. We haggled a while longer, but then I gave up—it was evident that Comrade Novotný had no intention of risking confrontation with one of his victims. "All right," I said finally, "you'll just have to do."

Comrade Jerman pulled out a printed text from his drawer and announced, platform-style, "In accordance with the instructions of the Party we shall now read to you a communication with which we have familiarized all members of. . . ."

"Don't bother," I cut him off, "I know it almost by heart."

"But that's impossible!" Both comrades panicked. "This is a top-secret document—who betrayed it to you?"

"Don't speak to me like that," I exploded. "Can't you ever treat people as anything but spies?"

With that all my good intentions about calm and dignified bearing went to the winds. The comrades sat at the table, pale, shocked, and only occasionally managing to stutter some answer. I told them just what I thought of Party policy and of the character and intelligence of its representatives at the time of the trials, for the first time speaking publicly, without any reservations.

"But they did not realize that those people had been innocent," Jerman strained for words.

"How could they help realizing it when they worked with them for years? When the confessions were prepared ahead of time? A whole staff of experts helped prepare them. Why didn't Rudolf's superior, Minister of Foreign Trade Gregor, speak up for him? He knew all the accusations were false!"

"But you must understand," Jerman stuttered, "he, too, was afraid."

"What did a member of the government of a presumably sovereign state have to be afraid of? Of truth? Of responsibility? Wasn't he afraid of his conscience? And what of Bacilek, who made such a show of promising my husband that he would look after me and my child, in order to get him to accept the sentence—and then he did everything to destroy us! How could he lie to a man who was to die in a few hours? How could anyone be such a monster?" I banged so hard on the table that everything jumped up, including the Party representatives. I raged and raged until I ran out of breath. Comrade Jerman seized the pause:

"Please calm yourself. Here is a detailed document, especially prepared for the Central Committee; I was instructed to let you read the passage relating to your husband."

He got out a thick volume, opened it at a marked page, and let me read a single paragraph:

"The innocence of Rudolf Margolius has been established beyond a shadow of reasonable doubt. His activities did not in the least harm state interests, quite the contrary. A thorough review of his case leads to the conclusion that he met his duties in an exemplary manner. Had his proposals and plans been realized as he put them forward, our national economy would have benefited significantly."

Comrade Jerman looked at me, almost pleading. Surely such a magnanimous admission must soften my heart. The Party admits it erred; what more could I ask?

"There's simply no point in speaking with you about the past," I said. "But tell me, what next? How can you make sure that something like this won't happen again?"

"I beg your pardon, how can you even think such a thing? It cannot happen again, ever. The collective leadership of the Party itself guarantees. . . ."

I shrugged him off. "You can skip that. But hear this: I want a retrial of my husband's case. I want the accusations examined publicly, in detail, and want them refuted. And I want a public investigation of the ways in which the confessions were extracted, on whose orders, by whom."

"Out of the question! The Party has decided that there will be no retrials. The sentences will simply be set aside."

That meant that the whole affair would be papered over; nothing would come out into public view.

"Then tell me, how long will it be before you make public at least that much?"

"Publication is out of the question. The party has decided to handle all this internally. Nothing can be made public."

"But that is monstrous! You made so much noise about the trials, you almost brought the world down, and you want to rehabilitate its victims on the sly? Can't people learn at least a tiny part of the truth? Is my child supposed to live out his life as a criminal's son?"

"Oh that. Don't worry, the word will get around. . . ." The responsible Party official tried to put me at ease.

That old, desperate sense of utter helplessness returned. "Then at least give me a letter, with a letterhead and a Central Committee seal, so that if my son needs it, he can prove that his father was innocent and has been fully rehabilitated."

"No, we are not empowered to do that."

I started to shout again, but it was clear it was in vain.

I now got up to leave. "You can keep this kind of rehabilitation. But wait, the truth will come out. You can't prevent it. And then you'll have to give account. I have waited for eleven years, I can wait a few more."

They stood there, dull, immobile, pale as statues encrusted with pidgeon droppings. Comrade Jerman added, "Lady, I just don't understand you. The wives of all the others who were executed came here to thank us. . . ."

I spun about, shot out of the room and slammed the door with a bang that echoed through the whole long corridor. I ran all the way to the nearest bar where Pavel Kovály was waiting anxiously, scheming to take the Central Committee building by storm if I should not come out.

Soon thereafter came an invitation from Dr. Boček, the chairman of the Attorneys' Association, who had been charged with the legal aspects of rehabilitation. I went to his office, prepared for the same kind of comedy as the one I had attended at the Central Committee. But this time it was different. It did not take me long to realize that I was speaking with an honest lawyer who was trying to serve truth and justice, at least within the miniscule bounds permitted by our crippled legal system. If he had had a free hand, the truth and the whole truth would have come out. He proved it five years later, in 1968 when, as the Chief Justice of the Supreme Court, he won the genuine, honest rehabilitation of many who had been unjustly sentenced, both Communists and non-Communists. In 1963 his efforts brought him into disfavor and cost him his job. He was the only honorable man among all the officials with whom I had dealings at the time.

When I returned from Boček's office, I decided that there might be a point in one more attempt. I filed a formal complaint with the Prosecutor General:

> I request that legal action be taken against all those who are guilty of the death of Dr. Rudolf Margolius, executed on December 3rd, 1952, because I am convinced that all concerned knew that they were sending an innocent man to death and so are guilty of murder.

The "all concerned" included almost the entire Central Committee of the Party, headed by President of the Republic and

First Secretary of the Party, Comrade Antonín Novotný. Once again friends cautioned me to be careful when crossing streets so that there would be no "accident." But there was little cause for concern. The comrades did not have to pay heed to a solitary voice, and the prosecutor general—even though the law required that he investigate every complaint and file a report on his findings —did not even bother to acknowledge my letter.

My final visit took me to the undersecretary of the Ministry of Justice, Dr. Čihal. His invitation said, roughly:

Report to the Ministry of Justice to discuss the losses you suffered due to the arrest and conviction of Dr. Rudolf Margolius.

Comrade Čihal's reputation made any illusions about the results of the interview ludicrous. Consequently, I sat down at my typewriter and composed a list:

Losses my Son and I Suffered Due to the Arrest and Conviction of Dr. Rudolf Margolius:
  (a) Loss of father
  (b) Loss of husband
  (c) Loss of honor
  (d) Loss of health
  (e) Loss of employment and possibility to complete studies
  (f) Loss of faith in the Party and in justice.

There were some ten items on the list. Only at the very end did I mention:

  (j) Loss of property.

I dressed in my best clothes and borrowed two lovely gold bracelets from a friend—I did not want the comrades to think that they were rescuing some pathetic wretch who would be grateful for any crumb of largesse.

Beside Comrade Čihal, there were two men waiting in the office—a representative of the Ministry of Social Care and one of, I believe, the Ministry of Finance. All three wore studied expressions of compassion and responsible sympathy, though all of them obviously were already tired of the whole charade. "My dear lady," Čihal started out, "We have invited you to discuss the losses that you suffered. . . ."

"Here is a list of my losses," I interrupted him. "I prepared it in writing."

Čihal took the document, but before he finished reading it he turned red as a lobster. "I do beg your pardon," he started out peevishly, "no one can make up these losses to you."

"Precisely," I said. "That is just why I wrote them out for you, so that you would know that no matter what you do, you cannot undo what you have done."

"Look here," the representative of the Ministry of Social Welfare tried a conciliatory tone, "We want to help you, give you compensation for lost property. You have lived in misery for years. . . ."

"You murdered my husband, you threw me out of every job, out of the hospital, out of my apartment, you moved us into a hovel where we survived by a miracle, you ruined my son's childhood—and now you think you can wipe it all out by giving me a few crowns of compensation? You think you can buy me off? Silence me?"

There was some compensation in watching the same dumbfounded embarassment as at the Central Committee spread over the official faces. The comrade from Social Welfare tried again, "I can see you are tired and wrought up. That is understandable. Look, what if you took a vacation, perhaps somewhere by the sea; we would pay for it. Understand, not that we want to do you favors. . . ."

That brought me to my feet. "You do me favors? The nerve! I'd do you a great favor if I took anything from you at all!"

I floated out of the office, leaving the comrades staring after me, speechless. Later I learned that Čihal called Dr. Boček right after that and raged at him for failing to warn him against me. Boček received strict orders to make sure I'd never cross Čihal's path again. It was fortunate that at that time no one could afford to have Margolius's widow arrested.

But as I walked out of the Ministry, I had an idea. I caught the first tram to the CEDOK State Travel Office and put my name down for a trip to the Black Sea in Bulgaria. I had to borrow the money for it, but the vacation was marvelous. Ivan, who had been depressed and troubled, could swim in the sea for the first time, got tanned in the sun, and revived. Every evening we would sit together on the café terrace, watching the albatrosses and the silver path that the moon threw across the waves, and then went to sleep to the regular whisper of the sprinklers in the flower gardens below.

Sometime in June the Party finally yielded, again unwillingly, and decided to publish a brief notice to the effect that the people convicted in the Slánský trial had been rehabilitated. Not a word more.

Comrades at the Ministry of Justice received instructions to limit the financial compensation granted to the next of kin strictly to the value of the confiscated property, at the lowest possible valuation, which was to be further reduced by projected wear and tear that would have occured if it had been used over the years. Comrade Čihal won special honorable mention because he managed to pay out only the absolute minimum to the widows, many of whom were old and ill, and returned to the Treasury a substantial portion of the funds that had been allotted for restitution.

Three Cabinet ministers were demoted. Two of the most notorious torturers from the Ruzyň prison were given short prison sentences—though a year later they were amnestied and placed in good, well-paying posts.

ii. The Spring

For me the Czechoslovak Spring of 1968 began that January—with a poster I saw, announcing a public discussion about crime in our country, to be led by a panel of lawyers answering questions from the floor. I had the evening free and decided to go. The panel proved a mixed bag: it included both Boček and Čihal, an officer from the Army's legal department, and some lawyers I did not know. The hall was filled with ordinary people, mostly middle-aged, the kind of people

I met every day in the street. I found a seat near the exit, resolving
to slip out at the first decent opportunity.

There was a brief general introduction about the rising crime
rate among the young, and then the panel called for questions
from the floor. A stocky older man, obviously a factory worker,
stood up. "That's all real interesting, but what I'd like to know
is just how was it with all the people they hanged in the 'fifties?
For eleven years all you could read in the papers was how they
were traitors and criminals and trash and then suddenly they
tell us these people were innocent, and then again not a word.
I want to know, what kind of justice it is when innocent people
get hanged? Now we feel like damned fools. Why can't you
tell us what's really going on? When somewhere in the West
they arrest a convicted spy, we have protest meetings, and here
at home we let innocent people get hanged and even pass resolu-
tions approving it. How do you think we feel now?"

The man spoke with vehemence, but that was only the
start. Questions and shouts flooded in from all parts of the hall.
Most of the gentlemen panelists now were sweating and uncomfortable. I was overwhelmed by it all. I had thought that everyone
had long forgotten about the trials—now almost sixteen years
ago. And these were ordinary people, those who never seemed
to care much about anything except their own good life.

At that meeting something started growing, the solidarity
of decent people that reached its climax eight months later during
the Soviet occupation. I sat with a friend, a newspaperwoman
who also had endured much suffering in the 1950s. As soon
as the discussion started, she frantically took notes and I tried
to help her. About half an hour later a young man in the balcony,
who had a good view of the hall, put up his hand. "People,
watch out, I can see well from up here, and there's a couple
of stoolies down there, writing down every word you say."

Both of us looked up, and Boček, who recognized me, broke
out laughing. Then we realized that the young man was speaking
of us. Boček said, "No friends, you don't have to be afraid
of those two." The young man understood, gave us a conspira-
torial wave and the whole hall started laughing.

Boček summed up the discussion; his remarks were factual,

cogent, solid. Čihal slinked off like a whipped dog. But it was typical of the mood of the time that no one attacked him personally, no one threatened him. Everyone understood that violence and revenge, no matter how understandable, could not be part of the rebirth we were living through. For it was a rebirth: it was the beginning of the Spring of our people, our brief Spring of 1968.

And the same spirit prevailed at all our meetings during that Spring. Whenever someone spoke up to defend the old order, people listened with patience, even if contemptuously, answered his arguments, and then ignored him. On one such occasion some nervous *apparatchik* lost his self-control and started shouting, "What do you expect from me? I have been a Party official all my life—am I supposed to look for a job now?"

I shall never forget the first large meeting of young people, workers and students, sometime that March. The Trade Fair Hall was jammed with some twenty thousand students and workers. There were thousands more in adjoining halls and outside, where confused, disgruntled policemen tried in vain to provoke some conflict that would give them an excuse to break up the meeting.

These young people had been born and brought up in a country walled in by censorship, in a society where any independent opinion was punished as a crime: what could they know of democracy, how could they know what they wanted? But as the evening progressed, we older ones were more and more impressed. Not only the precision and clarity of the ideas they expressed and the high level of the discussion but the very calm and discipline of that mass of young people proved to us that the young knew exactly what they wanted and what they did not want—where they could compromise and what they could never surrender.

The Czechoslovak Spring of 1968 had all the intensity, anxiety, and unreality of a dream come true. The narrow streets of Prague's Old Town and the courtyards of Hradcany Castle were constantly alive, teaming with people until late into the night. If anyone came alone, he would soon join others, exchange a few words, a joke, and everyone listened with relief as those ancient walls once again echoed with the sound of human laughter.

At night, long after the Castle gates had closed, people would remain on the battlements outside, looking at the flickering lights of a city that could not sleep for happiness.

Every morning, on the staircase of the once-dreaded Central Committee building, women waited for Dubček to arrive at work. They brought him a piece of home-baked cake or a bunch of flowers; children brought him their teddy-bears for good luck. No one missed the opportunity of seeing him on television: he was so unlike the Party potentates of the past. We delighted in the way he stuttered occasionally and the way his glasses kept sliding down his nose.

The day after President Novotný's abdication, I walked into a store, crammed as usual with hurried, harried people, but this time there was no pushing, no quarreling. The girl in line before me turned around and said, "Look, today they are all smiling. . . . !"

Late one evening I was coming back with a friend from a meeting at the Strahov Library, high above Prague. It was a cold night, and as we hurried down steep Neruda Street we decided to stop in one of the little wine cellars to warm up. The place was jammed as all public places were in those days. After the long years of isolation, people were seeking out each other's company. We couldn't find a place to sit and turned to leave, but two young men at the nearest table got up: "Don't go out into the cold again; you look frozen. Take our places, we've stayed long enough." We sat down at the table around which some six people were crowded already, and the whole company started searching for a waiter to order us hot mulled wine.

My friend, whose husband had spent six years in jail and had died shortly after his release, told me, "We've paid an outrageous price for this moment; but if this will last, it was worth it. I want to make peace with all the horror. Not forgive, not forget, but come to terms with it. I never dreamed that life could be as magnificent as it is now, that people could feel so strongly that they belong together, that they are not living in vain. Just look around you, you'll see it too, the same joy, the same happiness . . . on every face."

". . . and the same fear that they will lose it all," a strange man next to us said, and smiled.

Groups of students now used to sit around the John Hus monument at Old Town Square all through the night, softly playing their guitars. Our people and tourists from abroad, spending the night wandering through the Old Town, would pause beside them, listen, and gaze thoughtfully at those beautiful, deceptive words carved in stone—TRUTH PREVAILS. Does it? Truth prevails only when people are strong enough to defend it. . . .

The night before our delegation was to go the Čierna in the mid-summer of 1968 to negotiate with the representatives from Moscow, no one in Prague was asleep, and the streets were crowded as at mid-day. We knew our new independence would be at stake in that confrontation. People clasped hands, shouting out to each other, encouraging each other. The next day, printed petitions appeared at streetcorners and in the arcades. People stopped to sign their names below the declaration of loyalty to a socialism that does not murder, does not intimidate and lie, does not demand bent backs, silenced consciences, and the denial of human dignity, before it deigns to bestow a minimum of material security and social equality. This was the socialism Rudolf had sought, the socialism whose promise had misled him to join the Communist party, the socialism in which he had believed so stubbornly that when his faith failed, he did not want to and couldn't go on living. Twenty years ago it had been an illusion, now it was becoming a reality. The declaration ended with the words, "As long as we live, we shall not abandon the path on which we now set out." I signed twice, once for myself, once for my son, who had been in England for two years, and said to myself, "If we are faithful to this path, Rudolf, you will not have died in vain."

As the negotiations in Cierna dragged on, anxiety throughout the country grew day by day. Every scrap of news spread through the city in a matter of hours. Airplanes delivered tons of paper with our signatures to Čierna—the declaration of confidence and hope that our delegates would not yield, that they would lean on the will and support of their people. In the tiny frontier village, confronted on the Russian side by massed armed might, the consultations took place in special trains, and the Russians had their train driven to their side of the border each night. I heard that once, when the negotiations came to a standstill, a rumor in the village had it that Dubček had gone alone into the Russian train on the siding at the Czechoslovak station, to speak with Brezhnev personally. At that moment people stopped work, strolled from their houses and fields to the railway and stood silently on the tracks behind the Russian train. If you take him away, and our freedom with him, it will be over our dead bodies.

The negotiations ended with a joint declaration that resolved nothing and satisfied no one, but the constant tension exhausted us so much that, still, we hoped for the best. They will push us against the wall, we said, perhaps we will have to compromise here and there, but at least the danger of armed intervention has been averted. Shortly after Čierna, what we thought were the last troops holding "maneuvers" on Czechoslovak territory were withdrawn. So far, so good, people sighed with relief and took off on vacations that had been postponed since the spring.

On the twenty-first of August, Petr, a journalist acquaintance of mine, was sitting at daybreak with his fishing rod by a pond. The float bobbed on the water, the fog rose slowly, and the birds began to chirp. Petr made himself comfortable, pulled out a hefty slice of buttered bread and turned on his transistor radio. He listened for a while, shook his head, then listened some more. What an odd broadcast! He stuck the rest of his bread back in his pocket, secured his fishing rod with a couple of stones and slowly returned to his cottage where his wife was still asleep. He sat at the edge of her bed and shook her awake. "Helen, Helen, wake up," he said, "The radio is broadcasting the oddest play, about the Russians occupying us."

Helen yawned and sat up. She listened. Then she screamed, "You idiot, a play at five in the morning! It's true! Occupation!"

About that time I was already sitting behind the wheel of my tiny Fiat, breaking every speed limit between Prague and the border. The phone had awakened me at three in the morning. "Heda, the Russians have crossed our borders. Airborne troops are occupying Prague. Call all your friends, make sure they know before they go out in the morning."

I gripped the receiver and howled, "No, no, no, it must be a lie."

"It isn't," said the tired voice on the phone. "It would be a hideous lie, but unfortunately it is the far more hideous truth."

For a while I just stood by the phone, my mind frozen. Then I dialed the police. An agitated voice answered at the first ring.

I asked, "Is it true?"

"Turn on your radio."

I leaped to the radio. ". . . Armies of five powers have crossed the Czechoslovak frontiers. . . . Tanks are patrolling the streets of Prague and other major cities. . . ."

I returned to the phone and called one friend after another. At the other end of the wire, I heard always the same cries, "No, no, no. . . ." At that hour, perhaps every phone in Prague was ringing.

I was home alone. My husband was on a lecture tour in America, my son was studying in England. As soon as the Russians reach the Western border, they are sure to close it. It will be like the 1950s; perhaps I'll never see my husband and my son again. My son.

I grabbed a small bag, tossed in a few essentials, and half an hour later was driving away. I have no recollection of how I covered those hundred and sixty miles to the border, but I arrived there at daylight. A huge billboard confronted me, prohibiting entry into the border zone without valid exit documents on pain of strict punishment. Naturally, I had no exit permit. I turned the car around and parked some hundred yards further back. Then I took my bag and tried to look casual as I walked into the forest.

They caught me some twenty minutes later. The border zone was several miles wide, the forest sparse, offering little cover. Two border guards appeared among the trees, ordered me to halt and to get into their jeep, then led me to the highway and drove me to my car. One of them got in with me and commanded that I drive to the nearest village, where there was a Border Guard command post, complete with a mini-jail to which two soldiers were just leading a bewildered-looking man. At the post were several other Border Guard soldiers with their young commander. They all were as excited as I was. I told them who I was—the name Margolius was enough to provoke a reaction. But the commander stood his ground. "Understand, I am a soldier, I have my orders. I really ought to arrest you on the spot for breaking the law. But I am merely entreating you to go home. I'll be delighted to let people pass when I receive permission. But if I don't obey one order, I cannot be trusted to obey others—for instance an order to resist the enemy."

The discussion dragged on. In the end all the soldiers pledged themselves to accept no orders from anyone except their supreme commander, President Svoboda, and to keep faith with their country. The commander took me back to my car and asked, "Aren't you afraid to go back alone? I could send someone with you."

I thanked him, but told him that I did not think any of us would be alone now.

The following day the Border Guard stopped their watch and thousands of people streamed out of the country without documents. But by that time I would not think of leaving.

On my way back to Prague I picked up three soldiers who had been home on leave, and now urged me constantly to drive faster, so they could get back and join their units. Now we would fight! But the order to fire never came.

All the cities through which we passed that early morning were already covered with printed posters and proclamations. Local radio stations were calling on the people to defy the invaders, people lined the streets, with clenched fists.

I reached Prague shortly after noon. I had to detour through side streets because the main thoroughfares were blocked by tanks. Crowds of people clustered around them, trying to communicate with the Russian soldiers. "What's your business here?

Do you even know where you are?" someone said, in broken Russian. "In Germany," one soldier grunted. "Imbeciles," the people screamed desperately, "Can't you see? You're in Prague!" But the soldier sneered and turned his back. As I started off again, I saw a blonde girl come dancing to the rear of the tank and toss a flaming torch under it.

At the next intersection a young woman stepped up to my car tossed in a bag of tricolors and a stack of leaflets through the window. "Pass them out!" After that I stopped every hundred yards; people clustered around my car, eagerly grasping the leaflets and pinning the tricolors on their lapels. Inevitably, someone would also stick another poster or flag on my car. Before I reached home, my car was covered from fender to fender with posters —"Murderers Go Home!" "Death to the Invaders!" "We Will Not Yield!" "Bring back Dubček!" Words, words against tanks. Fourteen million people tried to defend their freedom with their bare hands while bloodied flags covered our first dead.

At Wenceslas Square at the center of Prague, under the bullet-scarred facade of the National Museum, tens of thousands of people with transistors pushed their way through streets blocked by tanks, gutted cars, and pieces of masonry shot down from surrounding buildings. Prague's walls were covered with posters, paintings, slogans. Trucks festooned with flags challenged the tanks; the air rang with frequent shots.

Standing there in the crowd I felt that this was, somewhat paradoxically, the climax of our lives. In that night of the occupation, when we lost everything, we found something that the people of our world barely hope for—ourselves and each other. In all those faces, in all those eyes, I saw that we all thought, felt, and yearned alike. Prague resisted every way it could. Street signs disappeared; the licence plate numbers of Soviet Security cars were painted large on walls. Radio and later television broadcasts came from makeshift facilities, eluding frantic Russian search—while the train carrying Russian radio-station detector equipment was being shunted from siding to siding by Czechoslovak railway men. And hungry Russian soldiers wandered through our streets where all signs pointed in one direction: MOSCOW.

It was not hard for the Russians to locate our official television studios. Our commentator, still projected onto our TV screens, merely observed, "Well, well, so here we have them." Then the camera focused through a window on Russian soldiers in the vacant lots behind the studios, approaching the building in regulation manner by fire-and-maneuver, even though there was not a single Czech weapon in sight. After the camera had followed the soldiers playing war all the way to the back door, it switched back to the announcer who winked at his audience and walked out the main entrance to his car, parked in front of the building. Meanwhile the soldiers broke into the studios, where the cameras were still running. The Czech audience watched them on their screens as they cut every cable except the right one, and finally, battle weary and worn-out by victory, bedded down on the studio floor.

By then our technicians were installing their equipment in every possible hiding place. Our television system, which before the occupation had consisted of one channel, suddenly acquired twelve—and one commentator observed, "At this rate, we'll soon be broadcasting in color." An apocryphal story had it that the following day an elderly man in a worn overcoat arrived at the studio with two huge suitcases full of mysterious gadgets and started fussing about. When the surprised TV crew asked him what he was doing, he turned to them with a trace of annoyance, "You said you wanted to broadcast in color, so I've come to rig it up for you."

The third day after the occupation I heard a broadcast appeal from a district town asking for volunteers able to broadcast in English, German, and other foreign languages for audiences outside our country anxious for news other than the TASS releases. I called a journalist friend—"will you come along?"

The Russians stopped us three times but did not come upon the stacks of leaflets we had hidden under the seat and passed out all along the way. But we never reached our district town. In one of the small towns through which we passed a group of young people asked us to stay. They were patrolling the highways on motorbikes and had the whole district so organized that they knew every strange person and car that came along. At intersections, pensioners signaled the approach of the enemy and directed drivers to detours—in one village, an old man in a wheelchair directed us with his crutches.

Now the young men led us to the local National Committee. "Don't go on, we need your help more." Units of the Polish army were approaching, and the mood of the town was grim. We set to work, speaking over the town's public address system and composing flyers and proclamations, which the young men promptly distributed throughout the district.

When the first Polish units entered the town, their commander sent word that he wished to negotiate with the National Committee. The Chairman of the Committee turned to those of us working in his office: "How do we communicate with them? Can any of you speak Polish?"

I recalled the long-unused Polish I had learned in the concentration camps during an earlier occupation. "If there's no one who can do better, I think I can manage."

The Polish delegation consisted of a perfumed colonel in dress uniform, a sweaty major in rolled-up shirt sleeves, and a silent adjutant. The confrontation was icy. We sat at a table, the three Poles to one side, four of our people and I on the other.

The colonel began: "First of all I wish to emphasize that we have not come to interfere in your internal affairs. But you have let your Party slip into the hands of rightist opportunists and even zionists, to whom we in Poland have given short shrift long ago. . . ."

I translated in the juiciest terms I could manage. The chairman responded: "If you did not come to interfere, what are you doing here, anyway? Tell us what you want, and skip the preaching."

"We need water," the major announced curtly. "For the troops and for the trucks. Order the people to let us draw water from their wells."

The chairman threw up his hands. "I wish I could, I know your soldiers are suffering from thirst and that you can't move your vehicles. But we have no water. This is a dry region—we cannot spare a drop. But we ask you to clear the highway where you've halted. It is our only road to several villages, and we need it for food deliveries."

The major spread out a map. "Impossible. This is a crucial strategic location."

The colonel added, "We are not about to negotiate that. Give us water."

"We have none. Clear our highway."

So it went, back and forth, until I did not even need to translate.

"My proposal," the colonel said finally, "is that you give us water and we'll go back to discuss your request with the rest of our comrades and let you know the result."

"Fine," the chairman responded, "clear the road and we'll go back to discuss your request for water with the rest of the comrades and let you know the results."

Everyone got up. On the one side, sleek, arrogant soldiers of an occupying army, on the other, canny, plain Czech farmers. How many times in our history have we acted out this confrontation?

In the end we won that particular skirmish. The Poles were unsure of themselves—their common soldiers carried out orders unwillingly. Some of them had thrown away their ammunition, showed our people their empty weapons and shouted, "We won't shoot at you." Besides, Moscow was anxious to avoid unnecessary clashes. But little did all this matter; our fate was being decided in the Kremlin. If our captive government could not hold out there, our small victories would avail us nothing—and we'd pay for them bitterly later.

On the evening of the seventh day the voice of the only man we trusted came over the radio. We sensed the defeat and the helplessness in that voice. The long pauses, the heavy sighs told us more than the words. From Moscow, darkness settled over our land. It was over. I drove back to Prague. Whitewash letters shone at me from a board fence near my street, ,,*Doubečku náš drahy, my ti rozumime*"—"Dearest Dubček, we understand."

There was little left to do, there is little more to tell. The Soviet occupation blocked the hope that had sustained us for years and that had blossomed in our Spring; it blocked the road we swore never to abandon. There remained the hard choice—to submit and sink back into silent acquiescence, or to leave my country and try to keep alive, at least within me, the hope whose destruction we could not accept as final. For weeks, I could not decide. Exile is never a happy end, it can at best be the lesser evil. I wandered through Prague, talking with friends and strangers, trying to assure myself that no one, no one can ever forget, that the future will not be surrender, only waiting.

I could wait, but I did not want to be silenced again. At the end of September, I got on the train to Paris, with two suitcases, twenty American dollars, and a four-day French visa. The train was full. In the seats facing me sat two students, a young man and a girl; they were headed for Holland. We spoke of books and of life, but we were still numb from shock. The girl regretted that she had left a new hat behind—at that moment, exile would have seemed less dreadful in a new hat. . . .

At Mariánské Lázně, a middle-aged German tourist got on with her daughter. The little girl kept examining us curiously and finally asked her mother, "Mother, why do all these people look so sad?" Her mother hushed her sharply, "You dunce, don't you understand that the Czechs love their country?" I was grateful to her for her consideration and thought back to the East German tourists in Prague a month earlier, when East German troops joined in the invasion—the tourists wore placards reading, ,,*Ich schäme mich für Deutschland.*"

Just short of the frontier, our train halted briefly in the fields. An ancient railwayman walked past our car, waving his probe rod jauntily and shouting to us, "Don't be afraid of the Russians! We have a hospital full of them. Their rations gave out and they could not manage to get anything from us. They picked mushrooms and now half of them are sick to their stomach. Don't be afraid, you'll come back!"

The train did not halt long at the frontier. When it moved again, I leaned out of the window as far as I could, looking back toward our land. The last thing I saw was a Russian soldier with a fixed bayonet.

Part Two

THE VANQUISHED
Perspective of
Erazim Kohák

-I-
Preparing the Ground

October, 1938. *France and England abrogate their treaties and ask Czechoslovakia to surrender its border fortifications to Hitler in the name of "peace in our time," in exchange for great-power guarantee of independence.*

March, 1939. *The guarantees fail as Hitler occupies the western part of Czechoslovakia and transforms it into the German Protectorate of Bohemia-Moravia. Slovakia becomes a German puppet state, Hungary annexes Ruthenia.*

September, 1939. *"Peace in our time" comes to an end as Hitler concludes a nonaggression pact with the U.S.S.R. and declares war on Poland and the West. Czechoslovaks in the West form a government and an army in exile; at home the underground cooperates extensively with Western military intelligence.*

June, 1941. *Hitler attacks the Soviet Union, transforming the "capitalist war" into the "Great Patriotic War against Fascism."*

September, 1941. *The Germans resort to mass arrests and executions to crush the Czechoslovak resistance. Deportation of Jews to concentration and extermination camps begins.*

May, 1942. *The Czechoslovak underground assassinates the German "Protektor" Heydrich. The Germans respond with further mass arrests, level the villages of Lidice and Ležáky. The Underground shifts to guerrilla warfare.*

August, 1944. *Slovak National Uprising overthrows the Nazi regime and declares Czechoslovakia restored. Soviet armies halt their advance and stand by while Germans crush the rebels.*

April, 1945. *The Soviet army liberates the Czechoslovak town of Košice (most important town in eastern Slovakia), where President Beneš proclaims a coalition government and the "Košice Program" of democracy, socialism, and Soviet alliance.*

May, 1945. *Prague Uprising. The American armies halt their advance and stand by while Prague fights and waits for Soviet aid. The War ends with Soviet liberation of Prague.*

i. The Descent

What happened to Heda Margolius, to me, to our nation, had all happened before and promises to happen again. The alluring vision of freedom and justice gives human lives their uniquely human dimension of hope. It is as universal as its counterpart, the fascination with power. Again and again, humans have struck out to overcome the pain of oppression and the drabness of the everyday in the hope of taking Utopia by storm. Invariably, their achievements prove ephemeral and the terrifying logic of power crushing. All that changes for a time is the proportion between those who are willing to disregard human lives in the quest for Utopia and those who are prepared to accept the loss of hope and vision rather than strike out for the risk of hope. Over the wreckage of their hope, the visionaries proclaim its validity and the need to try once more while their victims foreswear hope and wish for peace.

The facts are familiar enough, and so are the fantasies. Neither suffice to break the vicious circle of victors and vanquished. For that, we need imagination and understanding. In the thirty years that followed the Munich dictate of 1938, Czechoslovakia, for the third time in its history, served as a laboratory of social dynamics. Its story is universal—its value lies less in the facts than in the analogies they evoke.

Czechoslovakia's revolutionary cycle did not really begin in 1938. It began much earlier, perhaps with the rise of the factories of the industrial revolution, belching up dirty brown soot and transforming uprooted peasants into an anonymous, totalized mass. Perhaps it began even earlier, with the emergence of a literary vernacular and the rise of national consciousness. Or perhaps it really has no "beginning"—it may be that the danger of totalization is a perennial one, rooted in the fact that human beings can be individuals only in a social context. Let us fix, here, the beginning of our story in 1938, because after the Munich dictate for us in Czechoslovakia totalization no longer was simply a perennial danger but became the dominant fact of our existence: the safeguards of humanity broke down under the impact of occupation and war.

This is the first, necessary step in the rise of revolutionary consciousness. Totalization evokes in the victim a totalitarian ideology, conceived as a necessary self-defense. The totalized workers of the Industrial Revolution turned to Marxism in the defense of their humanity. Similarly, Czech nationalism was a defensive response to Nazi Germany's attack on our individual identity.

The revolutionary cycle does not begin with the perennial danger of sinking into a totality—a faceless mass—or the perennial temptation to respond in kind, but rather with the transformation of necessity into virtue. It begins when the oppressed, again for understandable reasons, come to regard a holistic ideology no longer as an unfortunate necessity but as a positive good, and see their aim no longer as the restoration of human values, but rather as the "victory" of that ideology.

The victorious act of revolution invests the collective abstractions of the age of struggle with all the power and self-righteousness of brute force. The thermidor, necessarily, must follow. Though its original intent may have been to free the people from oppression, once in power the revolutionary ideology becomes yet another totalizing force, destructive and antihuman as its defeated predecessor. It is the loss of the human perspective,the submergence in the values of totalarianism that destroys human beings—not this rather than that set of abstractions.

If a genuine victory that upholds human values is possible, it can come only once the fury of the revolution is spent, the hollowness of "victories" obvious, and the bruised, exhausted humankind begins to discover once again the values of bread, freedom, and dignity. In our time these values no longer seem obvious. We have grown accustomed to making virtue out of necessity, to look for victory rather than reconciliation. We are, notoriously, a generation for which the inconceivable has become commonplace. The bombing of a provincial town in northern Spain in 1937 still could overwhelm a Picasso with unspeakable horror. Since then, we have learned to speak of such and even greater horrors in detached historical categories—the exigencies of war, of revolutionary violence, all in the name of ideals.

We excuse ourselves by saying that we have been radicalized by war and revolution. Undoubtedly, we have been, as had the generation that fought the wars of religion or the generation that fought the Napoleonic wars. Although this is true, it explains nothing. It only acknowledges the shift from the categories of concrete human joy and suffering to the inhuman categories of an anonymous History. Such terms as radicalization or brutalization simply acknowledge the shift from the perspective of persons to the perspective of movements, classes, and races. These terms do not make that shift any less vicious. Nor do they explain the mind of a generation that acquiesced to the shift and convinced itself that, in direct contradiction to the Apostle James's caustic comment, the wrath of man does work the righteousness of God.

Yet the call for violence as a way of survival and being human,—the total violence of war or revolution—in human terms remains fundamentally incomprehensible. Being human is caring. It takes an infinite amount of work and tenderness to make a human life, to raise a child, to build a house, to harvest a crop. A bullet does not just kill a man—it wipes out a lifetime of care and effort. Violence is viciously parasitic upon work and caring: it destroys, it cannot create. Not by the standards of social convention, but because of the very nature of what it means to be human is the call to violence as fundamentally inhuman as the failure to resist it. This is as clear as the anguish in Picasso's *Guernica*, yet we are the generation that has lost that clear perception.

ii. Defiance

Czechoslovakia and the West, facing war in 1938, seemed strangely innocent of its realities. Perhaps all societies, invoking the slogans of totality, of war or revolution, share that innocence. Strangely so, for history provides ample warning, and it did so in our generation. In the midst of the Versailles peace, that lovely illusion built on good wishes and vicious policies, Germany had acted out the revolutionary cycle before our eyes. A series of upheavals—starting with a defeat in war, followed by a ruinous inflation aggravated by historically justified and politically unjustifiable reparations, followed in turn by a depression—had reduced the value and meaning of individual life to a hollow shell. Martin Heidegger, voicing that malaise of his nation, wrote of the bankruptcy of what he contemptuously termed "the average everydayness" and called for a rebirth of the deep instincts of "anticipatory resoluteness." Adolf Hitler echoed the same feelings in popular terms, in a "challenge to national greatness" which would redeem the soured pettiness of bankrupt private lives. Many Germans responded to his call to totalization. In the main, the last days of the Weimar Republic no longer were a struggle between the values of freedom and humanity and the call to totalization, but between the calls to totalization from the Left and from the Right. In 1933, the Brown Shirts prevailed over the Red Shirts, and by 1938 Nazi Germany stood in locked ranks, exhilirated by the new-found sense of collective identity, ranged first against the Left and against the Jews, then against the Czechoslovaks, and eventually ready to defy and vanquish the whole world.

That onslaught caught Czechoslovakia and the West psychologically unprepared, incapable of comprehending the totalitarian mentality. Czechoslovakia was the showcase of Versailles, the only humanistic democracy east of the Rhine. Its leading philosopher was no Heidegger, but Tomáš Masaryk, theoretician of democracy and apostle of humanity. Its leading writer was Karel Čapek, who extolled the precious, tangible goodness of ordinary life in its joys and sorrows. Czechoslovakia in 1938 was incapable of comprehending the lure of totality and the appeal to violence, though it stood ready to resist it. It saw itself, with every justification, as the front line of humanity against the appeal of totalitarian violence. The soldiers who responded to the mobilization on the May 21, 1938, and again in September of the same year were no fanatic phalanx: they were individuals, free men prepared to defend humanity with their very lives.

That dedication suffered its first staggering blow at Munich. France and England served notice that they did not regard resistance to violence worth disturbing their comfort. Without consulting our government, our allies abrogated the treaties on which Czechoslovakia had based its foreign policy for two decades, and they smoothed the way for Hitler in his quest to occupy Czechoslovakia's border mountain fortifications—while appealing to the Czechoslovaks to surrender in the name of "peace in our times." Perhaps we should have fought, in a vain, gallant gesture of defiance, but the spirit of reason was too strong. We were still a reasonable, democratic country, committed to the preservation of human lives rather than to national gestures. Our strong and well-trained army, which might have nipped the Second World War in the bud, lay down its arms and, in the name of "peace in our time," surrendered our borders.

The bitterness of Munich and the self-doubt of surrender sowed seeds in our land that were to grow in years to come. Yet, even in the early years of the war the spirit of reason still prevailed. When the occupation came, nine months after Munich, it met no resistance. The signatories of the Munich dictate, having given preference to peace over justice, had made sure that the token country, now renamed Czecho-Slovakia, would be stripped of the means of armed resistance.

Life in Czechoslovakia in the first years of the war had an air of unreal normalcy for all but those directly affected by the German occupation. The visible horrors of the war were far away. The Slovaks, in a puppet state of their own, celebrated independence while, for the Czechs, in the entity created by the occupation, "the Protectorate Bohemia-Moravia," the immediate need was to survive from day to day under the increasingly difficult circumstances of occupation and oppression.

To be sure, in the first days of the occupation, the universal Czech response was to resist. But then the war was not to start for another five months and, after the rapid defeat of Poland, it was to drag on for another nine months of stalemate along the Western front and faraway. In those days the primary goal and activity of the resistance was to preserve our national identity. The Czech government of "the Protectorate Bohemia-Moravia" sympathized with that aim. Its president, a gentle jurist named Hácha, and its prime minister, General Eliáš, were in contact with the resistance and with President Beneš who now was in exile. They saw their task in minimizing the impact of the occupation. The Czechoslovak flag continued to fly from the flagpoles for some three months after the occupation, and when it was finally replaced by a "Protectorate" flag, the design selected was that of the old Czechoslovak tricolor, a white, red, and blue horizontal stripe. Meanwhile, the resistance organized protests: there was a boycott of streetcars when the Germans imposed regulations consigning Jews to standing room in the last car; flowers were placed on the graves of Czechoslovakia's great figures of the past; student demonstrations were held on the anniversary of the founding of the Republic.

In retrospect the early resistance seems naive. It was still so civilized, opposing the German war machine with peaceful protests. Perhaps it was naive—but, in our country, the reality of total war had not yet sunk in. Czechoslovakia had not faced an all-out war, like Poland. The Germans occupied our country without initial destruction—but also without the galvanizing effect of a war making clear that all is lost, that the peoples' lives are forfeited, and that any act of heroism can only save an insignificant part of what is really already lost. We had not yet learned to think of ourselves as condemned to death.

There was, to be sure, an active resistance movement as well. But it was still predominantly clandestine, consisting of urban resistance rather than of groups of desperate men hiding out in the woods and fighting guerrilla actions. That was to come later, but in the first years of the occupation the style of resistance was different. The intelligence network of the Czechoslovak army continued to function. It still had its agents, among them at least one highly placed German officer, and it continued to supply critical military intelligence to the Czechoslovak government-in-exile in London and through it to the Allies—including detailed advance warning of impending German attacks on Norway, France, and the Soviet Union.

We also developed a civilian resistance network in our country. It drew heavily on intellectuals, on the national gymnastic organization Sokol, as well as on courageous individuals throughout the nation. All its various members had one thing in common: they chose to resist. They did not have war forced upon them—they were not the remnants of an army fighting on in the forests. Their decision required a special kind of courage. Unlike the guerrillas, the members of this civilian resistance had the alternative of surviving the war in inaction, and they bore the full range of responsibilities for families that had to be fed, jobs that had to be kept up, identity papers that had to be kept in order. There were exceptions, daredevils like Colonel Mašín or Major Morávek, who reminded the Germans with high explosive that they had not yet won—and who reminded their fellow Czechs that we were not yet consenting to defeat. But for the majority, the early resistance consisted of men who still had much to lose yet chose the risk of fighting on, with all the dangers of war without quarter but with little of the drama that props up men's courage in wartime.

The military contribution of that early, first phase of the resistance may well have been greater than that of the far more spectacular dynamitings of ammunition trains or ambushes of German patrols in later years. Accurate intelligence in wartime can cause far greater damage than the loss of even a considerable number of fighting men. Its psychological value, however, was limited. Precisely in order to be effective, the members of the first resistance had to maintain a low profile—to accept humiliation, to avoid overt protest against the increasing ferocity of the occupation, to resist the urge for violent affirmation of our identity in a gesture of defiance. Such gestures are costly in human lives as well as in the effectiveness of intelligence networks. Once again, the Czechs were asked to accept the unreasonable in the name of reason.

In addition, the effectiveness of that resistance was waning from day to day. Had the Nazis been willing to play by the rules of hide-and-seek associated with the phrase "going underground" in civilized countries, it might have been successful. But they were not: for them, the war began and was fought as total war. The Vice-Protector of Bohemia-Moravia and General of German Security Police Reinhard Heydrich—appointed on September 27, 1941—was perfectly willing to arrest and execute a hundred men and women to save himself the trouble of finding out which among them, if any, were active in the resistance. Even the prime minister of the Protectorate government was not immune to arrest and execution. The deportation of Jews, which the Protectorate government had tried to resist, now began in earnest. So did massive arrests of Czechs, not on grounds of resistance activity but as a preventive measure—to strip the nation of its intelligentsia.

The Czechs did not choose to follow the German example of totalization and dehumanization. They sought to oppose Hitler with reason and humanity at Munich, during the actual occupation in March 1939, and in the first years that followed it. But the weapons of reason and humanity proved increasingly ineffective. By the end of 1941, the core of the clandestine resistance was destroyed by mass arrests and reprisals. In the calm light of reason, it remained true that the only real alternative to Hitler was humanism and justice. Mass arrests, however, leave little room for reason. To survive, we had to change, to oppose the Germans with their own weapons. The war now had come home to us—and with it the first stage of the revolutionary cycle.

On May 27, 1942, the Czechs struck back. A team of Czechoslovak paratroopers, working closely with the resistance, assassinated Reinhard Heydrich in broad daylight, near the heart of Prague. It was not an act of reason; its military value was negligible and its cost in mass reprisals staggering. Colonel General of the German Security Service Kurt Daluege, who replaced Heydrich, intensified Heydrich's policy of total war.

The Heydrich assassination was a crucial act. We had been reasonable at Munich, surrendering in the name of peace. We had been reasonable at the time of the occupation, yielding to save our country from destruction. We had been reasonable in the first years of the occupation, swallowing insults to save lives. But now we had served notice: we would be reasonable no longer. This still was our country.

Heydrich's assassination signified, too, that the days of the civilized, individual resistance, defying the Nazis with cunning and individual enterprise, were irrevocably gone. There was retaliation: over ten thousand persons were arrested in the few days following the assassination alone. Two weeks after the assassination, the Nazis singled out the small mining village of Lidice, near Kladno, though a hundred other villages might have served as well. Selected troops surrounded the village, shot all males over sixteen, hauled away women and children, leveled the buildings and, in the words of the report, "erased the name of the village from the map." Two weeks later another village, Ležáky, followed. But Lidice was enough to serve notice. There was no longer any illusion of normalcy. This was no longer a war fought by individual men: it now was a total war.

The second phase of the resistance, which began amidst this terror, was of another breed, different from the first, republican resistance. It was no longer primarily a clandestine organization of individuals, aimed at gathering intelligence and rescuing prime victims. Nor was it geared to purposeful activity guided by cool calculations of military advantage: it was desperate, armed defiance, the brute expression of a will to resist, regardless of cost, regardless of gain. It fought primarily a guerrilla war. Its partisans were based in the hills and forests, or focused on preparing armed uprisings in the cities. The stereotype of the first resistance had been the patriot of the First Republic, whose dedication to humanity had distinguished him from his German opponents—living an ordinary life on the surface while keeping the ideals of the Republic alive and serving it, perhaps, as an espionage agent undercover. The second phase of the resistance produced a different stereotype: the partisan, strong, forthright, matching his opponents in total ruthlessness and determination, emerging from a forest hideout to strike back with the fury and weaponry of guerrilla warfare. Statistically, those stereotypes may well have been far from an accurate description, but their very emergence testified to our changing consciousness. The day of the courageous humanist had passed. The ideals of humanity had been rendered impotent by the realities of total war and our enemy's ruthlessness. The nation that rose up in defiance from defeat had to be a nation cast in the mold of totality.

The Communists played a far more prominent role in the second phase of the resistance than they had in the first. Perhaps not in percentages: the resistance was still drawn from a nation that was not predominantly Communist. But the Communists now had definite advantages. In part it was simply that the Party, following the Soviet line, for the first two years had regarded the war as a capitalist war. And though many individual Communists had been active from the start, as Czechoslovaks rather than as Communists, the Party organization did not join in the resistance until Hitler's attack on the Soviet Union changed the "capitalist war" overnight into the "great patriotic war." The German sweep against the members of the early resistance had decimated the non-Communists who had been its core, yet had left the Communist clandestine organization reasonably operational despite some painful individual loses.

The increased prominence of the Communists in the resistance was partly geographic. With the opening of the Eastern front, the Soviet Union became our nearest combatantally, and soon escaped Soviet prisoners of war and Soviet commissars formed a steady influx into our underground organization. The Soviet Union, at least as much in propaganda as in fact, assumed the role of the official sponsor of the resistance. Besides, whenever Communists took an active part and played a significant role in the second phase of the resistance, they invariably did so as Communists, prominently displaying their political allegiance. The various non-communists, in contrast, fought simply as Czech patriots, indentifying their resistance with the nation as a whole rather than with a specific political orientation.

But the chief reason for the increased prominence of the Communist party in the second phase of the resistance was psychological. The Communists fit its stereotype far better than anyone else. The second phase of the resistance required totalized men, purged of the respect for individual lives, their own or that of others, which motivates ordinary human beings in ordinary times. It required men who found a new identity in the will to struggle and to sacrifice. They had to be men of iron discipline, capable of total self-sacrifice. I know of at least one man who carried out an impossible mission, escaped from captivity after inhuman torture and returned as the wreck of a man. When he came for help to the Communist party which had sent him out, he was greeted with the wry comment, "The Party is not a social-welfare institution," and he was given another brutal assignment. Finally, this second phase of our resistance required men who would not be deterred by the ferocity of Nazi reprisals, as the paratrooper who turned himself in and betrayed his comrades after Haydrich's assassination in the hope of puttin an end to the cruel reprisals.

The Communist party did not invent their rules. The same rules had been imposed months before Heydrich's assassination as Nazi German rules by Heydrich himself. They were the rules of total war. But the Communist party was uniquely equipped to play by those rules. The discipline, the self-sacrifice, the ruthless readiness to sacrifice oneself and others, even the image of the partisan for years had been familiar in Party lore. The very training and conditioning of its members for "class struggle," revolution, the perspective of wholes, and masses rather than of individuals fitted the conditions of total war far better than the humanism of our First Republic.

It is by no means obvious that the spectacular defiance of the second resistance required greater courage or greater determination than the quiet defiance of the first. Perhaps just the opposite is true: the second resistance had the courage of desperation, reinforced by a sense of belonging to a group; it conquered individual fear with collective courage. The first resistance had tested the mettle of individuals. I think of the men I have known from that period—inconspicuous, gentle, reasonable men, committed to human dignity and self-respect. I have often tried to imagine the courage it took for such men, alone, bearing the full weight of moral considerations, to confront the beastiality of the Gestapo. Theirs was a doubly difficult task: they sought not only to confront the Nazis, but to remain different from them—to preserve an ideal of humanity that would contradict and withstand the needs of total war. Theirs was not the courage of soldiers, but the courage of citizens tried to the breaking point. They defied and died choosing not to avail themselves of the psychological props of their opponents.

But no matter how heroic or reasonable, their defiance became anachronistic in an age of total war and totalized them In the latter half of the war, the resistance could no longer try to distinguish itself from the Germans by its commitment to humanity: it had to match them in determination and fury. Our nation, too, had to become totalized—and incidentally also polarized between those who fought and accepted the new total determination, and those who sought to preserve their individual lives.

At that time, it was easy for the Communists to create the impression that it was simply a distinction between those who resisted and those who did not. Thought it was never completely accurate, there was some justification for it. The humane, cautious resistance that tried to preserve human values had been rendered ineffective to a considerable extent by the conditions of total war. Preserving one's life had ceased to be a different way of resisting, and now it had become hard to distinguish between preserving the value of life and simply protecting one's own life. It had become difficult to risk within reason: all risks now were unreasonable. There was some truth in the allegation that those who risked had to risk everything—and that those who were not willing to risk everything simply took no risks. There also was some truth in the allegation that those who risked won total freedom—while those who tried to avoid exposure had given up not some, but all freedom.

But this simplification was not and never could be the whole truth. Even in the resistance there were a great many men, quite possibly a majority, who were willing to accept total risk and risk total courage for the duration of the war, but were not willing to identify the totalization the war demanded with ultimate self-realization. There were a great many people who were willing to fight in the resistance—but refused to become "resistance fighters" as a matter of personal identity. Most of these were non-Communists—people for whom the war was finite, not simply an intensification of a perennial struggle but something that had a beginning and would have an end. The freedom they sought was the freedom of humans fighting for the sake of humanity, which makes it possible to return home to live once more among human beings—not simply the freedom of the defiant that condemns them to the loneliness of perennial defiance and the exclusive fellowship of fellow fighters.

The war rendered this distinction much too fine. The other distinction was obvious and visible—the distinction between those who fought and those who cringed. It was all too easy to make it into a firm, permanent distinction between the fighters and the cowards. After the war ended, the distinction lingered on. The cowards retained their perennial place in society. The fighters retained their defiant image of the dedicated, self-sacrificing idealists. They never came home, they could not come home: now that the war ended, they could find no place: they had become fighters, and home to them had become the place of cowards. For those who fought but had no desire to become fighters—those who fought for the humanity of human life rather than for struggle and victory—there was little room in the clash of totalized dedicated men. There seldom is. In this confrontation, to give up the status of the defiant seemed tantamount to treason, to associating oneself with the cringing cowards who in the time of need had let themselves be humiliated rather than forsake their comfort. Yet to retain the posture of defiance meant exclusion from precisely what the resistance had fought for: a home, a place of peace, dignity, self-respect, and freedom.

This polarization, perhaps more than anything else, prepared the ground for the seed of revolution. Perhaps the greatest success of the Communist party in the early months after the war was precisely that it preempted the image of defiance and courage, because it had no scruples about identifying whole heartedly with the totalization most of us had been willing to accept only as necessary expedient. The Party now made it the test of idealism—as perhaps it had been in the war.

The Communists had fought and died, fought bravely and contributed much to our defiance, but they were by no means the only fighters, not even the majority of those who fought. Yet at the end of the war, the sole distinction appeared to be the one between fighters and cowards. Though now the war was over that was no longer an adequate distinction, psychological momentum kept it alive—and the Communists presented themselves as the defiant ones.

Czechoslovakia had survived the war; we had risen anew from defeat in the midst of the struggle. But we had changed: we had been brutalized, "radicalized." The appeal to a person's humanity had come to appear as tantamount to admission of cowardice. We no longer faced each other as human beings: we had come to think of ourselves and others in terms of hostile blocs. The ground was prepared: the revolutionary cycle had run through its first stage.

-II-

Sowing
the
Seed

May, 1945. *Liberation. The Coalition government of left-of-center parties affirms the Košice Program of Soviet alliance, socialism, and democracy. The Czechoslovak province of Ruthenia is annexed by the U.S.S.R.*

August, 1945. *With Allied approval, the Czechoslovaks begin massive deportations of the German minority to Germany.*

October, 1945. *The key industries are nationalized.*

May, 1946. *The Communists, in competing with the Catholic and democratic socialist parties in a relatively free election, win 39 percent of the vote.*

August, 1947. *The Soviets veto Czechoslovak participation in the Marshall Plan.*

November, 1947. *Democratic faction prevails over pro-Communist faction in the Social Democratic party, depriving Communists of the majority in Parliament.*

January, 1948. *Public opinion polls show a significant decrease of popular support for the Communists. The Communists secure control of the police.*

February, 1948. Non-Communist Ministers resign in protest over Communist manipulation of the police. The Communist party uses the occasion to seize power in a coup d'etat carried out by the Workers' Militia and police units.

i. A War Ends
The basic issue in the second stage of the revolutionary cycle is universal: the clash of the actual and The Ideal. The dislocation of the first stage wipes out the certainties of an earlier era that had both safeguarded and constrained human life. Individuals as well as society as a whole must choose whether to constrain the violent passions and actions of the first stage in order to protect the preciousness of human life—or whether to spur them on to take Utopia by storm.

The thrust of the age is always toward Utopia. Amid the upheaval of the first stage, human life becomes cheap and human happiness trivial. To survive the wholesale destruction of the first stage people have to learn to scorn the everyday, to pin their lives and hopes on an ideal that transcends the destruction of the actual. The dynamics of the second stage is a race between the rediscovery and restoration of the value of the actual and the vertigo of Utopia.

The rules under which that race is run differ widely. There are situations in which external forces impose limits on the messianic thrust and force the society to return to the concerns of daily existence. The Revolution then goes down in history as a noble, suppressed hope, cherished in the memories of the faithful. Alternately, external forces may either preempt the Utopia or make it the official program. The Revolution, imposed from above, then can attribute its failure to its official sponsors. Perhaps the utopian vision endures because the race is so rarely run in its own terms, as a confrontation of the value of life and liberty of everyday existence with the messianic dream of perfection.

Perhaps in the first three postwar years our country lived through one of these rare phases. Between the end of the war in 1945 and the Communist coup in 1948, Czechoslovakia was a reasonably free country, and neither democracy nor revolution had an exclusive official sponsor. Unlike other governments in exile, clearly committed to the East or the West, the government of President Beneš, which had been based in London for most of the war, returned to Czechoslovakia via Moscow, with Stalin's blessings. Beneš's government could claim continuity with the democratic humanism of Masaryk's prewar republic, but it included representatives of the old opposition parties, and among them the Communists, too.

Besides, by the first postwar Christmas, Czechoslovakia had become a European anomaly in another sense as will: it was an unoccupied country. Other former combatants became hosts to their respective conquerors or liberators. By an accident of geography, however, Czechoslovakia had been liberated in part by the Americans, in part by the Soviets. As a former ally, it could not be simply divided into zones of occupation, like Germany or Austria. Goegraphically, it fell into the Soviet sphere, and the Soviets were most anxious to see the Anericans leave. The Americans, however, in the one lone gesture in behalf of the victim of Munich, refused to withdraw without a reciprocal Soviet withdrawal, avowing a noble principle that unfortunately was not applicable to Central Europe as a whole—even though thirty years later such reciprocal withdrawal remains its only hope. Six months after the war had ended, the Russians yielded and took a calculated risk. They annexed Ruthenia, the easternmost part of prewar Czechoslovakia that forms a bridge over the Carpathians to the Danube basin, and then agreed to withdraw their forces from the rest of Czechoslovakia simultaneously with the Americans.

The Soviet's risk in annexing Ruthenia was hardly very great. This narrow 500-mile widge of Czechoslovak land was surrounded on three sides by Soviet-occupied countries. Only along a part of its narrow western border did Czechoslovakia touch on the American zone of Germany—and there the Americans demobilized frantically, leaving a few battalions of lightly armed constabulary troops to face the full might of the Soviet

Army. There was no point along all of Czechoslovakia's borders where Soviet troops would have had to march more than a hundred miles before encountering other Soviet troops marching in the opposite direction.

Yet in a sense the Soviet withdrawal was a gamble, though a heavily insured one. The Soviets, in 1945, were not planning an armed reoccupation of Czechoslovakia, and they did not resort to it until 1968. Czechoslovakia was to be an experiment in an entirely native "revolution." Here, without the cover of a Soviet army of occupation, the native Communist party was to seize power.

There was no chance of victory for the democratic forces in postwar Czechoslovakia. Any decisive development that would place political and social power in the hands of the Czech and the Slovak people—beyond the control of the Communist party's *apparat* that was responsible to Moscow—would have been countered by an armed Soviet move, as in fact was to happen twenty years later. But though the democratic forces could not win a decisive victory, they could avoid defeat by effectively blocking a domestic coup and forcing the Soviets to resort to overt armed intervention.

When the coup finally came, the presence of Soviet Ambassador Zorin in Prague and the Soviet armies poised along the entire open Czechoslovak border may well have been the decisive factors. Still, for almost three years the Czechoslovak Communist party prepared the revolution on its own, and in February 1948 it did seize power without Soviet intervention, relying for support on its own apparatus within the police, on its Workers' Militia, and on its considerable popular support. It was, for once, a genuine Communist revolution, and in the twenty years that followed, Czechoslovakia provided a test-tube experiment in the social dynamics of the dictatorship of the proletariat, unburdened by foreign occupation.

Similarly, the two years between the Soviet withdrawal and the Communist coup of 1948 represented a test-tube experiment in the dynamics of a revolutionary situation. The interim regime was not a reactionary one: it approximated rather closely all the overt aims of prewar leftists. The Communist party assumed a leading role in a coalition government committed to a socialist program. The parties of the Right had been banned: the Communists, together with the Social Democrats, did command a majority in the Parliament. Something like a censorship, exercised by person-to-person calls rather than by law, did develop and proved quite effective: while this tacit censorship permitted a variety of "progressive" views, it effectively prevented all dissemination of antisocialist or anti-Soviet views. Industry, except for very small enterprises, had been nationalized, Communist-controlled trade unions had acquired a dominant role, and the entire economy now was geared to central planning. All the traditional prerequisites for "building socialism" were there.

Yet Czechoslovakia did retain many distinctly democratic features. Its borders remained open both to people and to ideas. The press, though of course constrained by the Soviet alliance, retained considerable initiative and independence. The tacit censorship proscribed all views overtly critical of the Soviet Union and the Communist party, but it did not prescribe the content and orientation of news coverage. Similarly, the courts retained considerable independence and in fact thwarted numerous Communist attempts at using the police to destroy opponents. Individual citizens retained a considerable sense of security, had freedom of association, of travel, expression, and choice of employment. Elections remained pluralistic, with a choice of parties. Altogether, while the Communist party effectively assumed a leading role in the state, it had not acquired a monopoly of unrestricted power. Unlike in the Soviet Union and countries where the Communists came to power through a revolution, the power of the Czechoslovak Communist party remained restricted by the principle of humanity—legal guarantees of civil and human rights—and by the principle of democracy, the need for popular support and the possibility of losing it.

All in all, life was good—and getting better. There were shortages and inequities as the administrative apparatus tried to cope with the human and economic freedom, security, and hope. Czechoslovakia, simply, had not been driven to revolution by oppression and suffering. Nor was the situation "revolutionary" in the sense of the time-worn Marxist dogma about rulers who are no longer willing to rule and the ruled who are no longer willing to be ruled by them. In a very real sense, Czechoslovakia's short-lived postwar socialist democracy gave its people a real sense of participation: for all the bureaucratic inefficiency, its administrators from the local National Committees to the Parliament and the commissions governing its nationalized industries were administrators, not rulers and, conversely, its people were citizens, not a mass of the ruled. If there was a favored class, it was that of the workers.

Yet there was a revolutionary impetus and a revolutionary situation, and it came to a head in February of 1948. Only this revolutionary situation, as usual in liberal societies, was the reverse of the revolt of the ruled against their rulers. It was far more the grasp of dedicated men for power over a majority of their fellowmen. The revolutionary situation was not one of resolute will confronting unbearable oppression, but rather one of doubt and guilt seeking self-justification in radical faith and act.

Our people's profound self-doubt was perhaps an inevitable product of the occupation. Czechoslovakia had not resisted in 1938—perhaps for perfectly valid reasons, but still, it had submitted to the occupation. Except for a handful of resistance fighters, Czechs and Slovaks had survived by accepting humiliation and injustice, by maintaining a low profile and standing by while the Germans trampled on their pride and dignity. For our people the war had been above all an experience of impotence in the name of reasonableness. Quite understandably, this had created a powerful need for forceful self-assertion, for strong, determined acts that would reaffirm a sense of self-confidence and identity. The sense of self-doubt and need for self-affirmation may well have been most acute among those who had suffered most, but it was easily matched by an unacknowledged sense of guilt that called out for justification.

At that time, we did not admit either the self-doubt or the guilt. Quite the contrary, we had to insist on our confidence and righteousness—and those, after all, were also real: we had survived Hitler, we had suffered and triumphed. But the neurotic pitch of our acts and opinions of those days betrayed both doubt and guilt—and perhaps the most far-reaching effects were our willingness to expell the German minority.

The Republican party had been the strongest political force in prewar Czechoslovakia. It had been an agrarian party, basically conservative and individualistic in its orientation, far more committed to safeguarding the established values—and injustices—than to do battle for new achievements. It was, in temperament and policy alike, a fundamentally antirevolutionary nonheroic party, advocating conservative policies at home and conciliation with Germany abroad. Because of the latter, it became a convenient scapegoat for our sense of defeat and failure. At the same time, its demise eliminated the one force that would have challenged the slogans of revolutionary self-affirmation, and also rendered a significant portion of the electorate politically inert. Certainly, the Republican party represented outdated, outworn policies and opinions—but the fact that we did not feel confident enough to deal with these aspects of the Republicans did not bode well for our future.

Then there was the deportation of the German minority. None of us questioned it at the time, yet while quite possibly justifiable and defensible, it was an act that should have been debated, not simply accepted. The German minority made up some 20 percent of Czechoslovakia's prewar population. For the most part, it consisted of Germans whose families had lived in Bohemia for some three or four hundred years. The prewar Republic scrupulously observed the personal rights of its German citizens as well as the national rights of its German minority as a whole: German was used alongside with Czech and slovak in public life. There were German schools up to university level, and there was a lively German press and cultural life. Still, the Germans—for centuries part of the privileged nationality in Bohemia while our country was a part of the Habsburg Empire—now resented the loss of their former status. In the late 1930's, most of them had opted for Hitler. German irrendenta, its rights protected by Czechoslovak laws, became the instrument of Hitler's expansion and the immediate cause of the fall of the Republic—and many individual Czechoslovak Germans became Hitler's most willing and cruel servants.

In Chechoslovak eyes, the deportation of the German minority unquestionably appeared necessary for the future security of Czechoslovakia and morally justified by the role the German minority as a whole had played in the war. The move was sanctioned by the allies—by the British and the Americans as well as the Soviets—and even had legal justification: Czechoslovak authorities claimed they were not deporting Germans as Germans, but as collaborators who during the war had taken advantage of their nationality to claim German citizenship and the advantages it offered. In deporting them, we could with some justice claim that we were merely respecting their choice of citizenship.

Still, for all the historical and moral justification, the deportation represented a wholesale, drastic step against more than two million human beings whose families had lived in our land for ten or more generations. It may have been justified, it may have been necessary, but our ready consent to it betrayed our own sense of insecurity. It also established a dangerous precedent: that citizenship is not a matter of birthright, but something that must be earned by right actions and opinions, and can be denied—just as the Republican party could be banned if in the judgement of the regime it had not earned their right to function.

It would have been one matter if we had tried individual Germans, as Czechoslovak citizens, for wartime collaboration, or attacked the opinions and policies of the Republican party in public discussion and by vote in an election. But killing a scapegoat always perpetuates guilt. The decision to deport the Germans and supress the Republicans in the name of state interest and public passion testified to and reinforced a very real revolutionary situation: the reality of unacknowledged guilt and self-doubt fostered our search for self-justification in forceful gestures and our desperate need for symbols of rebirth and self-affirmation.

In this context, the most basic failure of Czechoslovakia's democrats was the generic failure of democrats in the second stage of the revolutionary cycle: the failure to appreciate the need for symbols of self-affirmation and the failure to offer such symbols. Czechozlovakia's democrats were surprisingly effective in coping with the incredibly complex task of coping with postwar society, but they were ill-prepared to provide symbols of rebirth. While the Communists were burdened with their heritage of utopian Messianism for which the country was to pay heavily in future years, the democrats were no less burdened by a heritage of bourgeois pettiness against which Masaryk had already protested two generations ago.

Bourgeois pettiness is by no means an exclusively bourgeois characteristic. The working class has a stifling "respectability" all its own, which Shaw satirized so effectively. Nor is bourgeois pettiness exclusively democratic: quite the contrary, it is fundamentally undemocratic, and the Communists soon established a far more coercive version of their own. Rather, stodgy pettiness is the spirit of mediocrity—a failure of imagination that infects men of all classes and all persuasions. It is the spirit of the fearful, who in the name of respectability and order stifle anything that sparkles, anything that seems alive, imaginative—and unpredictable.

Throughout its modern history, Czechoslovakia had always been the country of the reasonable and orderly. This is what made it one of the freest, most humane countries in Europe, but it is also what made it frequently a petty, stodgy country. There were countervailing forces, free to express themselves, but the spirit of stodginess always played a significant role. In the aftermath of the war, the spirit of pettiness stood out in all its dreary absurdity.

The revolt against stodginess, against the petty, shabby, vicious mediocrity that masquerades as respectability is a perennial life-spring of freedom. But the revolutionary cycle, as it enters its second stage, leads to an identification of imagination with power, an alliance of rebels with true believers—an alliance of militant imagination with militant dogmatism. As in the Weimar Republic, in postwar Czechoslovakia an autocratic, totalitarian movement somewhat ironically came to serve as a symbol of revolt against drabness and mediocrity—a symbol of the revolt of the imagination.

As the undramatic, steady work of the socialist democratic government started to take effect, the appeal of the dramatic posture of the Party decreased. After its peak in the first postwar election in 1946, in which it won 39 percent of the popular vote, the Communist party steadily lost support. The factor that triggered the coup may well have been the prospect of a sizable setback for the Communist party if the scheduled elections were to be held. Nor did the Communist party, even at the peak of its appeal, ever stake its power simply on popular support. While preaching popular revolt, it also systematically took over the police, organized an armed militia, and infiltrated the army. The anvil of popular support served the hammer of a disciplined power structure. But at the time when the anvil was needed, it was there: the Communists did have sufficient popular support to seize and exercise power. The outcome of Czechoslovakia's postwar attempt at democracy may have been preordained by Soviet might and the Communist party power *apparat*, yet the course of the experiment remains a study in the dynamics of the second stage of the revolutionary cycle: the dynamics of hate and hope that forge the popular anvil of revolution.

ii. Uneasy Peace

"Those Who Made The Revolution" inevitably make a depressing study, especially when that revolution is an unsurpation of power by True Believers in a liberal society. There is always the same patological mixture of paranoia and megalomania, the compulsive need to rule coupled with a sublime confidence in one's own divine mission, which Stalin shared with Hitler—the differences are only in organizational competence and mental agility. But there must be the millions who make revolution possible: the men and women who want to be ruled, who want to believe, who convince themselves that humanity can be won by cruelty, and self-realization by self-surrender.

Any society at any stage of its history has its share of Those Who Make the Revolution, and Czechoslovakia was no exception. There was Klement Gottwald, who upon his election to the prewar Parliament announced, "We are here to cut your throats" —and had enjoyed parliamentary immunity for the attempt. There was Rudolf Slánský, veteran combatant of the Spanish Civil War and of our wartime resistance, impatient even with

Gottwald's kind of moderation and straining to impose the Soviet model in its full brutality. There was Zdeněk Nejedlý, the intellectual autocrat who was prepared to provide ideological justification for the vicissitudes of power. There were others far too many others.

But not they alone made the revolution possible: the revolution needed its anvil, the millions of people willing to be ruled. Those millions, who gave the Communist party its 39 percent of the vote in our one free postwar election and whose inertia blocked any effective resistance at the time of the coup, make the interesting study.

Our active Communists, generally fell into three categories—the egotists, the gullible, and the idealists. The egotists were perhapsthe easiest to understand. They had a definite personal stake. For many of them, it was simply a matter of personal safety. during the war, a great many people, while by no means actively collaborating with the Germans, proved not above taking advantage of a special situation. Many of them rose to positions vacated by persons who had been dismissed, jailed, or killed by the Germans. Others acquired abandoned Jewish property as "Aryanizers," or, after the war, won a tenuous title to abandoned German property as "National Administrators." Every one of them had a good reason for not wanting his personal record examined too closely.

A Communist party card provided excellent protection. Communist propaganda repeatedly hammered in the theme that the party is the hard-fisted, uncompromising enemy of collaborators and profiteers—and the insinuation that the democratic parties harbor both, if they are not actually composed of them entirely. This propaganda was quite successful: even three decades later, former Communists, disillusioned with their erstwhile faith, frequently continue to believe that the confrontation of the Communists and the democrats was a confrontation of misguided idealists with collaborators and profiteers. Quite understandably, a great many men whose conscience was not quite clear concluded that membership in the Communist party would afford them the best possible protection against unpleasant investigation. They were tight: at the height of the Stalin terror and again after the Soviet occupation, a surprising proportion of those rising to power and prominence, or often simply to modest affluence, were comrades who during the war had anything but clean records—while an equally surprising proportion of comrades who found themselves behind bars or on the gallows were veterans of German concentration camps.

The sense of personal righteousness that Party membership gave, not only was a convenient cover, but frequently an inducement in itself. Every society has its self-appointed Guardians of Virtue: the tight-lipped, virtuous matrons of small towns, watching the comings and goings of their fellow citizens, the gossips of old Salem; the pious old maids of Calvin's Geneva. Communism produced the socialist concierges, whose censorious virtue it endowed with the righteousness of The People's Cause. Perhaps every revolution that sets out to give power to the imagination ends up giving it to the Guardians of Virtue. The only difference between the socialist concierge and the small-town bourgeois gossip is that the petty vindictiveness of the Communist concierge acquires the force of law.

Many rank-and-file members of the Party, however, did not fall into the category of the egotists but simply into the category of the hopeful and the gullible. In any society, there will be some social friction and reason for discontent. In our postwar society, there was an infinite number of these problems, and the administrative apparatus, weakened by the war, often could not cope adequately. The bulging bureaucrat is the oldest stereotype cited in justification for revolution: how beastly is the bourgeois! how beastly is the bureaucrat! Undoubtedly, many were. But in the heat of the moment it is easy to overlook that the bungling bourgeois bureaucrat remains vulnerable to human pressure. Not only can he be dismissed for corruption and incompetence, he also can be moved by personal appeals to pity or forced by the threat of passive resistance—including those of a young woman who threatens to go to sleep on his office sofa. The revolutionary Communist administrators proved to be men of a different mettle, beyond dismissal from their jobs and immune even to the thought of letting a sick young woman and her child die in an unheated hovel. The bungling bourgeois bureaucrat remained human, bunglingly human, and continued to deal with human beings; the revolutionary administrator was a prophet doing battle with the class enemy.

Communist propaganda focused on the incompetence of the bureaucrats, and avoided all mention of the inhumanity of the Righteous. It would be harsh to blame the gullible: they had real grievances, and the men whom they trusted, the idealists and intellectuals, had convinced them that all their grievances could be traced to the same source: that power was scattered in the hands of bungling and fallible human beings rather than concentrated in the hands of the Pure. That was the Platonic part of the argument. The Marxist codicil held that the Pure are necessarily and inevitably members of the Communist party, endowed with all the omniscience and omnipotence of philosopher kings, while the non-Communists are bungling, human, and incompetent at best, but for the most part collaborators and profiteers. . . .

That was and is the Communist intellectuals' basic article of faith: to be an idealist means to be a Communist, to leave the Party means to give up idealism—to give up hope and conviction and resign oneself to the recognition that not only Communism but all idealism is in vain; to admit Communism had failed is not to admit that another ideal might succeed—but that the smug and self-contented, the defeated and the resigned are right.

This is a peculiar faith, though a persistant one, and it requires a peculiar kind of gullibility. The gullibility of Communist intellectuals was an expression of a will to believe and an unwillingness to give up the security of the conviction that there is a kingdom of god on earth and that this kingdom can be achieved here if only we shall will and believe hard enough.

In 1946, this was an understandable desire, but it also had the effect of legitimating the most transparent propaganda. Above all, it gave a stamp of validity to the most important belief on the doubtful and the guilty, the disbelief in historical justification. In a "historical sense," what we had suffered in the past justified all our acts. The suffering of the war justified the revenge we took; the doubt, guilt, and frustration justified a revolution. No one could blame us, after what we had been through.

But blame is socially irrelevant. Social decisions do not need the justification of blamelessness, but the justification of efficacy. Whether the act was the deportation of the Germans, the destruction of the "class enemy," or the concentration of power in the hands of the forceful stalwarts of the Communist party—it remained socially irrelevant whether the motives that led to the act justified it. Social acts require social justification in terms of their social effects. Revolutionaries invariably stress the "historical" justification of their acts in their rhetoric, but avoid the question of social justification: it is an article of their faith that a "historically" justified act will produce desirable social results. The essence of Communist idealism, and of all revolutionary idealism, is the unshakable faith that any "historically" justified act—that is, any forceful response to past wrongs and sufferings—will lead to the elimination of injustice. To the Communists, regardless of personal or Party characteristics, theirs is the Party of the Pure and the Just because their acts and policies are the genuine response to existing injustice.

Perhaps the crucial, most difficult recognition in the second stage of the revolutionary cycle is that the experience of suffering, no matter how much it deserves respect, is by no means universally ennobling. It does not automatically strip away everything that is petty and mean, leaving men pure and idealistic. Its effect is simply an intensification of good and evil alike. Suffering destroys leeway: the idealists become more uncompromising in their idealism; the greedy, the cruel, the mean become more unscrupulous—and they all believe that their earlier suffering now justifies them in turn. After the war, the Communist party was not the party of the pure—it was the party of the intense, and it attracted the idealists and the villains alike.

Psychologically it may be a difficult recognition, but it is a crucial one, that not all the intense are pure—and not all the idealists intense. Even after the war, there were other, no less sincere idealists, who recoiled from the intensity of the Communists. Many of our people who passed through the experience of resistance, jails and concentration camps saw only the intensity of the Nazis and the passivity of their victims. They admired the Communists precisely for their ability to match that passionate intensity, even in dying. But many others saw something quite different: the ruthless intensity on the one side matched by no less ruthless intensity on the other producing much the same rusults. While we could only defy the Nazis by matching them, we, too, were becoming dehumanized and totalized in the process.

There remained one difference: for the Nazis, inhumanity was a matter of national policy—and years before Hitler, Schlieffen's German army manual had discussed terror as a means of controlling conquered populations with a minimum of troops. The cruelty some of our people vented against our oppressors and collaborators in the last days of the war was the eruption of pent-up emotions—emotions we resolutely tried to disown and did our best to control. Later, many men whom the Communists accused of lack of zeal and dedication turned against the CP not out of a lack of idealism, but because of the recognition that for the Communists, as in the past for the Nazis, hate was again a matter of policy. To be sure, it was being justified by injuries suffered, but it resulted no less in cruelty and ruthlessness: in the class war, in the elimination of anyone who could be called a "class enemy," all the emotions and strong-arm tactics of fascism were being reintroduced, in the name of "historical justification."

In comparison with the Communists, the democratic opposition might well have appeared weak and vacillating. It had talented men, but no dynamic leaders. In part, that was a consequence of the war. The democratic intelligentsia, closely identified with Masaryk's democracy, was active already in the first resistance and took frightening losses in its liquidation. But more than that it was a function of the democratic program. The democrats were committed to liberalizing our society, making it more free and just, not to transforming it to conform to a definite model. They offered little of the righteousness and fury which could make up for the experience of the war. The young men I knew, at the University, in the YMCA, or simply as friends of the family were no less idealistic than the Communists, nor did they constitute a smaller percentage of the democratic parties than the Communist idealists of their party. But the democratic idealism was not of the crusading variety. Even in its genuine commitment to socialism, it remained the humanistic idealism of Masaryk, dedicated to humanizing power rather than the revolutionary idealism of Lenin and Stalin, dedicated to seizing it. For the democrats, socialism remained a means, the goal and criterion of progress remained human freedom and human welfare. Perhaps the basic tragedy of the second stage of the revolutionary cycle is precisely that it makes it so difficult to distinguish between idealism and fanaticism on the one hand —and between the idealism of humanity and simple complacence.

Under "ordinary" circumstances, the passionate faith of the Communist idealists and their willingness to sanction violence as a historically justified and socially effective solution to the society's various problems would appear as little more than yet another intellectual abstraction, with little relevance beyond the lecture halls of the university. But ordinary life was slowly returning. The war had unmasked, mercilessly, all the anachronistic pettiness of our daily life: we all needed something new, we all needed to believe. The mood in Czechoslovakia between 1945 and 1948 was rather like that of the Western intellectuals in the late 1960's. There was the same sense of disillusionment—but there was also a longing for a new start, with little conception of what that new start could be. There was the pervasive sense that the world ought to be other than it is—that it ought to be reborn.

Thanks to the willing faith of Communist intellectuals, the Party was able to capitalize on that mood. The slogan painted above the stage of the E. F. Burian Theater summed it up well. *"Komunismus je mládí světa"*—"Communism Is the Youth of the World." The Czechoslovak intellectuals had fashioned a kind of Communism that would be hard to reconcile with actual Communist ideology or practice—to them Communism was a symbol of rejuvenation, a birth of new freedom.

The Communist ideology, in fact, was really as irrelevant to our condition then as it is in the West today. We were beginning to solve out concrete economic and social problems, steadily and quite effectively. We had built a socialist economy, had brought about a profound social transformation, our democracy was sinking roots. Our problems were tangible, daily problems, not the problems of struggle for power. The communist conception of autocratic "revolutionary" power smashing the villains of reaction was quite beside the point: what we needed was hard, competent work rather than the strong-arm methods of the Czars and the commissars or their exhilarating slogans.

The other idealists were not fossilized remnants of the prewar Republic, but were willing to forgo the luxury of slogans for the reality of social progress. We, too, felt that Czechoslovakia had been betrayed by the Western democracies at Munich. We were not reactionary bourgeois: most of us were young and idealistic, sympathetic to the idea of socialism and social justice, and convinced, no less than the Communists, of the need for a national rebirth. But we could not simply equate the ideals of progress with the ideals of Communism—and especially with the Communist party. Each of us had his own experiences during the occupation and the war, about which one did not speak but which we could not forget. We were acquainted with prewar Russian refugees who, after the war, mysteriously disappeared into the Soviet Union. Many of us remembered the initial years of resistance, when the Communist party, against the feelings and convictions of its members, submitted to the Moscow line and stood apart from the "imperialist" war and the "bourgeois nationalist" resistance to Hitler. Only when Hitler attacked the Soviet Union did the Party *apparat* begin to support the resistance activities of its members. It did so ruthlessly, imposing Soviet "advisors" on resistance groups and sacrificing their Czech members. And even then there were cases in which the Party leadership used the disjointed wartime conditions to rid itself of men and women who might stand in the way of its plans once the war was over.

Already then, we were quite aware of a contradiction between the self-sacrificing idealism of ordinary Communists and the Party *apparat*. Or, more precisely, at the time we already recognized the difference between the idealists and the fanatic fighters, between the people for whom the ideals of Communism remained the measure of the Party and Party policy—and people willing to subjugate their conscience and conviction to the Party's ambitions to power. A friend who had been in the resistance and then in a concentration camp told me of a guerrilla, hard-line Communist, whom he had met in Brdy. The man told him quite openly, "This war will be won, with us or without us. What matters is what comes next: to win the class war."

The opposition to the Communists, in my experience, was not composed primarily of old reactionaries, but of idealists from the other side: convinced democrats who could not bring themselves to believe that the ideals of social justice or personal idealism and heroism of individual Communists justified the power claims of the Party *apparat*. These democrats sensed that the unquestioning dedication and discipline, which the Party demanded and its members gave freely, was a double-edged weapon that could be used not only against the Germans but also against our own people—or even against fellow Party members. They proved to be right: in the coup of February 1948, that dedication and discipline were used against other Czechoslovaks, not only against the "reaction" and the "bourgeoisie," but against all who stood in the path of the Party's ambitions to power—including idealistic socialists. A few years later, in the purges, this method was used again, this time against Party members who only a few years ago, in the February coup had justified dictatorial methods by their effectiveness against the "enemy"

Yet for many people the concepts of progress and of Communism had become virtually synonymous—even for some who were aware of the price we would have to pay in freedom and democracy. Among them were people whose hopes I shared and whom I respected. Yet the Communist cadres—autocratic, dogmatic, primitivistic—were such unlikely prophets of rejuvenation. And Party Communism—just as autocratic, dogmatic and primitivistic—was such an unlikely ideology of progress. Masaryk had warned us long ago that violence is not a suitable vehicle for social progress. Once the Party was in power, it bore him out: it was the violent reality of the revolution and not its idealistic value as a symbol of rebirth that shaped our lives.

But the reality of rebirth takes time to mature, while the myth of revolution offers the vision of instantaneous liberation.

The second stage of the revolutionary cycle is a race between reality and myth, and in the postwar confrontation between East and West, time proved too short.

iii. The Party The cabinet crisis of February 1948 broke while I was skiing in the north. It was a perfect weekend, sunny and crisp, with dry, powdery snow over the old base. On the train to Prague people spoke freely and seemed generally confident. My fellow passengers were ordinary workers—the presumptive "anvil of the Revolution." They were clearly aware of the mood of the people, of the decreasing appeal of the Communist party and the increasing support for our democracy. The country, they knew from firsthand experience, was not Communist, and was becoming less rather than more so. They could not believe that the government could become Communist.

The mood in Prague was different. Here it was the "hammer of the Revolution" that mattered. Worker's Militiamen, equipped with red armbands and new Soviet rifle patrolled the station and the streets all along the way from Dennis Station to my home in the Letná district. I was to repeat that walk in a dream again and again for twenty years of exile. With every step it became more obvious that the anvil had ceased to matter: the hammer had swung into action.

I spent that night lying sleepless beside the radio, waiting for President Beneš to act, to order out the army, to stand up to Gottwald's demands, to meet the force of the Communist hammer with the force at his disposal. But the weapons of out democracy no longer sufficed. They were such naive weapons! The university students tried to march to the Castle, to let the President know that he was not alone: the police and Workers' Militia blocked their way and scattered them with clubs. The editors of the non-Communist daily, *Svobodné Slovo*, had hoarded newsprint so that they could put out the paper behind barricaded doors—reminding me of the sandwiches the non-Communist Russian deputies brought with them to the Parliament in 1917 in order to hold out against a Communist blockade. Our Cabinet ministers counted on their parliamentary majority—but by that time the Communist militia had occupied the offices of the democratic parties and destroyed the parliamentary majority with clubs and guns.

The army could have made a difference. All night, I waited for the President to give the order to mobilize; by morning, it was clear that he would not. Our army, which had not fought in 1938, remained in the barracks in 1948. Our democracy proved too humane to defend itself by force of arms.

The Communists' struggle that preceded the coup was of a different order. One of its aspects was covert, the process in which the Communists forged the hammer of the revolution. That process lay largely beyond our ken and power to interfere. Step by step, the Communists took over the machinery of power. The Ministry of the Interior, which controlled both the secret and the uniformed police, had been in their hands since the end of the war—that had been one of Stalin's conditions, and the Communist party made good use of it. Non-Communist police officers were gradually pensioned off, dismissed, or transferred to distant parts of the country. A similar process went on in the labor unions, in the organs of local administrations, even in social organizations. The iron discipline of the Party helped: while non-Communists were increasingly eager to return to a normal existence, the Communists were always willing to take on responsibilities and do the work that in a democracy would be trivial but because crucial to a struggle for power. By the time of the coup, throughout the country as a whole, the Communists had markedly less support than they had when the war ended. But our country, though still not Communist-controlled, was to a great extent Communist-dominated; the hammer had been forged.

Soviet pressure helped, too. Although an independent country, Czechoslovakia was within the Soviet sphere of influence. In 1947, the Soviets made the point. The Czechoslovak government, under Communist prime minister, had voted to participate

in the Marshall Plan—but Stalin summoned the government
to Moscow, and he pronounced his veto. Jan Masaryk commented
upon his return, "I went to Moscow as the foreign minister
of a sovereign state—I am coming back as Stalin's lackey." For
a time, Moscow was prepared to tolerate a degree of autonomy,
but it would not permit any serious challenge to its policies.

Under these conditions, the democratic parties were in no
position to challenge the Communist drive to forge the hammer
of the revolution. Instead, they took the only route open to
them: to dissolve the anvil by eroding the CP's popular support
before its hammer could be prepared to strike.

It was not an easy task. The war destroyed much more
than buildings, more than men: it destroyed much of the spirit
that makes a free society possible. We had come to take strong-arm
measures for granted—and to think of people as expendable.
Now we had to build up, and we were achieving a great deal.
We had created a basic, functional administration; supplies were
being moved, people housed, crops harvested, and goods
purchased. But we were doing far more than that. We had created
a socialist economy in which the democratic process would not
be at the mercy of economic interests—and a democratic social
structure in which men, consumers and producers, would not
be at the mercy of a state appatatus. Through the Ministry
of Justice, we were painstakingly reestablishing legal conceptions
of fairness, justice, and human rights which, during the time
of occupation and wars had been replaced by that era's rough-
and-ready norms. In the press, we were building norms of objec-
tivity and freedom of information.

To the average man in the street, it often seemed that the
democratic parties meant well but had no program. Although
they were in fact acting in a thousand ways, they seemed to
him ineffective, incapable of taking the kind of radical action
to which the war had accustomed him. It was hard for him
to understand that the democratic parties were trying to build
a new life, not win battles.

The Communists were psychologically in a far stronger position. They did have a militant program—seizure of power. To
each of our problems, and they were legion, they had the same
answer: all power to the Communist party; remove all restric-

tions, all safeguards on power; focus it in the hands of the Party—and in a few years all our problems will be over. They spoke of purging the impure: removing "reactionaries," bureaucrats, "enemies of the people"—and quite incidentally also such bourgeois trivialities as civil rights—so that the Pure could build a new society unhindered by the past. Their program was clear and simple: to take the Kingdom of Heaven by storm.

To a people weary of putting up with a thousand frustrations this seemed an attractive program. The democratic parties tried to ask how giving power to the Party would solve the problems of supplies, social organization, housing—all the problems that still were to remain unresolved twenty years after the Communist coup. But too many people had become convinced that all our problems stemmed from insufficient will and courage, and that the Party, which made much of its role in our wartime resistance, had both. Only the outworn fetishes of democracy stood in the way.

President Beneš had proclaimed his government's first post-occupation program when he returned from exile and came to Košice—right after the Russian army had liberated this first major town on Czechoslovak territory. It was on of the sad results of the Košice program that it had become virtually impossible to speak objectively of the Soviet Union. The Soviet Union supposedly was a paradise on earth; in the Soviet Union the sun was always shining and there were no problems—obviously, the Soviet approach must be right! But even if it had been possible to speak objectively of the U.S.S.R., many people would not have listened. We were so tired of problems, and many of us had to believe that simple, unambiguous solutions are possible, that there is a place on this earth where human life is joyful and unproblematic. When I hear the paeans of praise Westerners today, with far less provocation, heap up on China or on Cuba, I think much less harshly of our naivete in 1948. We yearned to believe.

Yet we made progress in those three years. The Communists had reached their peak of popular appeal at the time of the first elections, right after the war. Perhaps it was the power they had won then that changed their fortune. In positions of responsibility, the Communists were far less impressive than in opposition. And now that life was returning to a state of normalcy, our people had less confidence in strong-arm tactics, were less ready to ride roughshod over each other. People now were more anxious to live than to fight. The Social Democrats committed themselves decisively to the democratic process at their 1947 congress, and in municipal elections the Communists made far weaker showings. The Institute of Public Opinion, which traditionally was highly reliable, estimated that their proportion of the vote in the next general election would drop to 20 percent or less. The anvil was eroding.

We were fighting a difficult battle. We battled against the war mentality of strong-arm methods and of disregard for human rights. We were gaining in that war—although painfully slowly—and we were forging a democratic nation. We still had the vision of the millennium, the wartime impatience with ordinary solutions to ordinary problems, the hope for a radical, drastic change. I suppose that, given time, we would have developed, like Sweden, toward a democratic society with a strong Communist opposition prodding us on. Given time. . . .

We were not given that time. The election that could have effectively dissolved the Communist anvil was scheduled for May 1948. On the level of popular sentiment, we had every reason for confidence. Results of local elections, of public-opinion polls as well as party-menbership statistics, and the tenor of the daily press clearly indicated that the Communist party had lost much of its charisma and was losing support. Our Communists—and the Soviets—knew it, too, and knew they had to strike before the election.

The moment came by end of February. With the erosion of the anvil, the Communists concentrated on the hammer of the revolution. In the fall of 1947 they had initiated a campaign of open intimidation, including bombs sent to non-Communist cabinet ministers. By January 1948 their campaign to transform the police into an instrument of the Communist party was in full swing. In February, another large group of non-Communist police officers was dismissed or ordered to outlying provinces and their places in Prague were filled by loyal Party members, many of them with dubious qualifications.

Ever since the end of the war, the non-Communist parties

had followed a strategy of avoiding confrontation with the Communist hammer in order to buy time to dissolve the Communist anvil. The May election was to be the payoff for that strategy. But by mid-February it had become clear that the non-Communist parties had to challenge the Communist hammer as well—or there would be no election.

The challenge took the form of vigorous protest in the Cabinet against the Communist manipulation of the police, followed by the protest resignations of non-Communist ministers. On constitutional grounds, it was a feasible plan. The Communists, lacking parliamentary majority, could not form a government without non-Communist support. The President would have to dissolve the Parliament and call for a new election, in which the Communists would lose their virtual stranglehold on the country—though they would remain a major force. Our democracy would be safe: Czechoslovakia could become the Finland of Central Europe.

Yet the Communists were not prepared to accept a defeat within constitutional limits. Now Gottwald mobilized the Worker's Militia. Their units, in cooperation with the Communist-controlled police, occupied the offices of our newspapers and of the non-Communist parties. Communist action squads attacked known non-Communists. Several Social Democratic members of Parliament, who held the balance of power, were beaten up or disappeared. At the same time, Soviet Ambassador Zorin arrived in Prague and held several extended conferences with the President. Beneš, cut off from all non-Communist support, held out for a day against the reports that the Communists had seized control of the country, that the Soviet army was ready to march across the borders, and that his one recourse, calling out our army to restore order, would only result in a brief, bloody and futile civil war. On February 25, the President broke down. Instead of dissolving the Parliament and calling for an election, he accepted the non-Communist cabinet ministers' resignations and let Gottwald form a new Communist cabinet.

I remember walking the streets of Prague the day after, seeing the broken display cases and torn posters of the democratic parties, the gruff, unshaven Workers' Militia patrols, feeling the fear in the air. It was so much like the German occupation:

once again we were helpless; power had shifted from the hands of the people to the hands of the revolutionaries, and once again there was no recourse. But this time the ideology was different, this time it was a socialist ideology—and though the power structure was similar, this time many people believed that the change was for the good; others held their breath and hoped. For better or for worse, the second stage of the revolutionary cycle had been resolved in favor of the revolution. We had entered the third stage—the revolution had come.

Years later, when the country was slowly beginning to recover from the trauma of the coup and the period that followed, it became fashionable among some Communists to hold that the coup, for all the devastation that resulted from it, had been necessary: that it had laid the foundations for the socialist democracy that finally began to emerge in the Dubček Spring of 1968. We were all eager to believe it then: the rebirth of that Spring held out so much promise. We wanted to come to terms with the twenty dark years, and this seemed a way to do it. But that Spring ended in the Soviet occupation and a return to the regime of the Stalin years. The coup may have been inevitable, but today the question arises again: was it necessary? Or, in a much broader sense, is a revolution a necessary, painful perhaps, sut still necessary step on the way to socialism?

The Communists continue to believe it—even many of the chastened Communists who now, since the Soviet occupation, are living in exile in the West. Many of them are too honest to deny the disastrous results of the coup for a whole generation of Czechs and of Slovaks. Some are even honest enough to admit that the coup made Czechoslovakia a Soviet vassal and created preconditions for the occupation of 1968. They admit the terror, they admit the injustice, they admit the destruction of human beings and social institutions, but they insist that the revolution was necessary for the creation of the economic and social infrastructure of a socialist society.

Yet socialism was not at stake in the revolution: socialism was the common goal and program of the coalition government. The coup, as any revolution, was a struggle for power. It did not make our country socialist: it concentrated power, unchecked and unopposed, in the hands of the leadership of the Communist party. The question was not one of socialism or capitalism, but rather whether our people could rule themselves on their way to socialism, or whether they had to be ruled.

The Communist belief in revolution in ultimately independent of the Communist belief in socialism. What justifies the revolution in the conviction that people cannot be trusted, that society cannot save itself but must be saved, even against its will, by the elect—the leaders of the Communist party. It is based on an elitist distrust of the people, and on a corresponding, naive trust in the wisdom and incorruptibility of the elect. The revolution must take the control of their own destiny out of the hands of the people, and place it in the hands of the Righteous few who will save the people from their own folly.

The Righteous may, of course, fail: they have failed consistently. But that is no argument against the attempt, which must be repeated again and again until the right Righteous have been found. The victims of the revolution, both its opponents and its supporters, die in a good cause: in the attempt to find the right Righteous rulers who alone can build the Kingdom of God on earth.

The touching, desperate hope that there are somewhere the right Righteous, completely pure and dedicated, who can be trusted with absolute power is obviously the weakest link in the argument. Even Plato gave up his search for the philosopher king, and settled for a "second-best state," best under human conditions, in which power is not concentrated in the hands of a savior but strictly circumscribed by the rule of law and popular suffrage. The revolution fails necessarily because it gathers power in the hands of a philisopher king—and there are no philosopher kings.

But for those of us who shared the Communists' commitment to socialism but dissented from the revolution, another consideration is more important. Socialism, after all, is not simply a matter of economics. A socialist society is first of all a free society, in which the full freedom of its members is not restricted only by political but also by economic privilege. It is a democratic society, in which the people are free to govern themselves, in the economic as well as in the political realm. It is a society based on complete trust in the people, on the confidence that people do not need Guardians. If a revolution is necessary—that is, if power has to be concentrated in the hands of the Righteous—then socialism is impossible.

The Communists have tried to avoid the inevitable conclusion by an appeal to education: the revolution is necessary because the people today need Guardians and cannot be trusted to make their own decisions. Socialism is possible—or will be possible—because the new socialist men, educated by the revolution, will be as trustworthy as the people of today are not.

The argument devolves to the value of the revolution as an educational instrument. But here the record is most dismal. Human beings do not learn freedom and cooperation by being endowed with absolute power on the one hand yet totally disenfranchized on the other. The corruption of masters and slaves alike is notorious: neither power nor servility equips men to live as free and equal citizens.

Masters can only raise slaves—or new masters. Human beings learn freedom and cooperation only by being free and working together, by being able to make decisions and accept their consequences, by having to work together and respect rather than command and obey one another. Even if socialism required a reeducated "new socialist man," revolution remains counterproductive: democracy educates far more effectively than a dictatorship—even if that dictatorship bills itself as "the people's democratic dictatorship" or the "dictatorship of the proletariat."

The Communist coup in Czechoslovakia in 1948 may have been inevitable. Given the sacrifices it exacted from our nation, it might be even necessary to believe that, in some odd dialectical way, it was not a total loss. But if we or any other society ever succeed in building a socialist society, a genuinely free society, democratic in economics as well as in politics, we shall have to give up the reliance on the Righteous and learn to trust a free people. Democracy, and freedom, are the only legitimate revolutionary slogans. Any slogan that begins "All power to . . ." is inevitably suspect: power is too dangerous an instrument to be trusted to any group of the economic or political elect, to anyone other than the people as a whole, the people under law. Democracy is and ought to be the most revolutionary slogan.

That is why we opposed the coup. We were socialists and

democrats: we were not defenders of an outworn economic order in 1948 or in 1968, and we are not that today. The alternative to Communism is not capitalism, but freedom—and freedom is not compatible with the rule of the Pure. We had fought, and we lost. In 1948, in its Victorious February, the Communist party triumphed: we were the vanquished. The dynamics of the second stage, the dialogue of freedom and Utopia, gave way to the dialectic of Utopia and power.

-III-

Bitter Harvest

February, 1948. *"Victorious February." The Communists seize all power in the state and establish their dictatorial regime.*

Spring, 1948. *Yugoslavia's defection from the Soviet bloc brings about open admission of the Cold War. The Communists consolidate their power.*

Spring, 1949. *Large-scale arrests of non-Communists, culminating in the execution of Milada Horáková and other leading democrats.*

Fall, 1951. *Amid the deepening economic crisis, arrests of Communists begin.*

Fall, 1952. *Series of "conspiracy" trials modeled on Soviet purge trials in the 1930s lead to the execution of many leading Communists, notably Rudolf Slánský and ten co-defendants, including Rudolf Margolius.*

March, 1953. *Death of Stalin, followed by factional strife in the U.S.S.R. and hopes of reform in Eastern Europe. Revolt in Berlin, strikes in Plzeň. Both are crushed and status quo is reaffirmed.*

Spring, 1956. *Khrushchev's admission of Stalin's crimes spurs hope of reform.*

220

Fall, 1956. *Soviet suppression of Hungarian reform and pressure on Poland stifles protest and again reaffirms status quo.*

i. The Revolution

The Communist coup of 1948, known in Party terminology as the "Victorious February," may well have been, for many years, the last free act of the Communist party of Czechoslovakia. A free act, unlike a happening, presupposes initiative, choice, and decision. In *seizing* power, the Party sacrificed its freedom of action. The chain of events that unfolded in Czechoslovakia after the coup, in strict parallel with the aftermath of revolutions in other Communist lands and impervious to the wishes of the Czechoslovak Communists, is far more in keeping with the necessities of Greek tragedy than with a series of free choices. The logic of the third stage of the revolutionary cycle, the relentless logic of power, had taken over.

Those who make the revolution seldom stop to take account of this logic. They tend to see the revolution in terms of persons and possibilities, and to explain its disintegration in terms of contingent choices and decisions which, most unfortunately happened to have been erroneous. At the time and later in retrospect, the Czechoslovak Communists were impressed by the divergent personalities of the Party leaders and the variety of views within the Party.

One of those views was genuinely humanistic. Among the rank and file of the Czechoslovak party and especially among its intellectuals, there were a great many people who honestly believed in the possibility of an individual and distinct Czechoslovak path to Communism. They understood the grim aspects of Stalin's rule as a reflection of a uniquely Russian situation and temperament, and assumed that in Czechoslovakia Communism would be humanistic and democratic, in keeping with our political tradition of the last hundred years.

But, contrasting with this first, there was a second view held by the Party's old Stalinists of prewar years, Klement Gottwald among them. They, too, sincerely believed in an independent Czechoslovak path to socialism. To be sure, to them this implied nothing whatever about humanism and democracy, but it did mean independence. Before the war they had accepted the primacy of the Soviet Communist party—though many, like the founder of the Czechoslovak CP Bohumír Šmeral, with great misgivings, viewing it as a necessary condition for securing Soviet help in seizing power. They estimated quite accurately that they could not prevail unaided—but were convinced that, once in power, they could dispense with Soviet aid. Gottwald was no humanist, but he also had no desire to become Stalin's vassal: like so many of the old Stalinists, he too wanted to be a Stalin in his own country.

There was a third view as well—the ultrarevolutionary alternative represented by a wing of old Bolshevik fighters and young zealots—among them the Spanish Civil War veteran Rudolf Slánský and the Slovak partisan combat veteran Gustav Husák. The comrades in this wing of the Party shared Gottwald's boundless contempt for humanism and democracy, but were no less contemptuous of the pedants and bureaucrats of the revolution. They fantasized about a permanent revolution, along vaguely Trotskyist lines, and advocated the "Soviet"—at the time also Yugoslav—model of ruthless, violent transformation of men and society.

Drab, ferocious, bureaucratic collectivism, however, was the one alternative none among the victors were willing to choose. Yet the coup that brought the Party to power made the comrades' preferences quite academic. Individual Communists, perhaps even a majority of them, may have envisaged a humanistic and even a democratic version of Communism—but a regime founded on power and a Party line rather than on the people's consent could not afford to tolerate dissent. The popular opposition that drove the Party to resort to force did not disappear with the coup: therefore the coup intensified rather than diminished the Party's dependence on brute force. Even if it had wanted to, the regime could not have been democratic.

Gottwald's hope of a domestic Stalinism proved vain. Having resorted to the use of force to seize power, the Party remained dependent on force, but the force it could generate thought their domestic organizations was hardly adequate to the new task. Over the years, the Party's success had been purchased largely with promises the Party really could not keep. The victors now desperately needed a new base of power, and the Soviet Union was willing to provide it—at a price. Again, even if it had wanted to, Gottwald's new Communist regime could not have stayed independent.

The vision of permanent revolution was hardest to kill. The zeal of a Slánský proved useful in destroying non-Communist opposition, and for some three years, it received official sanction. But continued social functioning, even in a democratic society, requires more stability than the spontaneous outburst that result from revolutionary élan. To maintain power over an unenthusiastic and often openly hostile population requires a spartan vigilance and discipline that is incompatible with spontaneity. Paradoxically, the revolution had effectively precluded even the revolutionary alternative.

There is little evidence that any of these possibilities can ever be realized. The attempt at national Communism in Yugoslavia succeeded only because Tito's broad popular support made a Czechoslovak-style coup unnecessary. (And our Gottwald was no Tito.) Yet in Yugoslavia, in spite of the domestic sympathy generated for Tito by Soviet pressure, the regime soon lost its Stalinist character, and only the continued Soviet threat prevented a full-fledged democratic development. The Chinese attempt at institutionalizing the revolution "culturally" had to be stabilized by the army to prevent internal disintegration. The later attempt at democratic socialism in Czechoslovakia in our Spring of 1968 showed every sign of promise, but it also proved that the days of the Party's "leading role" were numbered. It may well be that none of the various experiments of an "ideal Communism" are real possibilities.

In any case, there definitely were no possibilities for an "ideal Communism" in Czechoslovakia in 1948. For that matter, at the time of the "Victorious February" there were no possibilities at all—only necessities. That is the paradox of power: once it had seized power, the Party became powerless. In the coup, the Party did not, strictly speaking, seize power; rather, it created it. The unlimited, omnipresent power it claimed simply did not exist before the coup. Such power is never there to be seized—it is the product of the revolt of the zealots, required and justifiable only by an ideology that does not see the role of a government as one of public service, but rather as one of transforming men and society in its image. Certainly the non-Communist parties had not wielded or claimed such power. Nor did the remaining capitalists, nor the Church, nor even the state apparatus whose power was restricted by a democratic constitution and the rights of its citizens. Power in precoup Czechoslovakia was primarily administrative in nature and scope. As in any society, it had a certain functional autonomy, but, basically, it remained limited, decentralized and dependent on the consent of the governed. The Communist coup aimed to create totally autonomous power, not only administrative but sovereign power—capable of realizing the Communist program independently of the consent of the citizens and unrestricted by constitutional or legal limitations.

The Party realized this aim. In the coup, it created a sovereign, unlimited power independent of the people's wishes and views. But it was precisely this autonomous power that stripped the Party leadership of its freedom of choice. The basic truth revealed in the third stage of the revolutionary cycle is that the idea of sovereign social power is illusory. Perhaps a bully terrorizing a weaker companion by sheer physical strength could be said to wield power autonomously and even he only until he falls asleep. On the level of a society, power necessarily is dependent. It may be dependent on the consent of citizens who respect it when it represents their will and interest. But when it loses their consent, it does not become independent. Rather, it becomes more directly dependent, either on a small group that is willing to terrorize others in exchange for special privileges, or on a foreign power, or on both. In either case, power based on force and fear becomes radically dependent. Despite all constitutional limitations, a democratically elected president is far more a free agent than a dictator. A dictator by necessessity becomes the slave of his own slaves. That is the paradox of power: "independent"—autocratic—power is not free, it is determined by the needs of its own self-preservation.

This paradox defines the third stage of the revolutionary

cycle and the conditions in Czechoslovakia after the coup. The Party eliminated not only all actual opposition, but all potential opposition as well. Its power became independent of popular consent. But at the same time the Party took out a double mortgage, one from the Soviets, the other from the "shock troops of the revolution" in the ranks of the *Lumpenproletariat* and the *Lumpenbourgeoisie* which paid with revolutionary élan for special considerations.

This double mortgage defined the setting in which the prominent personalities of the time played out their roles. This may be irrelevant with respect to their individual guilt. The personal guilt of a man who willingly played the role a certain historical situation has created for him is in no way diminished by the fact that he did not take initiative in creating that role. The guilt of prosecutor Urválek is not diminished because Soviet demand had created his role of the prosecutor. But the nature of personal guilt is complex and includes many factors—reasons, intentions, convictions. In the case of crimes as monstrous as those committed against the people of Czechoslovakia in the 1950s, perhaps no one is in a position to adjudicate personal guilt. Neither human vengeance nor punishment can right the wrong. All men can do is strive that nothing that has been done should remain secret, that the whole nation shall know the full truth.

Yet we have to form a judgment on a different level, the level of objective possibilities and consequences. Here the question no longer is who is responsible for the road the revolution has taken, but whether under the conditions created by the revolution anyone, even the purest idealist, could have brought about a different course. Here, unlike to the question of moral guilt, the answer is unambiguous. The forging of absolute power transforms power from a tool of social change to a force beyond the control of individual men, governed by its own logic, annulling the significance of intent, good or evil.

The Party acted in order to create and seize power—after that, it had no choice. It paid off its debt to the opportunists with total surrender to the passions of the mob. In the months after the coup all considerations of economic and social rationality fell victim to the mortgage holders' insistent clamor for patronage—and for an opportunity to settle private accounts in the name of revolutionary justice. The economic and social effects proved disastrous: twenty years later, the country still was struggling to free itself from the bondage to imcompetent, corrupt officials whose tenure dated to the days after the coup and whose sole credentials were Party membership or their role in the coup. And twenty years later our country still was struggling to free itself from the lowest common denominator of primitive prejudice and petty vindictiveness, which had become the norm in our society in the early 1950s. The Czechoslovak Spring of 1968 was primarily an attempt to burn the mortgages on the revolution, which the idealists had handed to the opportunists in exchange for help in seizing power. Even twenty years later, the Soviets' Soviet armed intervention, which put an end to our Spring in 1968, was to remind the reformers of the second mortgage—which was held by the Soviet Union.

In the aftermath of the coup, that mortgage proved as disastrous to the Party as to the nation at large. The Czechoslovak Communist security organs, familiar with the domestic situation, did not consider the nationalist-Communist elements dangerous; they concentrated on eliminating the democratic and socialist opposition. But the example of Yugoslavia had convinced the Russians that national Communism was a grave danger. By now, in Poland and Hungary, there had been Soviet-style mass arrests and trials of Communists whom Stalin suspected of either the intention or the ability to defy Soviet demands. In the fall of 1951, it was Czechoslovakia's turn.

As Ambassador Zorin represented Soviet might at the time of coup the coup, so advisers from the ranks of Beria's secret police—men like Abakumov, Makarov, and Likhachev—represented it after 1949. As Zorin insisted in 1948 that all power must be concentrated exclusively in the hands of the Communist party, so the Soviet advisers in 1951 insisted that it must be concentrated in the hands of the Security apparatus, which was responsible only to Moscow.

At the Russians' insistence, Czechoslovak State Security was instructed to "uncover" an "imperialist-Zionist conspiracy." The trial of these "conspirators" would serve as an excuse for mass arrests and executions of those Party members whose long

Party membership gave them some standing in the country and whose past and views might suggest a loyalty to Czechoslovakia or to a kind of Communism that might conflict with unquestioning loyalty to Moscow. Hungarian Security already had staged its trials and could provide suitable stage props. On November 11, 1951, Ambassador Mikoyan confronted Klement Gottwald, then president of Czechoslovakia, with Stalin's demand to arrest and execute Rudolf Slánský. The startled Gottwald demurred: Slánský was an old comrade, had been one of the key men in the coup and a consistent advocate of harsh dictatorship on the Soviet model. Mikoyan gave Gottwald no reasons—Stalin does not argue, Stalin commands—and Stalin was informed of Gottwald's attitude. As Beneš before him, Gottwald broke down; a day later, he signed the order.

As in the demise of the Czechoslovak democracy so in the demise of the Czechoslovak Communist party's autonomy—the Soviets again played a decisive part. But this does not answer the basic question, Why was Soviet pressure so effective? There were no Soviet troops in Czechoslovakia. The Czechoslovak Party could have tried to resist—why did it surrender so easily?

Not all the reasons are sinister. There was a genuine element of idealism in the Party, a genuine desire to create a society in which social relations would not be constrained and cramped by relations to property. Even those Communists who had no illusions about personal and political conditions within the Soviet Union saw in the U.S.S.R. the only force willing, for reasons of its own, to support a radical challenge to the old entrenched powers and prerogatives of property.

Yet the same reasons that may have justified the Soviet alliance cried out for resistance to that alliance once the Soviet demands became contrary to those reasons. The surrender of the Party to the Soviets demonstrates, not its evil intent, but the powerlessness of mortgaged power, regardless of intent.

Effective resistance to Soviet demands would have required broad popular support, such as Tito's in Yugoslavia. The Czechoslovak Communist party had sacrificed that support in the way it had seized power. In the three years after its Victorious February, the Communist regime focused its policy on securing power by disenfranchizing its subjects. The regime demanded manifest enthusiasm and obedience, but barred its people, for good reason, from participation in determining policy. Three years later, the Party could not risk losing Soviet support; for, to win a free hand, it had deprived itself of popular support.

There was another—purely theoretical—obstacle to the Soviets' demands. In Leninist theory, internal Party supervision of judicial proceedings against its members is supposed to prevent any misuse of power after the revolution. But effective supervision requires some objective criteria of guilt and innocence—and those criteria, too, became victim of the coup. After the coup, the regime itself had given support to the ultraradical wing's merciless and extra-legal destruction of non-Communist components in the society. The trials of the clergy, of the small land-holders, the "kulaks," of tradesmen, of non-Communist and socialist intellectuals and politicians were not the work of "Beria's clique," but of the Czechoslovak party.

In the process of destroying possible non-Communist opposition the Party fostered the growth of an autonomous security apparatus before which, a year later, the Party itself stood power-less.

Years later, President Novotny tried to wash his hands of the trials in which he had played an active part by claiming that "Slánský made the wheels turn and got caught in them himself." But that is at best only a part of the truth. Slánský played out his role; the revolution that launched the third stage of the revolutionary cycle spun the wheels.

ii. Faith and Doubt
The men who seized power in Czechoslovakia in 1948 were caught by surprise by the harsh consequences of their own actions. Those of us who woke up to the revolution as a *fait accompli* on February 26, 1948, had no expectations. The human rather than the theoretical meaning of revolution, however, was something we all were yet to learn.

The armed patrols in the streets taught us our most basic lesson: whatever else it may have done, the revolution divided our society into two nations: the victors and the vanquished. Our country no longer belonged to *us*, all the people. It now belonged to the victors. Those of us whose social and political views and allegiances diverged had become the vanquished, aliens in our own land—and some hundred thousand Czechs and Slovaks now were to be exiles in foreign lands. The lines had been drawn.

Before the coup, I had known a number of Communists, some of whom I liked and respected a great deal, others not at all—but I had never thought of them *en bloc* as "enemies." They were individuals, some good and some bad. Our common commitment to a common good seemed much more important than our ideological differences. Though I disagreed with their views, I considered these views a valid contribution to the continuing discussion out of which social progress emerges. It may have been naive, but it was not inaccurate: within the framework of democracy, the vigorous Communist critique of existing institutions can contribute to common progress.

But with the coup all of that changed. Our discussion had been terminated by victory and defeat. Communism had become the official truth and the Communists its Guardians. We had ceased to be individuals, equal participants in the work of social progress—we had become the vanquished. The Communists also no longer were individuals: they now were the victors. They owned the land: we were the outcasts and the dispossessed, they the posessors. Their personal qualities, their intentions, their motives no longer made a difference. Anyone who supported the coup and shared its spoils, regardless of his personal qualities, became one of *them*, victorious and ranged against us, the vanquished. Conversely, anyone who had opposed the revolution or questioned its acts became a class enemy, to be silenced and destroyed. The idea of a loyal opposition had died with Masaryk's democracy. It was now the Leninist perspective that prevailed, which defines social interaction in terms of the class struggle.

The Communists' rule in Czechoslovakia was based on a lie—much as Lenin's rule was after the armed suppression of the sailors' and workers' revolt in Kronstadt: the Communists claimed that the coup had been an expression of the unanimous will of the workers.

The Leninist perspective soon prevailed in international relations, too. Stalin's coup in Czechoslovakia—as his supression in Poland, Hungary, and East Berlin—alerted the West much as Hitler's occupation had ten years earlier. When Stalin set out to test Western responses in Korea in 1950, the West fumbled, then held. The Soviet tide, unchecked in the years of euphoria of the wartime alliance, now ran up against determined resistance. Opponents became enemies, and different world views hardened in an irreconciblable struggle of worldwide proportions. The Cold War was in full swing.

The new rulers of Czechoslovakia put the Cold War to good use: it served as a justification for the crushing of dissent, and its slogans were brought into play to project the impression of unanimity that the regime deemed a pillar of its power. In the midst of the all-out struggle against an omnipresent enemy, full dedication is required—even a flagging of zeal aids the enemy. Even harmless, private interest, even privacy itself becomes treason. Nothing remains neutral, not even popular music, individual style of clothing or taste in sports: the ideological was is the most total war of all.

The spread of the Leninist perspective and the Cold War gave rise to a series of mirror images. While Party propaganda was constantly warning us against the class enemy—omnipresent, intent on sabotage, espionage, or dissemination of doubt—in the West U.S. Senator Joseph McCarthy was uncovering crypto-Communists behind every bush—in the branches of the U.S. government and even in the army. As in the war against Nazism so once again, the zealots had bred counterzealots. There were differences, to be sure: in Czechoslovakia, zealotry was an official policy with the force of law, while in the West the zealots ran up against the limits of law and democratic government. In the West the zealots' victims lost jobs rather than their lives. And the zealots in the West met with public opposition—which eventually was to destroy them. This is why the age produced a wave of refugees heading from East to West, and at most a tiny trickle in the reverse direction. But, for a time, there were similarities; the zealots had taken over.

For Czechs and Slovaks, the world of zealots and counter-zealots is an uncomfortable one. Both our geographic and our humanistic position made us a nation of conciliators for whom there was little room in a world in which, as Stalin and Dulles agreed, neutrality was treason.

There were, of course, a great many among us, both at home and in exile, who solved the problem by identifying with the one side or the other. Especially for those at home who were opposed to the Communist regime, exiled within their own country, and cut off from the rest of the world, it was easy to identify in their minds entirely with the West. It was simple: the Communists were the oppressors, the Soviets our masters —while the West resisted Communism.

It was not that easy in exile abroad, or for those at home who retained some contact with the outside world. We could not think away the Cold War polarization, at home or worldwide, and we had no desire to accept it. We had no love for the zealots of the West to whom socialism was treason, freedom suspect, and Franco a bulwark against "godless Communism." We had supported the socialist democracy of our postwar republic; it was freedom, not anti-Communism, for which we fought and for which we accepted exile, abroad or within our own land.

At that time, there was no place for us. Communist propaganda painted a picture of The Enemy who was surrounding us on all sides, without and within, dropping poisoned chocolate from balloons to poison our children and potato beetles from airplanes to damage our potato crop. The Party government justified its draconic suppression of freedom and justice by picturing the Communist East as a beleaguered fortress in which every potato harvested is a victory in the great struggle and every catnap treason.

On the other side, the propaganda differed in labels more than substance. It painted a picture of the oppressed nations, cowed by terror, filled with implacable hatred for their oppressors and living day by day in the secret hope and expectation of liberation.

There was some truth in that picture, a truth Western liberals of a later age, eager to dismantle the Cold War, are quick to overlook. We *were* oppressed: the victors were quick to claim the spoils of victory—our houses, furnishings, cars—and most of all there was their arrogance of power. We were silenced, citizens without rights or security. The terror was real: the arrests, the torture, the executions are amply documented in official Communist sources revealed in the fleeting moments of liberation. That, too, is a recurrent aspect of Communist rule, and recently, in the aftermath of the Soviet occupation of our country, it has acquired once again a measure of reality.

But, in the fifties, at the zenith of the Cold War, Western propaganda overlooked precisely the factor it seeks to see today, and perhaps with less justification. Unlike the regimes imposed in later years by outright Soviet intervention, the original Communist revolutionary regimes of Eastern Europe in the 1950s—and the revolutionary regimes of Cuba or China later—were in a peculiar, non-Western sense popular regimes. Not, of course, in the sense that the people had any significant say in their policy or operation. They did not: even the factory workers, deprived of labor unions, had less say at their places of work than before the revolution. Nor in the sense that the regimes were genuinely concerned about the civil rights of their subjects—to be sure they were not and are not now. But the revolutionary regimes did create a society in which the worker might feel at home: a state in the image of the proletariat.

"The proletariat" is a much abused, mystified term, and with good reason. At the time of the Russian Revolution, Russia had no proletariat to speak of, while at the time of Czechoslovakia's Victorious February the proletariat was well on the way to technological obsolescence, and a regime ruling in its name had to create it. As Hitler once had declared that the Magyars or the Japanese were Aryans, so Stalin now declared the Russians proletarians, and, more recently, Mao again bestowed that title on ideological rather than economic grounds.

Yet for all that, the proletariat—industrial mass labor—is sociologically definable. It is a by-product of the Industrial Revolution, specifically of the process of factory mass production. The metaphysical significance of this fact may be rather less than Marx, the inverted Hegelian, supposed, but its sociological impact is considerable. Factory production demands a distinct life-style, with a state of virtues, conventions, and values that diverge significantly from the requirements of democracy. The productive principle of early industrial mass production, after all, was not so much technological sophistication—an assembly line is technologically primitive—as the regimentation of labor. The unskilled industrial worker, the proletarian, was economically valuable not because of his individual skills or initiative, but rather because of his availability for rapid deployment in large, disciplined units, his ability to work as a well-coordinated part of a human mass, and his high tolerance to the degrading crudity of the factory.

In the proletarian, individual independence in thought or feeling would have been a definite liability rather than an asset. Industrial mass production was directly dependent on the worker's ability to accept and carry out orders, without questioning or understanding them, drudging on mechanically under utterly brutalizing conditions. Nor could the worker develop any particular sense of belonging to a particular home or community: that would have diminished his ready availibility for flexible deployment. Instead, he had to be able and willing to be utilized whenever and wherever production demanded—such roots as he could afford had to be portable, essentially spiritual, whether the spirit was destilled, religious, or ideological. The early industrial proletarian was and had to be a profoundly alienated mass man.

The appeal of the Communist party—and of the Nazi party in the Germany of the 1930s—was, to a great part, that they understood this. The social democrats may have been right in their conviction that the life-style of the factory was dehumanizing and inhuman, that the worker must be freed from it as much as possible. But, as long as the factory system remained unchanged, the worker had to function, in virtue of productive necessity, as a crude, disciplined mass man. Yet, the social democrats hoped that the society would reach a stage when the worker would walk out of the factory gate at quitting time and invert the entire scale of his workday's values: to become an independent thinker, with a meaningful private life, a sense of social responsibility, sensitivity, political discrimination, and independent judgement.

The Communists knew better. They recreated in the Communist party a mirror image of the factory. In its organization and life-style, the Party offered an equivalent of the factory, with a foreman responsible for thinking and decision-making, with personal relations approximation the familiar rough-and ready egalitarianism and collective discipline of the work shop, encouraging strong emotional loyalty and the comfort of believing and acting as a mass. In a very immediate sense, the Party made the worker feel *at home*, as he was at home at his workplace. Among the social democrats, the unskilled industrial worker might well feel ill at ease, in a strange world that followed unfamiliar conventions and made unfamiliar demands. In the Communist party, he found a world and a life-style he knew well and in which he was thoroughly comfortable.

Perhaps the Communist party's most grievous betrayal of the workers was precisely that the Party did not try to break and transform the crude, brutal life-style of the factory but instead gave it its blessing by incorporating it into the mystique of the workers' movement. It may have begun as a strategy, but it soon became an end in itself. Our regime of the Victorious February—like many other Communist regimes—recreated our society in the image of the industrial workplace.

In a very real sense, the workers were oppressed: the factory is oppressive and dehumanizing, and it became more so as the Communists rapidly destroyed the independence of the unions and guarantees of workers' individual rights, which the social democrats had won. As the state became the only employer, the worker lost not only the right to strike but even the freedom to quit. Yet thousands of men and women, who had felt alienated in a society whose normative life-style had been that of the bourgeoisie, felt at home in the crude egalitarianism and discipline, in the thought and behavior patterns of the new state—and could for the first time identify with it.

It would be a basic mistake to underestimate the importance and reality of that identification. Time and time again, workers who could be objectively considered disenfranchised and exploited, have defended a revolutionary regime as "their own," much as in other countries they had defended no less oppressive nationalistic regimes for the same reason. The regime may have been bad and oppressive, and the workers have always grumbled and complained about it, even in the years of greatest official enthusiasm but, nonetheless, they did identify with it. It took twenty years' experience and overt Soviet interference before the bulk of the workers realized that behind the facade of enthusiastic and devoted solidarity the regime had become an oppressor rather than a defender of the workers.

Yet, we must not underestimate the real, lasting contribution that the change of dominant life-styles made to Czechoslovakia's social development. Perhaps the biggest obstacle to communication between the men who carried out the rebirth of socialist democracy in 1968 and the men who, in exile, shared their political and social ideals was that the Czechoslovak Spring clearly claimed as its own the revolution of life-styles. That obstacle is no less real between the socialist democrats of the East as a whole, and the social democrats of the West. For all its ludicrous aspects, the cult of "the people" did sweep away a myriad of petty social cobwebs, of pomp and artifice that throttle and cramp human interaction in an inbred and tradition-bound society. The antimacassars came off the sofas, neckties disappeared, forms of address lost their formality. Had it been a free, democratic development, as it became in the Dubček Spring, it would have been an altogether salutary process, a social consummation of economic socialist democracy.

Unfortunately, our Victorious February of 1948 was not that. The de-bourgeoization of Czechoslovak society became a dogma, mechanically enforced and discredited by crude coercion. It created its own resistance—which in turn brought greater coercion. In Czechoslovakia, as in every country in which the Communists seized power, that pattern prevailed. The victors created a sense of liberation by making the life-style of the masses normative for the society. But because they did it by force, they froze our social development at the stage that was achieved in the days of the revolution—and so they sowed the seeds of new stress and alienation.

The vanquished experienced this immediately, but, not much later, the Communist intellectuals within the Party began to chafe at the bit of the new orthodoxy. Most of them had been led to Communism by a desire for freedom, for liberation from the petty constraints of bourgeois society. They had not bargained for a far more coercive new set of constraints, no less petty but more ruthless. Many of them went through a soul-searching crisis, blaming their discomfort on themselves, on their own bourgeois prejudices, rather than on the vicious pettiness of the regime. But such soul-searching could be effective only in matters of ideas and attitudes, and the problems that had to be faced were rooted in everyday reality.

The factory system, after all, is not only or primarily a system of social relations. It is an objective reality, geared to carrying out objective everyday tasks and, incidentally, to sacrifice the welfare of human beings if production needs demand it. When such a perspective is applied to the state, whose function is not production of goods but the well-being of its people, society suffers no less than productivity suffers when a factory is geared primarily to the well-being of its workers. In the latter case, the loss of productivity may well be an acceptable cost. In the former case, however, the society loses all justification. Masaryk had warned in 1898 that the Marxist vision of the world is one of a large factory, geared solely to the task of production. The Communists proved him right. The system established by destroying its opponents began to devour its own supporters.

iii. On Trial

Soon after the Victorious February, the arrests began. They surprised almost no one. It takes a government with the self-confidence of broad popular support to tolerate dissent. The Communists lacked that self-confidence and were aware of their vulnerability, and so they moved to destroy the seeds of protest. Perhaps the only people surprised by the first arrests were the Communist intellectuals, the genuine idealists who honestly believed that the Party would seize power to protect its people from capitalism but would use that power only to reeducate the opposition.

Anyone with such qualms about the early activities of the police of the new Communist state could readily be reassured by rhetoric and precedent. Communist rhetoric had always insisted that persons cannot be judged as individuals, but only as members of a class that is either friendly or hostile to progress. Though the treatment meted out to an individual may be unjust, it can and must be justified as an act of historical justice: the justice of the working class avenging itself on a defeated oppressor class and preventing its resurgence. Individual injustice, even if unfortunate, is inevitable. This rhetoric was sanctioned by precedent. The postwar deportation of Czechoslovakia's German minority also was justified collectively, by the guilt of the minority and by national interest. Individual injustice, even though unfortunate, did not seem important. After all, the German occupation had taken no account of our rights, not even our lives. The ground had been prepared well, the seed sown deep.

Still, the harvest proved far-reaching beyond our expectations. With the closing of the frontiers, we all became prisoners. The minimum requirement of a free society is the recognition of the right of the dissenter to leave. In the eyes of the Communists, even the desire to leave became a crime. The elaborate fortifications along the frontiers, with out-of-bounds zones, barbed wire, and machine guns made the point. For the subjects of the Communist state, whether victorious Communists or vanquished non-Communists, to attempt to leave the country was treason. A prison, no matter how large is the place the inmate is not permitted to leave; our country had become that.

Nor was the barbed wire physical only. A censorship omnipresent in intent and nearly that in fact together with a far-reaching purging of libraries and books was supposed to isolate us even from our past and from each other. Arrests and prohibitions rapidly eliminated or constrained all independent social organizations—athletic, social, or religious—which might give individuals an autonomous sense of identity. At the same time, an intensive campaign of indoctrination aimed to isolate us even from our own present. Reality had become a function of ideology:

it was up to the Party to determine, from its correct ideological standpoint, what was and was not real.

The social democratic economist Miloš Vaněk pointed out that for the internal functioning of the Stalinist economy there is no better model than that of a prison industry. Like the prison industry, the Stalinist economy was characterized by abundance of official exhortation coupled with a low and declining work morale. Like the prison industry, it was hopelessly wasteful of resources and especially of human labor—and committed to making good its technological defects by application of mass labor, from the harvest "brigades" to the various "voluntary" work projects. Like the prison industry, the Stalinist economy was capable of intensive concentration on any given, centrally determined project—but hopelessly incapable of flexible response to real demands. The analogy goes on, to all aspects of the economy and beyond, to the social structure of the country: the revolution, intent on transforming the nation, had to imprison it to carry out its experiment.

The analogy extends even to the paradoxical psychological asset of prison life. In a prison, the prisoner is the center and justification of all activity. He may be mistreated, restricted, oppressed, but he is important. Everything he does, even the most trivial acts, are the focus of attention. The entire apparatus exists because of him, for his sake. Freedom, by contrast, can be cold and uncaring. More than one refugee, free in the West, will unwittingly testify to the prison paradox: having left to escape the negative attentions of the Communist regime, he expects positive but no less careful attention abroad. In more than one case, the importance of a prisoner appears in retrospect far more reassuring than the loneliness of freedom. And so the regime had won some of its support, especially among intellectuals, not because of ignorance but because of the prison paradox: while taking away freedom the regime bestowed importance.

The prison paradox, however, operates only in the case of "trusties" and relatively favored prisoners whom the prison constrains but does not threaten to destroy. The stability of a Communist regime, as the stability of any prison administration, is dependent on the percentage of the population to which it can afford to extend such favored status. Czechoslovakia's revolutionary regime did not realize this: instead, it adopted a maximum-security approach. With every round of arrests, the number of those who could feel reasonably immune decreased.

The first category among those arrested was that of the men and women who had actively opposed the coup and made no secret of their opposition. Among these were Representative Milada Horáková of the Popular Socialist party in our Parliament, General Kutlvašr, General Pika, scores of Popular Socialist and Social Democratic party officials, leading members of the gymnastic association Sokol and the Scout movement, and hundreds of others. Most of them were veterans of our wartime resistance and survivors of German prisons and concentration camps who were not willing to stand idly by and watch our freedom trampled a second time in a decade. Their arrests did not appear particularily threatening to the favored segments of the new society: the arrested and executed were, after all, opponents of the regime, and the destruction of opponents was entirely consistent with the Communist approach to power.

The second, most numerous category of arrests was aimed at the non-conformists—men and women who, in the eyes of the regime, were not guilty by virtue of any overt acts of opposition, but simply by virtue of incompatatibility with the new order. This group included liberal teachers and intellectuals, peasant smallholders clinging to their five acres, a large proportion of the clergy, former members of the wartime Czechoslovak armed forces in-exile in the West, non-Communist members of the resistance, independent craftsmen—generally all people who, in the eyes of the Party regime or one of its local officials, were not conforming to the new life-style. Their crime was individuality and doubt; by their very existence they challenged the credibility of the zealots.

Some of these arrests may have troubled the consciences of the supporters of the regime—but they did not threaten their security. These people, after all, through perhaps not overt opponents of the regime, were not the creatures of the new order: they were the fossils of the old days, "class enemies" even if not personal enemies, and the Communists were used to accept the "liquidation of the class enemies" as a necessary part of building the new order. So far, these arrests did not challenge the faith of its supporters that Communism was building a better future, or the confidence that anyone who loyally supported the new regime with unflagging zeal and conformed to the new order remained safe from arrests.

The third category of arrests was aimed at people whom Party usage labeled, with unintended irony, the "honest Communists." This category included a whole range of individuals at all levels of the Party, old Bolsheviks and young idealists; veterans of Spain and the resistance; Communists who had lived or worked in the West and Communists who had lived in the Soviet Union and had come to know it a bit too well; Communists known for deviation from the Party line and Communists overly zealous in supporting that line at a particular time. All of them had one thing in common: they supported the new regime loyally with unflagging zeal, and certainly conformed to the new order.

This third category of arrests severely undercut the feeling of security of the favored segment. If "honest Communists" could disappear, without a chance of defense or fair trial, without appeal, who was safe? Many Party members continued stubbornly to believe in the guilt of anyone who was arrested—simply to reassure themselves that they, the innocent, were safe; but the pattern of arrests made it difficult to maintain that belief.

There have been many conjectures about the reasons for this category of arrests, none of them entirely groundless. In part, there was Soviet pressure: the shock of Tito's defection had reinforced Stalin's paranoia and sent him of a rampage of destruction against those whose very loyalty gave them access to power and opportunity to defy him. There also was the rivalry among competing grounds within the Party—and there was the dire need to find scapegoats for the failures—some of them inevitable—that could not be disguised. But behind all these reasons for the massive arrests there remains the logic of power: having seized power by force, the regime had no confidence in the security of its position. It was not willing to take the risk of relying on popular support, even Communist popular support. To maintain its position, it had to make sure than no one, not even within the most loyal ranks of the Party, would be in a position to challenge its power.

In a historical perspective, the first category of prisoners may well be the heroes, the second the martyrs. While compassion is the due of all who suffered and died, honor is the due of those who fought for freedon and dignity, whether they were non-Communists seeking to prevent the seizure of power or the Communists who in subsequent years tried to humanize that power. Compassionate respect is the due of those who suffered and died innocently—the thousands who may have done nothing to prepare the coup or oppose it, but sought only to live their lives, individual, human—and who were caught in the maelstrom of the revolution.

It is easy to conclude that the men who had actively dedicated their lives to the Party and so helped destroy our freedom were the victims of their own deeds when they in their turn became objects of persecution. At the time, after having been confronted with the second wave of arrests—with its torture, concentration camps, and executions only five years after the war—many non-Communists did in fact conclude that the due of the "honest Communists" was nothing more than the compassion that is the due of all who suffer.

Yet, paradoxically, in retrospect, the sacrifice of the "honest Communists" may have contributed most to the rebirth of freedom. Although the Party's opponents and the innocent won our people's honor and respect, the supporters of the regime could write them off with a clear conscience as enemies. But the suffering and death of the "honest Communists" destroyed the glib rhetoric about revolutionary Communism as a lofty ideal, a creative system that destroys only accidentally what obstructs the way to greater freedom. Their death made the point that any system that is based on a monopoly of arbitrary power, regardless of its ideological justification, is vicious and self-destructive. Masaryk had warned us, half a century earlier, that socialism must be humanistic and democratic—or it cannot be socialism at all. The death of the "honest" Communists proved the point.

The rebirth of freedom in Czechoslovakia—that brought about our brief Spring in 1968—did not begin with admissions of guilt or error. The first step to it was the general shock at the recognition of the suffering of "honest Communists."

This was to show up so clearly in the Piller report on the

trials of the 1950s, prepared at the peak of the liberalization of our Spring in 1968. After a compilation of a grizzly list of torture, perjury, duplicity and horror, and a statement that the "honest" Communist victims were innocent, the report states drily in one paragraph that a group of some two dozen social democrats, arrested, interrogated, tried, and executed simultaneously with the Communists, had not been tortured or mistreated in any way, that all requirements of due process had been scrupulously observed, that their confessions were free and genuine, their guilt established and their execution justified.

The significance of the death of "honest" Communists is precisely that it could not be written off in such a paragraph. It forced the admission that the use of arbitrary power is illegitimate and destructive—not only when used against supporters but also against non-conformists and opponents. That admission was crucial: it freed many socialist intellectuals from the curse of Lenin's "perspective of class struggle" and led them to the recognition that it is the dialectic of the social process rather than the "victory" on the one pole or the other that builds social progress. And so this admission—that the use of arbitrary power is altogether illegitimate—promised to lead socialism back to democracy.

That recognition in turn led to the next step in the redemption of socialism, the recognition that not only the arrests of supporters, not only the arrests of opponents, but also the fettering of a whole nation was illegitimate and incompatible with socialism. The coup itself, which had split our nation into the victors and the vanquished and fenced us in with barbed wire, was the ultimate reason for our tragic detour from the path of socialism. Finally, we had to recognize that socialism is incompatible with autocracy. The tragedy of the 1950s was in great part that our society had reached the point at which it could demand that idealists accept death while pledging loyalty.

The revolution of the Victorious February ended with death certificates. The regimes that ruled Czechoslovakia in Moscow's behalf in the aftermath of the trials no longer were revolutionary. Moscow could assure the survival of a facade, but it could not provide the substance that the cataclysm of the third stage of the revolutionary cycle had destroyed.

In the retrospective mood after the Twentieth Congress, some Communist revisionists put forward the thesis that the revolution, right in itself, had "fallen into the wrong hands." But had it? Every revolution claims that it is "putting things into the right hands"—and the hands of Gottwald, Slánský, Bacílek, and others certainly were anything but right. They brought to power the infinite greed of the nouveau riches and the ruthless, self-righteousness of zealots. They were liars, perpetuating a vicious lie, because they did not admit to ruling in the name of power and greed—but proclaimed they were governing in the name of socialism. The old capitalists may have lived off the sweat of the workers—the new elite lived off their faith and hope.

Did the revolution fall into the wrong hands? On the rare occasions when some of us met abroad and could speak freely, my Communist friends were completely convinced of it. I doubt it. The revolution did not "fall" into the hands of Gottwald & Co., it was placed there by the idealists who handed it to them. Not for reasons of wickedness or folly but by the very nature of the revolutionary ideal, even the purest ideal, they could do no other. The Communist ideal was not an organic extention of the democratic, socialist ideals of our heritage. It was revolutionary—it had to be imposed by men willing and able to weild power ruthlessly. Justice, legality, freedom had to be sacrificed so that force could impose the ideal.

That was just the devil of it. The intellectual idealists could not themselves realize the ideal. They rarely can: their task is to present it as an alternative that men can choose. When men remain unconvinced, the ideal cannot be realized and if the idealists attempt to impose it by force they can do it only by alliance with the Gottwalds and Švábs of this world, who invariably make use of the ideal for their own ends.

The revolution did not fall, accidentally, into the wrong hands—only the wrong hands, quick with a gun and a knife in the back, could carry it out successfully. Perhaps the most tragic aspect of the Communist revolution, and not only in our country, is that the idealists placed the tyrants in power, and for so many years continued to support them for the sake of an ideal that died as soon as the revolution succeeded.

The death certificates of the executed announced to the victors the end of the revolution. At the same time, their vanquished opponents in exile received different kinds of certificates—certificates of naturalization from countries all over the West. This, too, marked the end of an era.

The men and women who had dedicated their lives to the Party only to be destroyed by it felt very much alone, yet their experience was not altogether unique. In an obvious sense, it was shared by the non-Communist victims of the coup: the dramatic arrests, the searches, harassment and torture, prison and execution followed an unvarying pattern. In a way, the non-Communists had it easier: they did not lose an ideal. A woman like the Socialist member of our Parliament Milada Horáková went to her death on a Communist scaffold no less defeated, but not betrayed.

Nor was the experience of the exiles totally different from that of the rest of our people. Certainly, it was infinitely easier. They did not have to bear the fear, nor the overt pain and suffering. But the exiles shared something with the Communists. Their lives, their indentities, their very being also was defined by the coup, by an ideal faced with conflict. I am not thinking of the emigrants, who for entirely good and sufficient reasons decided to forget the country that had treated then so ill and to build new lives and identities as citizens of other lands. I now am thinking of the *exiles*, whose basic commitment was and remained to Czechoslovakia. In the years following the coup, they, too, lived with a sense of struggle and dedication. To them, too, just as to the committed Communists, the daily reality of their lives seemed secondary. They bore the deprivations of exile without much concern: what mattered was their concern for the ideal of freedom and social justice in their homeland.

In a far less painful, dramatic sense, after years of living abroad, the naturalization certificates signaled to them the same thing as the delayed death certificates at home: the end of the revolutionary era. The whole detour out of the ordinary in a thrust for "authentic" existence had ended: what remained was the reality of the ordinary.

That, more than anything, is the meaning of the end of the third stage and the beginning of the fourth stage of the revolutionary cycle. It is, genuinely, a fourth stage of a cycle, marked by a quest for meaning. It is not a return to meaninglessness—it is marked by a radical shift in strategy. The revolutionary strategy defines the quest for meaning as an alternative to the ordinary. From Martin Heidegger's utter rejection of "average everydayness" in favor of the anticipatory resoluteness of the SA, through our wartime contrast of the partisan fighter and the surviving bourgeois, down to the caricature in the statements like "How could you go on a date when there is a war in Korea?"—we had seen significance and daily existence, authentic existence and simple human life as mutually exclusive, opposite alternatives. Revolution separates the ideal from the actual: the fourth stage of the cycle begins with the end of that separation, with the search for meaning in existence rather than for an alternative to it. The heroes of the fourth stage of the revolutionary cycle are poets rather than revolutionary ideologues, its triumph is not victory or martyrdom, but life.

This is a far more difficult search, one that men seldom undertake when the far more simple "revolutionary" alternative seems available. But now we knew that this simpler alternative was no longer open to us. At the time of the certificates, the sole heritage of the revolution was that it had discredited the whole mode of struggle as an alternative to living. For better or worse, we had passed beyond the dominant mood of the two generations who had preceded us. The sole task and the sole possibility that now remained was to live—with hope, perhaps, but without illusions.

-IV-
The
Shoots
of
Hope

1956. *The East European regimes stabilize in the Soviet mold following a brief period of liberalization. Economic and social stagnation.*

1960. *First large-scale releases of prisoners in Czechoslovakia.*

1963. *A Communist party commission secretly reexamines records of the Stalin era. Further releases of prisoners and rehabilitation of some Communists who were convicted in the 1950s.*

January, 1968. *The Soviets permit the fall of old Stalinist President of Czechoslovakia, Antonín Novotný, and sanction the rise of Alexander Dubček. The Czechoslovak Spring begins.*

April, 1968. *The Action program of the Czechoslovak Communist party sets out an independent program of socialist democracy. Censorship abolished. First rehabilitations of non-Communist victims of the 1950s.*

August 21, 1968. *The Spring ends as Soviet armies occupy Czechoslovakia. Unanimous passive resistance, followed by a large exodus into exile.*

Spring, 1969. *Self-immolation of Jan Palach marks last outburst of national resistance. Gustav Husák replaces Alexander Dubček.*

246

August, 1969. *The Emergency Decree of August 22 marks full consolidation of power in Soviet hands and puts an end to hopes for democracy.*

i. Stagnant Water There are in human history periods of necessity when the pressure of accumulated, unresolved needs seems to drive events along an inexorable course, sweeping men and women with it. There are other periods, when men feel free: the periods when pressing tensions and conflicts have been resolved and men are free to shape their own future. The years after the triumph of revolution in 1948 and its cataclysmic consummation in 1952 belong to neither category. They were years of exhaustion and stagnation. The trend of the preceding age was broken, but the new hope was not yet born. It awaited the rediscovery of personal reality.

The revolutionary cycle, after all, begins with the loss of personal categories—with the polarization that deprives humans of individual identity and pits them against each other as members of totalized wholes, whether nations, denominations, races, or classes. It begins when wholes replace individuals as subjects of history, when abstractions about the value, the rights, and the claims of a social whole, whether a class or a nation, come to guide social action in place of considerations of individual human welfare.

The element of truth and the appeal of such holistic analysis lie in the recognition that at times concern for individual human beings becomes an insufficient guide for social policy. Just to live a good, peaceful human life can seem trivial or impossible when individual destinies are lumped together in totalities, and decided en bloc. A Czech or a Jew could not simply live his own life when Nazi policy determined his destiny solely in terms of his allegiance to a totality, with no recourse to individual virtues or vices, rights, or qualities. Holistic analysis expresses the recognition that the power of the constraining totality must be broken before individual freedom becomes possible and meaningful.

The danger of holistic analysis is the perennial temptation of Leninism, whether as class struggle or cold war—that is, the temptation to lose sight of the goal of struggle, of the restoration of individual freedom, and to substitute for it the vision of a "victory" of one class or of one power bloc over another.

In 1940, individual Czechs could defend their identity against the Nazis only by uniting, as Czechs—but the triumph of "the Czechs" over "the Germans" is not yet a triumph of freedom. In the struggle for freedom, "victories" are no less hollow than "defeats." Freedom triumphs with the rediscovery of individual persons, with the withering away of the collectivist mentality. Class struggle may, to be sure, be forced upon persons, but even a "victory" in such a struggle fixates the collectivist mentality and so forges a new bondage. The effect of the first stage of the revolutionary cycle is to call attention to the reality of polarization and to the impossibility, at this moment, of going on living individual lives as usual. It represents a situation in which freedom requires conscious effort in order to remove the causes of polarization. With that recognition, two strategies become possible. The revolutionary strategy fosters totalization and commits itself to the "victory" of the "progressive" totality. The democratic strategy consciously seeks to remove rather than exploit the causes of polarization, and commits itself to the rediscovery and freeing of persons. The hope for freedom at the second stage is that the democratic strategy will succeed. If it does not, the polarization prevails, revolutionary strategy fixates it with a "victory" for one and "defeat" of the other pole, making the gap more difficult to bridge than ever.

This polarization prevailed in our country in the 1950s. The "Victorious February" was not a victory. A genuine victory would have required reconciliation, a withering away of holistic abstractions and the rediscovery of persons rather than blocs. The alleged "victory" was no less a defeat for the Communist party than for the democrats: it locked all of us more securely than ever in the vicious circle of power and submission, of victors and vanquished who mutually constrain each other. Similarly, a Western surrender and a Soviet victory on an international scale—or the reverse—would not have resolved the Cold War. Here, too, freedom requires not a victory, but a withering away of holistic abstractions and rediscovery of self-determination.

The fourth stage of the revolutionary cycle begins not with a victory and a defeat, as does the third stage, but rather with weariness, the infinite wariness with ideological abstractions and the rediscovery of the value of concrete human life, of persons rather than principles. It begins with the recognition that, perhaps, personal competence and dedication may be more important qualifications for a factory manager than political orthodoxy. Or it begins with the recognition that individual guilt or innocence may be more important evidence in a court of law than class profile; or that truth may be more important in newspaper reporting than the perennial Leninist question, "Whom will it serve?" Or, finally, it may begin with the recognition that national self-determination may be a far better guarantee of international security than the imperial principle of domination.

Yet such recognition grows slowly. The total faith of the true believers can collapse far more rapidly than a democratic consciousness can grow, which is free from reliance on an ideological dogma and based on respect for individual freedom. The interim period can draw on painfully long. In objective history, that interim might be said to have begun with the death of Stalin in 1953 and ended with the release of most of the political prisoners at the end of the 1950s. If there is a watershed, it is the year 1956, when Khrushchev buried the old by unmasking Stalin at the Twentieth Party Congress, and strangled the new by suppressing the Hungarian reform by force. In terms of human history, however, the parameters are different: this was the period of the bankruptcy of ideology and the triumph of momentum.

With Khrushchev's revelations, the power monopoly the Party claimed and exercised since the revolution lost all justification. Omnipotence can be justified only by omniscience, and the Party stood revealed as anything but omniscient and far from incorruptible. To avoid the inevitable conclusion, Khrushchev had to borrow a page from Stalin's book. In the official version, Stalinism and all it stood for was the work of one man, Josef Vissarionovich Dzugashvili—Stalin, and, at most, of a handful of his associates. The explanation was that of the peak of a cult of personality. In an utterly non-Marxist way, it does not see social superstructure as a product of objective economic and social factors, but rather explains the entire socioeconomic system in the exclusively subjective terms of Stalin's paranoid personality and lust for power. The Party may be absolved from blame—even if at the cost of the historical materialist ideology that had justified its existence. It stood revealed as impotent: its brankruptcy was both ideological and moral.

The year 1956 was a year of ideological bankruptcy for the West as well. Ever since the start of the Cold War, Western ideology had been couched in terms of liberation, of rolling back the Iron Curtain and championing the right of all peoples to self-determination. The revolt in Hungary gave the West the chance it claimed to be waiting for. Even a guarantee of Hungarian integrity and neutrality, for which Nagy pleaded, could have started a chain reaction leading to the rise of a tier of sovereign nations in central Europe in place of the Soviet Empire. The risk of war was minimal: the Soviets hesitated for a week before attacking the tiny, lone Hungarian army. Yet the West did not move. Its inaction declared the bankruptcy of its ideology far more eloquently than any official statement: the West was more interested in peace and order, even if Soviet-imposed, more than in freedom and self-determination.

With the double bankruptcy of both the Communist and the Western ideologies the only logical course seemed clear—radical democratization of the socialist states and fundamental reconciliation between East and West. The bankruptcy of the Communist party destroyed whatever justification it may have claimed for a monopoly on power, just as the bankruptcy of the policy of "liberation" destroyed all justification for continued confrontation. Democratization and reconciliation now were the only justifiable alternatives; they still are today.

Yet it was neither a time of democratization nor a time of reconciliation. Ideologies collapsed, but in the absence of an alternative possibility, life continued along its accustomed lines, carried along by its established momentum. Khrushchev suppressed the Hungarian reform at one stroke, and the West responded with Cold War rhetoric that was no more credible than the rhetoric of the Communist East. The regimes had wavered for a moment, but then momentum reasserted itself. The substance was gone—and the facade became more rigid for it.

Later, to be sure, the moment of indecision was to have long-range consequences. In Czechoslovakia, it provided a brief period of relaxation of censorship, which permitted the publication of such novels as Ptáčnik's *Border Town* or Škvorecký's *The Cowards*. None of the books that were printed—and they all were sold out within hours of publication and then disappeared again—was particulary revolutionary. When *The Cowards* appeared in English in 1970, it seemed to its readers just another novel about adolescence, well observed and effectively written, but not particular significant. Yet in Czechoslovakia it was a prophetic book precisely because it was ordinary: it spoke of real life, not ideology. By introducing the topic of human reality into a world of self-sustaining ideology, the writers of the period provided a far more radical alternative than any ideology could have done.

For the moment, in the 1950s, however, momentum prevailed: ideology, no matter how bankrupt, had become institutionalized. The autocrats, from the high and mighty in the Kremlin and Prague's Hradčany Castle to the petty bureaucrats and the concierges ruling over a cell of ten Party members, remained endowed with power. Now that they felt no longer justified by ideology, they became even more tenacious about the trappings of power and greedier for its spoils. It was an odd period, marked by a pronounced sense of unreality; it has been amply described in the books published during the eight free months of the Czechoslovak Spring. It was a period of aimlessness: the old slogans still retained a monopoly on public communication, and we repeated them dutifully, though few of us could believe them any longer. The increasing rate of alcoholism, the failing economy, the rise in divorces and drop in population increase are not unrelated—all these were symptoms of the basic malaise of a society that could no longer believe the old but could not yet shape the new.

The fate of the political prisoners was most indicative of that malaise. Beginning in 1956, many of them were being released—but they were not rehabilitated. Men and women who had passed through arrests, torture, and years in concentration camps were expected not to speak about their ordeal, to slip quietly into the ordinary life of some provincial town and forget all that had happened. Perhaps it was all a mistake—though even that admission was almost never made—but to speak of it would help the class enemy! The report of the Barák Commission, appointed in 1956 to review the record of the trials, made it official. The trials were fair, the guilt of the accused real, the executions justified—but it was not right to speak of all this. The 1950s were to be forgotten: on the surface, the history of the Party, beginning with the Victorious February, was one of a persistent struggle for an ever happier future.

With the enforced cover of darkness enveloping even events as recent as those of the 1950s, little liberalization was possible. There can be no future without a past, and Czechoslovakia's past had been officially erased, replaced by the Party version of history. Writers writing of the future could not speak of the most urgent tasks at hand, the resolution of our problems of the past. Not surprisingly, their offerings remained slim—as trivial as the official version of the past. And, again not surprisingly, censorship remained as rigid as in the days when all censors had believed the official ideology. Not out of zealous commitment but out of the necessity of momentum: the regime, though it may no longer have believed its own line, had to make sure that no incautious admission of what had in fact happened would cast doubt on the stereotyped description of its joyful building of socialism.

The gap between the Communist intelligentsia and the non-Communists, whether in internal exile at home or in exile abroad, by now had narrowed down considerably. It was no longer the gap between zealots of the revolution and adamant defenders of the old order. The Communists had been chastened by the experience of the 1950s, and the non-Communists had come to realize that, desirable or not, a return to the pre-Communist Republic was impossible. Our new democracy, if it was to grow at all, would have to grow on the basis and within the framework of the new socialist society. In 1968, the vanquished of 1948 were prepared to assume the role of a loyal opposition.

In the 1950s the need to maintain the myth of Party

righteousness made any such role impossible. To admit that loyal dissent is a valid form of social participation would have required the admission that the ruthless destruction of dissent and divergence in the 1950s had been unjustified. To safeguard the lie, the regime had to deprive itself of something it desperately needed: open criticism without which even routine human errors grow into major disasters of policy, unchecked and uncorrected. Even though the holistic principle of class struggle had lost both its objective and its ideological justification, it remained operative, for it shielded the regime from its own memories.

The stagnation of the time, locked between the loss of faith in the old and the inability to permit the new, is not uniquely Czechoslovak. This stagnation is the generic condition of revolutionary regimes that succeed and then maintain themselves in power by mystified ideology—by dictatorial control of the state bureaucracy, the army, and the police—long after they have outlived their social utility. It has been the condition of the Soviet Union since Stalin, of East Germany since the Berlin revolt, of Hungary since the Soviet intervention of 1956, of Poland since the throttling of the Polish October—and, most recently, of Czechoslovakia since the Soviet occupation. It is a condition that permits considerable fluctuation: periodically, the regime has to liberalize its policies in order to generate some movement and spontaneous activity on the part of its subjects. And equally regularly, the regime again curtails the freedom it had so briefly tolerated in order to reassert its control—even at the cost of creating new apathy, and in turn a new need for liberalization. This can be an endless cycle—as the official revolutionary faith remains an irrelevant but indispensible justification for the existence of the privileged ruling elite.

One factor, however, is noncyclical. Seen from without, this factor frequently appears as a rise of consumerism. The lean, taught revolutionary of early years becomes increasingly plump and contented; the citizens of ideologically oriented countries seem less and less content to be fed revolutionary slogans and more and more interested in better food, clothing, vacation cottages, travel, and, most of all, cars.

The zealots of yesteryear, preserved artifically in the West and in their heyday in the Far East, may well see the development as revolution threatened by increasing fetishism of goods. There is something to that criticism, though not much. The basic root of the fetishistic drive for consumer goods is not some metaphysical principle of greed, surviving from the capitalist era, but rather the limits imposed by the bureaucratic collectivist state. Its citizens cannot believe: the official faith has been discredited, a new faith is precluded by the need to maintain the myth of the old. The bureaucratic monopoly on power precludes initiative in arts and letters, the central-directive economy precludes significant participation in economic life. Private life is literally all that remains: as in the case of other disenfranchized groups, the acquisition of private posessions is the only ambition possible under these conditions. The desire to own a car, to be the master of a machine hurtling down an open road—even if in circles—is an expression of an urge for a better life, in the only form available.

The regimes may well be concerned to keep the material expectations of their subjects within limits they can hope to meet, for they are concerned to meet those expectations.

The fetishism of goods, however, is only an external expression of a deeper change, the change that signals the fourth stage of the revolutionary cycle. It expresses a rediscovery of personal life. In disenfranchizing its subjects to keep intact its power and ideology, the post-revolutionary regimes at the same time foster the growth of a very different mentality, to which ideological abstractions remain irrelevant. It often appears as a mentality of boundless individual greed, but it is far more than that: it is a profoundly humane and nonrevolutionary mentality, the mentality that recognizes the tangible reality of human life as the ultimate criterion and justification of all social action. It can be petty, but it can also express a democratic mentality—judging social policy in terms of human welfare and unwilling to sacrifice human beings to the abstractions of social movements and social wholes.

The postrevolutionary regimes, manipulating the swing of liberalization and suppression, have been largely successful, as the Czechoslovak regime had been, in preventing any political expression of the growing democratic mentality. The facade remains true to the design of the zealots. But they have not prevented its growth, within, to quote Marx, the womb of the old order. With its growth, the regimes have become not only irrelevant—they were that since the day the revolution died with the executions—but also superfluous. Beneath the surface of post-revolutionary stagnation, beneath the Kafkaesque, absurd institutions of a messianic movement, beneath the weary slogans of verve, there was a radical alternative to revolutionary fervor, waiting for an opportunity to express itself. It did not make revolution—the democratic mentality is not revolutionary—its essence is its concern for the reality of individuals rather than the grand revolutionary gesture. But it was no less real for it, that new life sprouting through the cracks of the ideological concrete of the regime. Unlike the Communist revolution of 1948, the social change of the fourth stage of the revolutionary cycle did not have to be carried out—it only had to be acknowledged.

ii. The Spring

When, amid the tumultuous rebirth of Czechoslovak freedom in April 1968, the Communist party of Czechoslovakia sought to provide a rationale for the new development of its Action Program, it did so in terms of the dynamics of the fourth stage of the revolutionary cycle. Class struggle, the introduction to the program argued, had been fought and won. The revolutionary regime had eliminated the capitalists as a class and had created a socialist society in which all citizens shared the same relation to the means of production, as users rather than owners, and so they all constituted *one* class. The differences among social strata no longer had a class character. The perspective of struggle and the dictatorship of the proletariat had become obsolete and counterproductive: the urgent task now was to draw the highest possible proportion of Czechs and Slovaks into active participation in the life of the society. The implication that the Victorious February coup of 1948 and the bloodbath that followed it had been necessary to create the foundation of socialist democracy was dubious, and some of the rhetoric remained reminiscent of an earlier era. But the spirit of the new program was clear—the rediscovery of the importance of human beings, the withering away of holistic abstractions.

The program was consistent with the best traditions of Marxism. The Marxists had, after all, always spoken of Party dictatorship in the name of the proletariat as a transitional device. It was to be dismantled as soon as the effective abolition of the class structure through the socialization of means of production would make possible genuine individual freedom and socialist democracy, unconstrained by privileges of ownership. The program was not only orthodox, but also relevant and timely: the organs of class struggle—especially the central-directive structure of the economy and the autocracy of Party officials from the censors with nationwide authority down to the petty local National Committee members—had ceased to serve any real purpose. Quite the contrary, these organs had become a serious obstacle to popular participation in social and economic life and they barred the society from profiting from the skill, initiative, and competence of many of its members. But most of all, the revolution itself the idea of righteous victors seizing power and cramming Utopia down the throats of the vanquished had become obsolete.

The development began inconspicuously. Perhaps the most important factor was our people's endless fatigue with revolutionary rhetoric and the desperate longing for normal human life, for freedom from the draining, perennial zeal, and for an opportunity to work and live freely. As the slogans came to carry less and less conviction, it became harder and harder to find individuals willing to maintain the facade against the urge to live, harder and harder to find censors and policemen who would dedicate themselves to maintaining the lie no one believed any longer. The administrative apparatus remained securely in the hands of the Party, but the way in which it exercised power became increasingly lax. As once before, in the waning days of the Habsburg monarchy, the system had become one of *Absolutismus gemildered durch Schlamperei*—absolutism tempered by sloppiness.

Perhaps nowhere was the effect of this sloppiness more evident than in the application of censorship. Although censorship was not officially abolished in Czechoslovakia until May 1968—and was promptly reinstituted by the Russians three months later, following the occupation—from 1963 on it had become increasingly lax. Czechoslovak literature and films had come to describe more and more freely the ordinary reality of our daily lives rather than the stereotypes demanded by "socialist realism." Once again, the dominant mode of our lives was genuinely socialist, but in a way for which orthodox Marxists, associating socialist realism with faithful perpetuation of the myth, were not prepared. The new wave of films and literature restored a vital relationship between ordinary experience and literature, holding up a mirror of concrete human reality to ideological abstractions. In these works, revolutionary heroes and class enemies once again became human beings, with human concerns, strengths and weaknesses, capable of human cooperation in dealing with mutual problems rather than being condemned to mutual destruction in a relentless "struggle." At no time did the idea of socialism itself become questionable to either these artists or their audiences: socialism was the framework making the new freedom possible. But it was a human not a class socialism, a socialism with a human face.

The exiles, both in the country and abroad, came to participate more and more in this process; but they did not play a leading role. For good reason: for years, they had been cut off from the foci of development, whether by geographical or by political distance. Influential positions, down to the most petty, had been reserved for Communists, and it was the Communists themselves who recognized the imperative need to dismantle this monopoly of power and involve non-Communists in the life of the society. Despite the twenty years of bitter memories of oppression and humiliation, the non-Communist Czechs and Slovaks proved their willingness to cooperate with the Communists in building a new, democratic socialism.

The exiles abroad took part in this process, too. Already in 1963 Pavel Tigrid, editor of the prestigious exile journal *Svědectvi* and perhaps the most capable non-Communist politician who had a chance to speak out, resolutely refused the role of class enemy to which the Party condemned him and for which many exiles praised him. Tigrid assumed the role of the loyal opposition. His journal spoke for no faction: it started with the assumption that the Communist society is the framework within which Czechoslovakia lives, and that the common concern of Czechs and Slovaks regardless of party allegiance is not a missionary one in the Leninist style of the Cold War but a *democratic* one, concerned to make the system as humane, free, and democratic as possible. In the West Tigrid was called many names— from fellow traveler to crypto-Commie, while in Prague he was tried and condemned *in absentia* in 1967. The fundamental premise of his policy was sound: the triumph of freedom requires the withering away of abstractions and the rediscovery of the value of the individual human being.

The Communist initiative found ready ground among Czechs and Slovaks at home and abroad, but its driving force may well have lain in the memory of the Czechoslovak show trials of the early 1950s. The memory of those trials, unmentioned and unmentionable, remained perhaps the most decisive factor in shaping the Czechoslovak national consciousness. Not simply because dedicated men had been destroyed by the very ideas they had professed: after all, every militant faith produces its *autos da fé*, and it cannot do otherwise. Having promised to set men free of all the ills of the flesh, it can only keep its promise by burning that flesh. The Inquisition had been most explicit about that. But ordinarily, such events are written off as the unfortunate errors of a misguided few. Great institutions, such as the Church or the Party, change—they do not apologize.

In Czechoslovakia change without apologies proved impossible. Perhaps it is because we are fundamentally a democratic nation: we are used to participating in history rather than leaving it to a handful of the mighty. And we treat it seriously, as the stuff of our lives, not as the antics of our politicians. In our country the whirlwind of the 1950s was not an aberration. It followed directly from ideals we accepted and believed in. Nor was it the work of a few. Many of our most idealistic men and women had supported the Party, in the repressive machinery there were thousands of people who did their work with conviction and initiative, and in the nation at large there were hundreds of thousands who made the hate and malice of the time their own. The 1950s were a national phenomenon, in the mainstream of our traditional idealism—a classic case of conscience subordinated to conviction, of reality subordinated to a "higher truth."

It was not the first time we had confronted this problem in its various forms. It was the problem of the period of forcible Catholicization in the seventeenth century, the problem of the suspect historical documents treated as genuine in the interest of our national revival, the problem of Slovak separatism hushed up for reasons of state. We needed to believe, and we were prepared to write off anyone and anything that did not fit in with our faith as unreal, untrue, treasonous in the name of a "higher truth."

But to us the ordinary strategies for dealing with uncomfortable reality were not available. The trauma of the 1950s was not a matter of an ideological diversion or of a misguided few. It was our basic problem, the problem of all idealists: conscience had been subordinated to conviction. The men who wielded power in the decade that followed the trials knew this. Part of the stagnation and stability of that period resulted directly from the realization that no piecemeal reform was possible. Any wavering in the insistence on the superior role of a "higher" truth, any concession to reality would inevitably bring the whole ideological superstructure tumbling down. We did not need a better "higher" truth, we needed the plain truth, the whole truth, without reservations.

When the Czechoslovak Spring came in 1968, it was so basically different from any earlier reform movement precisely because of the memory of the 1950s. The men who initiated the process of liberation that brought about our Spring may well have thought that "socialism with a human face" would be no more than a new version of the "higher" truth—and would make it tenable for a few more years. Moscow, in its initial support, was convinced of that. But the trials had cut too deeply into our consciousness: they did not discredit only this or that higher truth but the principle of "higher" truth itself. Socialism with a human face, controlled and orderly, became in a matter of days a full-fledged program of socialist democracy, a program of the whole, plain truth, flushing twenty years of white, grey, and black lies out of our system.

Foreign commentators told us after the Soviet occupation, with the wisdom of hind-sight, that we should have been more cautious, that we should have let the past lie, should not have looked back so intensely at our history from the death of Jan Masaryk through the liquidation of democratic opposition to the Slánský trials. They told us, in effect, that we should have respected the Soviet principle of make-believe. Theoretically, they might even be right. But it would have been impossible. There could be no new beginning until we had purged ourselves of the all-pervasive lie of the 1950s. The social and economic failures of the Communist regime might have led to a revision of this or that feature as in Poland or Hungary. But the trials put it all in a different light. We had to purge socialism of its dirty secret, set it free from the need to subordinate all other consideration to sustaining the lie of a "higher" truth.

The rationale of Party policy after the fall of Novotný in January 1968 acknowledged this need. The justification of the new policy was to purge the Party of its guilt and its suppressed memories, which were robbing it of popular support and freedom of action. And, again in a way that Soviet Communists found incomprehensible, it worked. Never in its history did the Communist party have such widespread popular support as in the period of the Czechoslovak Spring. The Party's First Secretary Alexander Dubček became a symbol and a legend as no one had been for centuries, with the exception of Tomáš Masaryk, Czechoslovakia's first president. Under Dubček's leadership, the Party for the first time became truly the vanguard of an entire people.

But now it was a different Party. Its new Action Program demonstrated that, and so did Dubček himself when he said, at the First of May celebrations in 1968, that he preferred engaged non-Party members to nonengaged Party members. The institutional development inevitably lagged behind the tumultuous transformation of our spirit, but in intent and in strength Czechoslovakia's Communist party had become a democratic party, one of the partners in the dialogue from which social progress grows rather than an autocratic institution with a monopoly on power. Few of its leaders were prepared to acknowledge this—they still curtly rejected all possibility of a reconstitution of the Social

Democratic party, which may well have come out as the strongest party in an election—but the indications were unmistakable.

The Dubček era lasted a few short months, and in retrospect it is easy to write it off as one of the perennial oscillations of Communist regimes between liberalization and repression. But it was not that. For a few months, in the late spring and early summer of 1968, Czechoslovakia was a free country. Censorship was abolished in May, the borders were opened, the Parliament was debating the passage of a law normalizing the status of the exiles. A multiparty structure was emerging—no longer class-based but rather reflecting our experience of the past twenty years: there now was the K-231—the club of former political prisoners, named for §231 of the Penal Code; there was the Club of Engaged Non-Party Men, representing those who had been the excluded of the Stalin years; there was the Communist party, and the new socialist democratic government. Most of all, the Czechoslovak Communist party had changed, so much so that after the occupation the Soviets could not simply "restore it to power" as they had expected to do, but had to purge it thoroughly and even disband many of its local organizations. Its program had remained socialist and pro-Soviet, but it had given up the principle of the monopoly of power—the principle of victors and vanquished.

Czechoslovakia in the summer of 1968 was still socialist, and still an ally of the Soviet Union, but it was also a free country. The Soviets recognized it perhaps more clearly than the leaders of the Czechoslovak Communist party. In the tradition of alternating liberalization and repression, the Soviets had authorized the fall of Novotný and the rise of Dubček as a tactic designed to secure the Party's and so their own control of Czechoslovakia. Instead, they found themselves gaining an ally but losing a vassal.

There were many reasons for the occupation. One of them was the amply demonstrated willingness of the West to let the Soviets exercise their unimpeded power in Eastern Europe. Another may well have been the continued pro-Soviet orientation of the Czechoslovak leadership, which made armed resistance unthinkable: the Soviets may have thought that their interference would prove a minor nuisance and a major aid to the Czechoslovak

Communist leadership in controlling what to the Russians must have appeared as an incomprehensible situation. But the major reason for the Russians' intervention was domestic. For years, the Soviets had justified their rule over other Communist countries before their own people by insisting that this was the only alternative to a virtually nineteenth-century model of capitalism. Now Czechoslovakia was demonstrating another alternative. For years the Soviets had justified the demands they made on their people by a merciless international confrontation between the Soviet Union and forces of "international imperialist capitalism" bent on its destruction—now Czechoslovakia, though still a loyal member of the Warsaw Pact, was demonstrating the possibility of self-determination and peaceful coexistence. Finally, for years the Soviets had justified their draconic police rule with the demands of a lingering class struggle—while Czechoslovakia served as a vivid demonstration that the building of socialism surges forward precisely with the withering away of the class struggle. The Czechoslovak leadership may have been scrupulously careful to affirm its loyalty to socialism and the Soviet Union; but, not unlike the "honest Communists" of the 1950s, Czechoslovakia by its very existence destroyed the credibility of the Soviet regime.

On August 21, 1968, the Soviets moved with a force greater than that which Americans deployed in Vietnam to put an end to our offending Spring. The step proved rather more difficult than they had anticipated. The armies of the five Warsaw Pact powers encountered no armed resistance, but no friendly welcome, either. The Soviets could not even find the dozen men required to form their planned "Workers' and Peasants' Government." Czechs and Slovaks, and this included the Czechoslovak Communist party, were defiant.

The Communist party, shielded by the Workers' Militia and universal anti-Soviet opposition that included even portions of the Secret Police, held its Fourteenth Congress under the noses of the occupation forces, and reaffirmed the ideals of the Czechoslovak Spring. The Soviets had to compromise. They had to bring back Dubček and his colleagues from the Soviet Union, and they had to tolerate a considerable measure of freedom for several months. Only slowly could they wear away the

Czechoslovak autonomy. It was not until eight months after the occupation that they dared replace Dubček, a full year before the Special Decree of August 22, 1969, stripped away the vestiges of individual freedom and reaffirmed the power monopoly of a purged *apparat*. It was almost three years before they dared resort again to more than occasional arrests and the routine forms of police repression. And, by then, they had not succeeded in gaining any semblance of popular support.

A little over a year after the occupation, a week after the promulgation of the Special Decree, I crossed the borders of my native land for the second time, bound for the West and a second exile. By then, the bayonets that had been so much in evidence the year before had become much less conspicuous and much more effective. The defiant signs with which the Czechs and Slovaks responded to the occupation had been covered over with whitewash on the side of a dilapidated railway shed. It read, *"Nedáme se oblbnout."*

Since then, I have tried to find an adequate translation, but that concise colloquialism is too much a part of our mentality. There is no equivalent, unless this entire book provides it. In place of a translation, I'd offer a paraphrase:

"They won't make fools of us this time."

-Epilogue-

Promise of Things To Come

The Czechoslovak Spring was a victory without vanquished. It was a time of reconciliation. After the vicious confrontations, the hollow victories and the bitter defeats, we had found a framework within which we could meet again as human beings, living and working together. Our Spring held out the promise of democracy untarnished by exploitation, of socialism unmarred by oppression. The ideals and aspirations whose conflict had made our history tragic fused in a vision of humanity.

To the Soviet Union, that was threatening enough to warrant risking open aggression, marching in fall across the border of a friendly socialist country. It was threatening enough so that the Soviets were willing to pay the price of transforming the one traditionally pro-Russian ally into a sullen, conquered territory, waiting for a chance to rebel—just to eradicate the idea of Czechoslovak socialist democracy from the airwaves and newspaper pages.

The Czechoslovak Spring was all of that—but what precisely was it all about? The original program of the January reform was really quite modest. Put through by a coalition whose only common ground was a dislike for President Novotný, it was at the very best a program of Communism with a human face, reminiscent of the hopes of the idealists of the days before the coup who had expected to seize power to guide their people along the one true path laid down by the Party, but to do it humanely, respecting the rights of their subjects. As such, it even had the blessing of the Soviets who had become concerned lest the longstanding twighlight Stalinism of Antonín Novotný provoke so much dislike as to make the country hard to govern.

But while not radical in intention, the program proved radical in execution. Respect for human rights includes a respect for free opinion, freely expressed. The Party may have expected expressions of gratitude for its more benign course—and it received them. It may have expected increased support, and it got that, too. What it did not get was popular approval of the principle of arbitrary rule, even though that rule had become benign. Czechs and Slovaks had had their experience with promises of benevolent paternalism after the Victorious February. What they spoke for, clearly and unambiguously, once the censorship had been relaxed, was not benign autocracy but a democracy that would transfer the government from the sphere of central-directive rule, no matter how benign, into the sector of public service, subject to popular supervision, direction, and recall.

Even among the reformers, probably the majority found that demand unacceptable. Most of them still hoped for power that would remain autonomous and independent of the popular will but would earn support and confidence by being benign. The Action Program of the Communist party, adopted in April 1968 and obsolete by May, stressed the leading role of the Party in the state, though it added the ambiguous proviso that the Party had to be worthy of that leading role. The leadership tended to read this conservatively, as meaning that the Party has both a right to rule and an obligation to rule well. The people—the rank and file of the Party as well as Czechs and Slovaks at large—gave it a different reading, and the people carried the leadership with them—it is up to the governed to decide whether the Party deserves to rule, and the Party's right to rule is contingent on the consent of the people. At the moment, that consent was forthcoming, freely and more enthusiastically than ever in the history of the Party, but that did not affect the point made by this democratic principle. What the reform leadership launched as a program of humane Communism had been transformed by popular pressure into a program of socialist democracy.

In 1968, such a program had little real hope of uninhibited realization. The idea of socialist democracy, which seemed so obvious to us, was simply too radical for a world dominated by a polarized past. It was far too radical for the Soviet leaders in whom bad conscience, reaching all the way back to Stalin and to Lenin at Kronstadt before him, gave rise to a basic fear of their people and an almost pathological need for the security provided by power. It was equally radical for the West, which was conscious of the fundamental discrepancy and its oligarchic economic structure. Most of all, the idea of genuine self-determination of a small nation was far too radical for a world dominated by the polarized mentality for which neutrality is treason.

Even then, there were men who understood us. In America, Norman Thomas and his miniscule Socialist party regocnized that what was happening in our country was neither a reversion to capitalism nor an East European version of a campus revolt, but a genuine step forward. There were also far-sighted men in the Soviet Union, apparently even in the Kremlin, who recognized that the Czechoslovak experiment was pointing the way out of a political and international impasse. But in the late 1960's such men were few. The counsels of the past prevailed, and the armies of the Warsaw Pact marched to preserve for a few more years a situation that had become untenable back in 1956.

The Czechoslovak experiment, however, was not simply one of history's hopeful offshoots that can be lopped off at a stroke. Such offshoots, which spring up and wither like the "revolt" of the flower children, reflect merely the perennial thrust toward freedom. As such, they are bright with perennial hope but inevitably doomed to failure because freedom is a goal, not a program. The goal of freedom can inspire men in times of overwhelming repression or weariness, but it does not solve the daily problems of social existence. Human freedom in the society can be affirmed but not achieved by such outbursts of protest: it is always a by-product, something that comes about when a society finds ways of resolving the problems of social coexistence without repression and develops safeguards of both social responsibility and human rights.

The Czechoslovak Spring could not be simply lopped off precisely because its resemblance to the effervescent outbursts of hope was only superficial. There was, of course, the thrust toward freedom that motivates both such outbursts and the first steps of concrete historical progress. But there was something more basic as well: a genuine attempt to find solutions to social problems that would remove the causes of polarization and repression and make freedom possible. In this sense, the Czechoslovak socialist democracy was not simply a protest, but an anticipation of the next step on the way of social progress, frozen since the days of Stalin.

Progress, the building of social foundations of human freedom, has been guided by numerous political slogans. In recent times, democracy represented and symbolized the most determined effort to solve the problems of social existence noncoercively and to create the requisites of freedom. Its insistence on majority rule.was designed first of all to take power out of the hands of vested interests, to make it serve society at large. Its corresponding insistence on safeguarding the rights of minorities, even against a popular majority, was designed to humanize power and assure the leaway of human freedom.

Democracy succeeded far more than we are ordinarily prepared to admit. It ceased to be a dynamic, inspiring program in the industrial West largely because its very success created internal obstacles to dealing effectively with a new kind of problem, that of economic power. Democracy has always found it difficult to differentiate between the inherent needs and rights of concrete men and women—and the abstract extentions of those rights to cover the claims of corporate entities.

Yet perhaps not always: American antitrust legislation in the latter nineteenth century, Roosevelt's New Deal, the Czechoslovak land reform, the growth of worldwide unionism —all these reflected a growing recognition that men and women have rights while economic entities have only privileges, which men and women extend to them for the sake of the public good, and which remain subject to public control.

Unfortunately, those instances tend to be exceptional. Far too often, democracy accorded to economic privilege the protection owed to human rights and so became an apology for oppression. Notoriously, the basic right of man to won the land he tills and the tools he uses became a shield for the privilege of large landlords and factory owners. The right to fair trial, again a fundamental human right, basic to all freedom, has frequently provided large economic aggregates with a veil of endless litigation for pernicious activities. Even the right of free speech, essential to a free society, was extended from the right of a man to speak his mind to an elaborate protection of fraudulent advertising and so to protecting not the interests of men but the privileges of economic aggregates. The irony of democracy in advanced industrial societies has been the paralysis of public power, which only too often became immobilized by the extention of human rights to inhuman aggregates to such a degree that the effective defense of individual rights became problematic.

The appeal of socialism, no less than that of democracy, was the promise of freedom. Socialism promised to wipe out the privileges that gave economic aggregates their stranglehold on society. But socialism was no less tainted by the vicious confusion of individual rights and corporate privileges. It, too, came to argue that the two are inseparable, that corporate privileges can be wiped out only if men are willing to give up thier individual rights as well. The young idealists who convinced themselves that the Communist seizure of power and destruction of civil liberties was justified—or, in the West today, would be justified—do so on the specious ground that privileges of corporate interests cannot be broken unless all rights are abolished. The revolution that abolished the privilege of a large landowner to control land he did not till also abolished the right of a man to own the land he tilled. It did abolish the freedom of fraudulent advertising—but it also abolished the freedom of speech and opened the way to a far greater fraud. The result was quite understandably a mirror image of capitalism, carried to its logical extreme of bureaucratic collectivism fusing political and economic monopoly on power to a degree capitalism never achieved.

The core of the Czechoslovak socialist democracy was the determination to restore the rights of men without restoring the oppressive prilileges of corporate entities. It was basically humanistic, concerned to propose an alternative to the impossible choice between democracy strangled by capitalism—or socialism strangled even more effectively by absolutism. In Czechoslovakia, we spoke of that alternative as "socialist democracy"—but labels mean little in this area of conflicting ideologies. Its fundamental principle was humanistic, the distinction between men and women who have inalienable rights and, on the other hand, the social wholes, whether political or economic, which can have only privileges. In the idiom of the time, we were convinced that economic aggregates, just as political ones, have no autonomous justification and must continually justify their existence by the public services they offer, whether in the productive sector or the sector of social services, and including the services of the government.

We were Socialists, but the twenty years since the Communists came to power had taught us that socialism and Communism, which the Marxists tried to reconcile as "two stages of socialist development," are two irreconcilable alternatives. They do have a common foundation: the recognition that social justice is not separable from economic justice. That, after all, is the great contribution of socialism to Western thought. Traditional social philosophy has tended to treat human relations as autonomous from their economic context. It focused on human rights and obligations as if men were pure spirits. Socialism recognized that men are incarnate in their bodies as well as their world, that they become actual in their relation to a physical world, and that their mutual relations are mediated by their concrete embodiment. Practically, this means that property relations are not accidental, but essential in any social ordering that all socialists have in common. Beyond that, however, two strategies are possible, and they are basically contradictory.

The first strategy, the socialist democratic one, seeks to resolve the problem of property by extending the principle of justice and democracy to economic relations. It starts with the recognition of the fundamental need of every human to translate his being into the concrete terms of material counterparts, which he makes uniquely his own in his life and labor—a place to which he belongs and which belongs to him. It is the right to be actual, not merely potential. In the name of that basic right the socialist democratic strategy takes the part of the slave to whom society denies even the right to his own body. It takes the part of the wretched ot the earth to whom society denies the right to the most elementary means of existense worthy of a human being. It takes the part of the worker to whom society denies the intimate relationship of owning the tools that he makes his own through his work. The basic socialist democratic principle is the right of each human being to become incarnate, to find a positive relation to his life and work. In that sense, it recognizes as the only basis for the claim to ownership the belonging established by life and labor, as the peasant establishes a claim to the land he tills and the worker to the tools he uses. It denies the legitimacy of any abstract posession—in the jargon, of *capitalist* ownership.

This strategy clashed from the beginning with an opposite thrust, which is also as old as mankind—the desire to resolve the problem of property by freeing man from it altogether. Marx to the contrary, it is not the next stage of socialist development—it is an alternative. In mythological terms, the first alternative is reflected in the perennial myth of the gods who sanctify human incarnation by becoming incarnate. The second alternative is Platonic, the myth of the god or reason that does not set a man free from the ills of the flesh, but rather liberates man's soul from the prison of the body. This is basically an ascetic alternative, which celebrates the freedom of poverty.

In more recent terms, the first alternative has been guided by the vision of a just and free relation between man and the material world. By contrast, the second, traditionally the Communist, alternative sees man, for all its materialist pretensions, as a pure subject. It understands property in aristocratic terms, as theft of burden—which, for an aristocrat, it is—rather than as the incarnation of a subject's life and work. Thus its political strategy is ultimately the abolition of concrete relation between man and his physical world: "the society," in fact the state, will be the sole owner, placing the tools at the disposal of individual humans. As the Inquisition destroyed bodies to free souls, the second strand of socialism has confiscated fields, tools, and labor to free pure subjects.

The Communist strategy bears a strong resemblance to that of the monastic orders, which wanted to enjoy both the virtue of poverty and the convenience of property: they had their lands, flocks, and chapter houses owned nominally by the Church at Rome and placed at their disposal. There is also a more ominous analogy. The slave, after all, is the person most free from property. He owns nothing, not even his labor, not even his body. He contributes according to his ability, and receives according to his need. In his more aristocratic moments, Karl Marx was convinced that the slave is indeed closest to freedom: all it takes is the magic dialectical moment of revolution in which the slave is the victor and the master the vanquished, and the slave and the master are subsumed in a new perfectly free being in whom the slavery of the slave is transformed into its dialectical opposite, freedom.

Our experience with masters and slaves since 1938 taught us that reality does not obey the rules of dialectical magic. Slavery does not prepare humans for freedom, nor does the slave and the master add up to a free man. We were not interested in one more inversion in the cycle of alternating slaves and masters. Our strategy was one of reconciliation, not victory. We wanted to build a democracy in the very basic sense of a state without masters or slaves, a state in which "the leading role" is delegated by a freely formed and freely expressed majority, within the limits of respect for human rights, subject to supervision and recall. It was socialism because we applied that principle to economics as well. What he had hoped to build was an economy based on the recognition of every human being's right to work, to receive the rewards of his labor, and to own the tools of his trade—whether individually as a craftsman, cooperatively as a farmer or a service worker, or socially, through elected representative councils, as the factory worker. Whatever the particular arrangements, the basic principle is the clear recognition that no man has the right to exploit the labor of another whether by claiming to "own" the means of production others use or by controlling those means in the name of "revolutionary" pre-rogative.

Perhaps what was at stake, philosophically, was a revision of the fundamental error that Karl Marx shared with his century's capitalists. Marx saw the operative principle of exploitation in the ownership of means of production. In the case of abstract "ownership," the two do coincide, though they remain distinct. But in the case of the ownership which acknowledges the bond a man forges between himself and his tools in his labor, they become distinct: here exploitation is depriving a worker of what he makes his own in his life and work. Ironically, Mark's succes-sors did nothing to change the principle of abstract ownership except to transfer it from an economic to an ideological elite. They did, however, expropriate one-man workshops and three-acre farms in the name of liberation. The basic critique of capital-ism, including the critique from Marxist quarters, was precisely that it alienates man from the tools he uses. Capitalism defended exploitation in the name of the right to own tools, incongruously extended from those who use them to abstract, corporate entities. Communism stripped men of their rights on the same grounds, assuming that because those rights had been illegitimately extended to corporations, those very rights had become illegitimate.

Twenty years of the kind of state capitalism against which Whilhelm Liebknecht had warned showed us that Marx was wrong. Private ownership of means of production is only second-arily the cause of exploitation: the operative principle of exploita-tion is abstract ownership, the ownership of another man's labor. A society can free itself of exploitation if it prevents abstract, anonymous ownership. Socialism can become progressive when it gives up the goal of a state monopoly and seeks instead to build a society and an economy based on consistent support of the rights of men and women against all claims of abstract social aggregates, whether political or economic.

This means the defense of the rights of speech against "interests of the state," but it means also the defense of the right to work and organize for the protection of that right, to own the tools a man uses and to receive rewards for his labor, both against corporate claims and the claims of state monopoly. A society becomes socialist when it recognizes that men and women have rights—and that only concrete, individual men and women have rights. Corporations and governments alike can have only privileges, justified by the service they perform for the society as a whole, and always contingent on the performance of that service.

Finally, socialism has the effect of making economic power public. In a democratic society, where public power is subject to democratic control, this makes economic power democratic. In an absolutist society, reactionary as Bismarck's Germany or revolutionary as Stalin's Russia, making economic power public has the opposite effect and makes absolute rule more pervasive. Economic power in Czechoslovakia had become public: when the flash of freedom in the spring of 1968 promised to make public power democratic, the promise we glimpsed was the promise of a socially democratic society.

Four years after the occupation, little is left of the institutions that were to make that promise a reality. The men who represented the Spring disappeared from public view, the Action Program of the Czechoslovak Communist party became treason, the movements that sprang into life dispersed and even the conception of human rights that make socialism democratic was abrogated by the Emergency Decree of August 22, 1969. On the surface, in the press, in official pronouncements and policies, the country reverted to the conditions of the 1950's.

But only on the surface. In the 1950's, the official passions penetrated deep into the body and soul of our nation. Since then, something basic had changed. We have found ourselves. The dogmas of the past can rule, but they can no longer deceive us.

The idea of socialist democracy and self-determination may have been premature in 1968, but it was no less basic for that, and with every year since the occupation it has become more obvious that it is the only way out of an impasse. The conception of the victors, of the leading member of the socialist commonwealth or leading role in the state, is necessarily only an interim one. It perpetuates a polarization that is ultimately untenable in the age of advanced technology and weaponry. The security the Soviet Union needs as badly as the West cannot be built on military occupation. It requires a détente, a separation of potential foes by autonomous allies. After all, even Czechoslovakia can have no interest in the "defeat" of the Soviet Union. A small country, faced at one of its borders with the power of Germany, requires the counterbalance of a strong Russia. Our long-range hope is reconciliation: and when the last Soviet soldier leaves Czechoslovak territory, we shall be able to become quite pro-Russian once more. Similarly, social progress is in the long range incompatible with polarization between domestic victors and vanquished. Here, too, we have no interest in a "victory" over the Communists. Here, too, our long-range hope is reconciliation, the chance to live and work together as free human beings.

This, to be sure, has been true since 1956. It has always been true: the difference is that today we know it. The people of Czechoslovakia know it. They can be forced to raise their hands in assent and repeat the magic formulas out of the past, but those formulas have lost the power to deceive. They are too obviously false and anachronistic. The mood of our nation is one of living and waiting, not one of hate. Even the part of the nation that is in exile abroad—even the exiles no longer see themselves locked in an implacable struggle with the ideology of our homeland. Today, we are a democratic opposition, which shares with its nation its hopes, its ideals, and its waiting. Finally, even among the men who have undertaken the ungrateful task of governing an occupied country, there are many who know it. Though their pronouncements and policies inevitably reflect our political reality, many of them, too, conform without conviction. In the not too distant future, even the men of the Kremlin will no longer be able to avoid the admission that their formulas have become irrelevant, and that the Communist party cannot depend on the ability of its bureaucracy, police, and army to supress the admission that the emperor has no clothes.

Repeatedly in our history, our hopes have run counter to the trends of the time. That was true in 1938, and again in 1948. Possibly it was even true in 1968. It is not true today. The Czechoslovak Spring did not defy history; it anticipated it. Today we are waiting for history to catch up with us.